Understanding and Promoting Access for People with Learning Difficulties

Seeing the opportunities and challenges of risk

Edited by Jane Seale and Melanie Nind

 Routledge
Taylor & Francis Group

LONDON AND NEW YORK

First published 2010
by Routledge
2 Park Square, Milton Park, Abingdon, Oxon OX14 4RN

Simultaneously published in the USA and Canada
by Routledge
270 Madison Avenue, New York, NY 10016

*Routledge is an imprint of the Taylor & Francis Group, an inform
business*

© 2010 editorial and selection, Jane Seale & Melanie Nind;
individual contributions, the contributors.

Typeset in Bembo by Saxon Graphics Ltd, Derby
Printed and bound in Great Britain by
TJ International Ltd, Padstow, Cornwall

British Library Cataloguing in Publication Data
A catalogue record for this book is available from the British
Library

Library of Congress Cataloging-in-Publication Data
Understanding and promoting access for people with learning
difficulties : seeing the opportunities and challenges of risk /
edited by Jane Seale and Melanie Nind.
    p. cm.
  1. Learning disabled-Education. 2. Inclusive education.
3. Learning disabled-Services for. 4. Social integration. I. Seale, Jane.
II. Nind, Melanie.
  LC4704.U54 2009
  371.9-dc22   2009005279

ISBN 13: 978-0-415-47947-9 (hbk)
ISBN 13: 978-0-415-47948-6 (pbk)
ISBN 13: 978-0-203-09212-5 (ebk)

ISBN 10: 0-415-47947-9 (hbk)
ISBN 10: 0-415-47948-7 (pbk)
ISBN 10: 0-203-09212- (ebk)

Contents

PART 1
Introduction

1 Access for people with learning difficulties: new rhetoric or
   meaningful concept?
   MELANIE NIND AND JANE SEALE

PART 2
Access to and through information

2 Access in mind: a review of approaches to accessible
   information for people with learning disabilities
   JAN WALMSLEY

3 Creativity, choice and control: the use of multimedia life
   story work as a tool to facilitate access
   ANN ASPINALL

PART 3
Access all areas

4 Access all areas: the use of symbols in public spaces
   CHRIS ABBOTT AND CATE DETHERIDGE

List of Tables

List of Figures

Acknowledgements

The idea for this book stemmed from a seminar series that we ran between 2005 and 2007 on 'Concepts of Access'. We would like to acknowledge the support of the Economics and Social Research Council, which funded the seminar series (RES-451-25-4145) and the School of Education at the University of Southampton, which provided the venue and supported our time. A large portion of the administrative support for the seminar series was provided by a patient and resourceful Nicki Lewin, to whom we are, as ever, extremely grateful. However, our biggest thanks go to the enthusiastic, creative, open and honest seminar participants who have inspired and stimulated many of the ideas and arguments presented here in this book.

Finally, a number of figures contained within this book have been reproduced with the kind of permission of the copyright owners, and we wish to acknowledge those owners here:

Figures 2.1, 2.2 and 2.3 are reproduced under the terms of the Click-Use License (Office of Public Sector Information).
Figure 2.4 is copyright of the Healthcare Audit and Inspection 2007 and is reproduced with kind permission of the Healthcare Commission.
Figure 2.6 is reproduced with kind permission of Beth Tarleton, coordinator of Plain Facts, Norah Fry Research Centre.
The *Valuing People* clipart contained within Figures 2.7 and 2.8 is reproduced with kind permission of Inspired Services Publishing Ltd (www.inspiredservices.org.uk).
Figure 2.9 is reproduced with kind permission of Helen Graham, Visiting Research Fellow, the Open University.
The Widgit Literacy Symbols used in Figures 6.1 and 6.2 are copyright Widgit Software 2008 and reproduced with kind permission of Widgit Software (www.widgit.com).
The photosymbols used in Figure 6.3 are reproduced with kind permission of Photosymbols Ltd (www.photosymbols.com).

Notes on contributors

Chris Abbott is Reader in e-Inclusion at King's College London, where he is also Programme Director for the MA in e-Inclusion (Learning, Disability and Technology). His research interests focus on aspects of inclusion, technology and disability. His recent publications include *e-Inclusion: Learning difficulties and digital technologies* (Futurelab, 2006) and he is Editor of the *Journal of Assistive Technologies*.

Ginny Aird, Alan Dale, Sarah Edgecombe, Louisa Jones, Trevor Rowden, Mark Sabine, and **Sara Wornham** are involved with Be Heard, a self-advocacy group for adults with learning disabilities run in Bracknell.

Ann Aspinall worked for 15 years at HFT (The Home Farm Trust Ltd) a national charity supporting adults with a learning disability; initially as ICT Service Development Manager and then as Project Manager for TATE (Through Assistive Technology to Employment) an EU-funded project in the second round of the Equal Community Initiative. Since August 2008 Ann has been employed as a Telehealth Project Manager for Gloucestershire Primary Care Trust.

Drew Bradley, Darren Grant and **Wayne Taylor** are involved with Choices Advocacy citizen advocacy project where **Judith Clayton** and **Claire Royall** work and Claire is deputy chief officer. They all took part in the Concepts of Access seminar series that stimulated this book.

Gary Butler was a presenter at the Concepts of Access seminar series where he spoke about his experiences of working at the medical school, St George's University of London. He works as a training adviser, helping medical students understand how best to work with people with learning disabilities. He has co-written a book about his experiences called *A New Kind of Trainer* (Royal Society of Psychiatrists, 2004).

Suzanne Collins manages a day service for people with learning disabilities for the Belfast Health and Social Care Trust. Previously she was a Research Associate at the University of Ulster working on a project investigating social inclusion across different accommodation options.

Cate Detheridge has worked for Widgit Software for the past nine years. She heads up the Accessibility Team, managing the development of the Widgit Literacy Symbols and accessibility and web projects. Pioneering projects include working with the Sensory Trust to enhance the access of the Eden Project, the UK's largest tourist attraction; accessible information with the police and local government; and work with charities like Home Farm Trust and the Children's Society. She is co-author of *Symbols, Literacy and Social Justice* and has presented on symbols and their technologies at international events.

Hazel Lawson is a senior lecturer in special and inclusive education at the University of Exeter. She was formerly a primary and special school teacher and has research interests in citizenship education, curriculum development and pupil involvement for children and young people with severe learning difficulties. She is fascinated by the exploration of methods and methodologies in researching people's perceptions and stories. She is co-author of *Access to Citizenship* (David Fulton, 2003).

Duncan Mitchell is Professor of Health and Disability at Manchester Metropolitan University and has research interests in learning disability nursing, advocacy and the history of learning disability research. His recent work includes *Exploring Experiences of Advocacy by People with Learning Disabilities: Testimonies of resistance* (Jessica Kingsley, 2006).

Roy McConkey is Professor of Learning Disability at the University of Ulster, Northern Ireland and has previously held posts in England, Republic of Ireland and Scotland. He has worked in the field of intellectual disability for over 35 years and has acted as a consultant to various United Nations agencies and international NGOs.

Melanie Nind is Professor of Education at the University of Southampton. She has worked in special schools and further education colleges where she developed her particular interest in interactive and inclusive pedagogy and issues of access to communication and curriculum. She is best known for her work on Intensive Interaction. Her books include *Access to Communication* (Routledge, 2005), *Curriculum and Pedagogy in Inclusive Education* (Routledge, 2005), *Witnesses to Change: Families, learning difficulties and history* (BILD, 2005) and *Implementing Intensive Interaction in Schools* (David Fulton, 2003).

Jonathan Rix is a senior lecturer in Inclusion, Curriculum and Learning at the Open University. His research interests relate to learning difficulties and issues of equality and participation, particularly in the fields of early intervention, intellectual access and simplified language. His recent books include *Policy and Power in Inclusive Education* (Routledge, 2005) and *Inclusive Education: Learners and learning contexts* (Routledge, 2004).

Jane Seale is a senior lecturer at the University of Southampton. She has worked as a special needs technology consultant in a range of settings including Social

Services Day Centres and Occupational Therapy departments. She coordinated the first ever UK Interdisciplinary Masters Programme in Assistive Technology (2000–2002). Jane's main research interest is the role of computers and assistive technologies in promoting independence, identity and quality of life for adults with disabilities. Her recent books include *E-Learning and Disability in Higher Education: Accessibility research and practice* (Routledge, 2006) and *Approaches to Developing Accessible Learning Experiences* (Taylor & Francis, 2006).

Amy Tyler and **Mary Waight** work as occupational therapists within Bracknell CTPLD, which is a multidisciplinary team made up of professionals from both health and social services, including occupational therapists, community nurses, physiotherapist, social workers, behaviour specialists, dieticians, psychologists, psychiatrists, team managers and speech and language therapists.

Jan Walmsley was, until recently, Assistant Director of the Health Foundation. She is Visiting Chair at the Open University and runs janwalmsley associates consultancy. Her research interests include participatory and inclusive research methods, oral history and the history of learning disability. She has recently written *Community Care in Perspective: Care, control and citizenship (Palgrave Macmillan, 2006)* and has worked on joint projects with people with learning difficulties including *Good Times, Bad Times: Women with learning difficulties telling their stories (BILD, 2000)*.

Foreword

It is a pleasure to provide a foreword for this important text. Reading this book has highlighted for me not only the complexity of the concept of 'access' but also reminded me of the smoke and mirrors of policymakers, theorists, providers, researchers and practitioners who hide the key human necessity for access behind complex philosophical questions, conflicting interests and measurable service outputs. The contributions to this book, from people with the label of intellectual disabilities and their allies, make significant inroads into the complexities and, conversely, the simple message of access. It is of course important to understand access as a troubling concept both theoretically and practically. Yet access is at its most understandable – at its most accessible – when we demand that it is viewed in the political realm. Since the 1950s, it is possible to trace a growth in potency of the disabled people's movement, through which people with the label of intellectual disabilities are challenging their exclusion from mainstream life. The key policy imperative in the UK, *Valuing People* (Department of Health 2001), is testimony not only to the emergence of a potentially more participatory worldview developed by policymakers, service providers and professionals, but is also a consequence of the agitations and activism of people with the label of learning disabilities who have demanded access to mainstream life. This book reminds us that we must keep their activism at the foreground of all debate. Without their involvement, access withers into a limited offering of well-meaning people, rather than a crucial element of meaningful community participation.

Access, then, is about recognition, inclusion and respect. It is also about humanity and the ways in which 'normate' cultures continue to exclude disabled people because they are deemed as the monstrous antithesis to what the critical psychologist Edward E. Sampson (1977) termed the 'United-Statesian' ideal citizen of contemporary life. Access is about challenging the norms of a society that privileges certain characteristics of human beings (autonomous and hyper-capable) and opening up more exciting, inclusive, connected, different (maybe disruptive and disrupting) ways of living life. Access is not simply about accessing the ordinary. It is also about embracing the diverse. This book shows that we should not forget the simple message of access that is often lost in wider debates of an increasingly marketised and globalised welfare system and the growing governance of families, schools, workplaces and health care systems. Access is a useful concept and term that gets right at the heart of calls for the dismantling of disabling society. It is about people, their families, their allies and advocates, their potential and their ambitions.

As Nind and Seale argue in their excellent introductory chapter, access touches upon all aspects of human and social networks including physical access, knowledge, power, relationships, advocacy and participation. The contributors to this book address these networks in a variety of exciting and novel ways. Knowledge production on the part of people with learning disabilities and their representative organisations is key to accessing wider society. When we make knowledge accessible then it can be reacted to, as in the case of accessible forms of policy and legislation, considered by Walmsley. Access allows critical appraisal of dominant knowledge (synthesis) and, when necessary, rejection of knowledge (antithesis). The contributions of Walmsley and Aspinall illuminate different sides of knowledge production of people with the label of intellectual disabilities. Access is not simply about learning about knowledge out there in the world but also about criticising it and developing alternative ideas that are more in tune with the aims and ambitions of disabled people. The role of technology has long been recognised in the social sciences. Recent philosophical work suggests that technology opens up possibilities for the flattening of social hierarchies and the extension of relationships and commonalities (Lash 2001). The impact of multimedia, described by Aspinall, is clearly being felt on the web. Voices of people, whose ideas and perspectives have often taken second place to those of experts, fill the web with new possibilities for thinking about not only accessing mainstream life but also the meaning of mainstream life. A personal favourite of mine is the spoof website set up by people who identify as neurologically atypical, which describes how one can find out if they have the diagnosis of 'neurological typicality' (http://isnt.autistics.org/). This site for the 'Institute of the Study of the Neurologically Typical' turns ideas of difference on their head and asks us to think about the conditions that mainstream society places on those that it *allows* access to. Related to this, Abbott and Detheridge's chapter clearly indicates that an inclusive culture is a symbolising culture. The input of resources such as Widgit, alongside the potential of the web, open up different access routes for all people including those who are labelled as having intellectual disabilities.

This book also makes some very significant points about *what* is being accessed. The inspirational chapter by members of the Bracknell self-advocacy group, Aird, Dale, Edgecombe, Jones, Rowden, Sabine, Tyler, Waight and Wornham, provides some excellent advice for readers in terms of how leisure, education, work and healthy lives can be accessed. I was particularly struck by their comment that meaningful access is associated with 'not being bored'. This is a fundamental part of life that we must keep in mind. While self-advocacy groups have added markedly to the level of interest in the lives of their members, other areas of the community continue to create non-stimulating and boring experiences for disabled people. Being bored equates with being disengaged. And disengaging with community often results in marginalisation. A way of addressing this marginality is through opening up culture and the arts through meaningful discussions with people with learning disabilities. The chapter by Rix with The Heritage Forum discusses not only the need for meaningful processes of participation but also the importance of cultural heritage in the lives of disabled and non-disabled citizens. The meaning of citizenship tugs at the very heart of the meaning of culture and access. Access to mainstream life might also be viewed as access to cultural and civic life. The history of people with the label of learning disabilities is a history associated with a questionable relationship with the notion of citizenship. Indeed, Manion and Bersani (1987) argue that the 19th and 20th centuries marked an increasing dehumanising of people with learning difficulties, to the extent that the status of citizenship conferred on people so labelled has increasingly become owned by disabling professionals and institutions. Even in these days of anti-discriminatory legislation, disabled people remain devoid of the rights afforded to all other citizens of society. I welcome Lawson's contribution on citizenship education because it tackles a key concern for us all: if we are accessing social and civic life, we need to be aware of the rights that this gives us as citizens. Being supported in this process of getting to know one's own citizenship is difficult and requires careful, thoughtful and facilitating modes of support described eloquently by Bradley, Clayton, Grant, Royall and Taylor. I enjoyed reading this chapter and found myself wishing that their identified areas of good practice be rolled out across a whole host of contexts: in work, education and leisure.

This book is also a timely reminder of the exclusionary and uncaring nature of the communities we still live in some 20 years after the major deinstitutionalisation of many adults with the label of learning disabilities was introduced in the UK. McConkey and Collins offer a sobering account of the meaning of community participation. While their argument is not all bad news, and points to the contributions that many people with learning disabilities make to our communities, the idea that access means communities letting in some and excluding others remains a strong tension. Community exclusion or inclusion is also a matter of life and death. As Mitchell notes in his chapter, the health needs of people with learning disabilities remain misunderstood and ignored. That is why the input of experts, such as Butler who describes his contribution in Chapter 11, is more necessary now than it ever was. I was reminded of Bronach Crawley's oft-used statement in her work in the 1980s, that people with the label of learning disabilities are often a lot more useful to the empowerment of people so labelled than the most committed non-disabled advocate. The final chapter of this collection, by the editors, takes up the lessons provided by the contributors to rethink access in terms of productivity, possibility, resilience and interconnectedness. This is a brave piece of writing that not only aims for theoretical coherence and innovation but argues for a new kind of attitude around access. Seale and Nind suggest, for example, a new model of risk that in itself takes risks, leaps of faith and tolerates serendipity. Theirs is a strong message of capacity: to view the potentiality of people with learning disabilities as they seek access to mainstream society. It is only right that all societal members start to think of how they support the access of all and to question exactly what it is that we are accessing.

Professor Dan Goodley
Psychology and Social Change, Manchester Metropolitan University
d.goodley@mmu.ac.uk

References

Department of Health (2001) *Valuing People: A new strategy for learning disability for the 21st century. A white paper*, London: HMSO.

Lash, S. (2001) Technological forms of life, *Theory, Culture and Society,* **18,** 1, 105–20.

Manion, M. L. and Bersani, H. A. (1987) Mental retardation as a western sociological construct, *Disability, Handicap and Society*, **2,** 3, 213–45.

Sampson, E. E. (1977) Psychology and the American ideal, *Journal of Personality and Social Psychology*, **35,** 11, 767–82.

Preface

The contributions in this book cover a range of different perspectives: from researchers, to advocates, practitioners and of course self-advocates. This variety brings with it differences in style and language. Readers will therefore notice that some authors use the term 'learning disability', others use 'learning difficulty' or 'intellectual disability'. However, rather than insist on uniformity we have decided to embrace the diversity and to interfere with the 'voice' of our authors as little as possible.

Part 1

Introduction

Chapter 1

Access for people with learning difficulties

New rhetoric or meaningful concept?

Melanie Nind and Jane Seale

Introduction

In this introductory chapter we set the scene for what follows in the book by discussing the ways in which access is conceptualised in the policy and research literatures. We show how calls for access from policymakers and others are not always matched by understanding of what this means in practice or in theory. This can turn access into unachievable aspiration at best and empty rhetoric at worst. As it would be hard to argue that access is anything other than a 'good thing' there is a danger that it could become the meaningless buzzword that Thomas and O'Hanlon (2001: vii) argue inclusion has become; made into a cliché that allows people to 'talk about inclusion (or access) without really thinking about what they mean'. Similarly, Benjamin (2002: 310) discusses the ways in which the term 'valuing diversity' has been used to 'lend a veneer of social justice and moral authority' to other agendas. The potential for access to be used likewise is self-evident.

We go on to briefly outline some of the failures of access and what this means for people with learning difficulties. These failures are acutely felt and described throughout the book (see for instance, Drew Bradley *et al* on struggling to live free of others' rules and Duncan Mitchell on failure to access health screening). Our intention here is to illustrate why better understanding of what we mean by access and how access can be promoted and achieved is fundamental to people's lives. We show how and why getting hold of access as a concept is both difficult and necessary. This involves a discussion of the ways in which access overlaps with other key concepts (and equally with other bits of rhetoric). This leads us into our multidimensional model of access (Nind and Seale 2009) and a discussion of the complex, layered nature of access drawn from multi-perspective narratives. In doing all of the above the chapter fulfils some key purposes:

- it goes some way towards communicating the kind of work that researchers have already done on access;
- it demonstrates why access is a topic worth dwelling on at this juncture in time;

- it shares some of the findings from the ESRC-funded seminars series on Concepts of Access that inspired this book; and
- it prepares readers for what the book goes on to offer, so that the accounts of research and experience and the reflections on the nature of the challenge can be read in context.

Unpicking access

The issue of access is frequently recognised as being at the forefront of the practical challenges facing people with learning disabilities and the people working with or supporting them. Despite this, it has received little theoretical attention; access has been much less picked over by academics than inclusion or participation, much less pondered by philosophers than democracy, social justice or citizenship. Like inclusion, access has become part of the fabric of our talk about education and community, pervasive and often unquestioned. In contrast to inclusion, however, there is nothing like the plethora of papers debating what the word means, illustrating how it is interpreted differently by politicians, practitioners, disability theorists; it has not become 'contested territory' (Clough 2000). Thomas and Loxley (2007: 1) argue that thinking about inclusion and inclusive education has 'billow(ed) out' into new terrains, sometimes so overused as to lose meaning, but also gaining in multiple meanings, concerns and discourses in its relatively short history. The term 'access' has not been on this scope of journey and it has acquired less baggage along its way; nonetheless it is used almost complacently at every turn.

There have been some attempts to unpick what is meant by access. This was one of our intentions when, back in 2004 we bid to ESRC for funds to run a seminar series. Our aim was 'to advance, through inter-disciplinary debate, our shared theoretical framework and understanding of the concept of access for people with learning disabilities' and our objectives were to:

- Bring together, in ongoing, focused discussion, people with learning disabilities, a range of practitioners including educators and health professionals, advocacy groups and rights campaigners, and new and experienced researchers.
- Engage in shared questioning of the concept of access. For example, access for what purpose? How do people with learning disabilities experience access? What is worth accessing? What kind of access do people with learning disabilities want? How can access be enabled and evaluated?
- Stimulate and enrich the debate about access for people with learning disabilities through input from presenters and participants working on access across a wide range of fields and disciplines.
- Enhance clarity around the concept of access for people with learning disabilities without oversimplifying what is involved.
- Foster the process of access through greater understanding.

We won the funding and the seminar series did indeed do something original and powerful in bringing together an interdisciplinary and diverse group of participants to break new ground in addressing the variety of ways in which access can be conceptualised and enabled for people with learning disabilities. We have shared some of the processes and findings of the seminar series elsewhere (Nind and Seale 2008; 2009), but in this book we enrich this by bringing together some of those diverse voices from the seminars on paper and by presenting further analysis.

Before going further we want to dwell a little more on why the concept of access needs unpicking in this way or indeed at all. Calls for access to primary healthcare, access to leisure, access to mainstream education and so on are familiar to us. Indeed access in these separate domains form the basis of separate polices and sometimes even separate struggles. But, while access has to be *to* something, we question whether this implies that access is different in each domain or whether we can identify something essentially the same across contexts that helps us to understand the phenomenon per se. Our starting point was that there is likely to be something about the essence of access that means that educators can learn from healthcare practitioners and vice versa about what access entails, requires, and leads from and to. Similarly, if people with learning difficulties 'do' access everyday across these domains we might see them as the real experts on what access means, although true access might happen so infrequently that what people with learning difficulties know best might be what access is not!

If we unpick the concept of access a little we can see the need for the unpicking. Talk of access captures elements of aspiration. 'It' (primary healthcare, leisure, mainstream education etc.) is out there, 'other people' have it and therefore people with learning difficulties must want it too. We owe much to normalization movements for this thinking. Access also captures elements of entitlement; not only must they want it but they should have it too. Disability rights movements have helped to enshrine the rights agenda in our worldview. Aspiration and entitlement lead us towards concepts of universal access, which Eng *et al* (1998) suggest has become some kind of gold standard; everything must be accessible to everyone. And then we get the rhetoric–reality gap and a void in understanding what we really mean by all this.

Shakespeare (2006: 46) has recently been an unsettling voice in the social model of disability by critiquing the 'notion of a barrier-free world' in which 'Universal Design can liberate all'. He provides examples for which access needs to be individualised and where compromises are reasonable and practical. Keen not to discount the interaction of impairment with social factors, he is one of the few people who dares to voice the idea that access to work, for example, is not feasible for all people with learning difficulties, notably those with profound impairments. Shakespeare (2006: 45) reminds us that 'architectural and communications barrier removal is often easier than the removal of social and economic barriers' and that 'progress on many of these latter issues has been much slower to achieve'. He also shows (building on Singer 1999) how addressing some barriers and making aspects of the social world accessible for people with autism begin to look rather like specialised, even segregated provision.

It is not surprising then that service-providers, politicians and campaign groups grapple both to visualise and achieve accessible provision. An example familiar to educationalists is the story of the National Curriculum in England and Wales. Government thinking in introducing the National Curriculum did not initially include pupils with learning difficulties, but in response to pressure from professional and voluntary organizations (Mittler 2000) there emerged a new discourse. Official publications and pronouncements began to give assurances about *all* children and to provide guidance on access to the National Curriculum for pupils with special needs. Questions were raised about what 'access' to the curriculum actually meant (Peter 1992) and about whether the access was to something worth having (Aird 2001). Nonetheless, teachers have adopted this language of access and guidance and various interpretations proliferate, often without clear conceptualisation of whether this access is about entitlement, participation or something different. In healthcare there has been a growing agenda of access to mainstream services (e.g. Department of Health 2001) but what this means in practice is equally complex (Hall *et al* 2006).

Policy and legislative change (e.g. Disability Discrimination Act 1995, Special Educational Needs and Disability Act 2001) has raised the profile of access issues for many services and institutions making it no longer an option to ignore them. It has energised debate about the quality of the access provided and about who has the power to provide it (see for example the Website Accessibility Initiative), but it has not brought with it answers to the multiple access questions. Sometimes the goal of access is specified without strategies to achieve it. Redley (2008: 376), for example, argues this is the case in regard to access to election processes:

> The 2001 White Paper *Valuing People: A new strategy for learning disability in the 21st century* (Department of Health 2001) included a specific commitment to supporting more adults with learning disabilities to vote. The White Paper did not, however, present figures describing the extent of their current participation in recent elections, nor did it make recommendations as to how more adults with learning disabilities might be supported to vote.

More often there has been a tendency for formal documents to present an oversimplified impression of what is involved in enhancing access. For example, the Electoral Commission for Scotland (2003, cited by Redley 2008) refers to improved physical access and an easy-read guide to voting as important in the goal of barrier-free elections. The *Right to Vote Information Pack* and *Supporter Fact Sheet* (Disability Rights Commission 2005) go further in providing information (easy to read with pictures) about registering to vote, casting a vote, and the legal position on helping others to vote but, argues Redley (2008), falls short of advising on the sensitive issue of judging capacity to understand.

With regard to education, following Part 4 of the Disability Discrimination Act 1995, every school must now have an accessibility plan and the guidance specifies that this plan must show how the school will improve accessibility for disabled pupils: how the school will improve the physical environment, make improvements in the provision of information and increase access to the curriculum. The impression given is of a straightforward task for which a staged process of steps is needed: barriers to access must be removed, technology and other resources used and access is facilitated. This, like much that is written about access, is based on a model taken from physical and sensory impairments in which basic adaptations make a huge difference.

Failure to access

We have argued that greater understanding of access is needed, but if more evidence is needed to support this argument it must surely come from the ongoing inability to make access happen. One example of important but largely unsuccessful access relates to education, employment and training, which is all the more significant because of the wide acceptance that this can in turn facilitate transition to adulthood for young people with learning difficulties and access to the life chances that flow from this transition (Caton and Kagan 2006; Further Education Development Agency 1997; Taylor et al 2004). Participating in education, employment and training is regarded by the Social Exclusion Unit (1999) and Department of Health (2001) as a key component of social inclusion. The evidence suggests, however, that this is hugely problematic (Affleck et al 1990; Florian et al 2000). Restricted access results not just from the profound impairment discussed by Shakespeare (2006) but from the limited choices and opportunities available to young people (Terlizzi 1997; Wistow and Schneider 2003) and from services with ineffective ethos and structures (Aston et al 2005; Dewson et al 2004; Riddell et al 1999). There are even considerable barriers to employment that arise from governmental systems and regulations themselves (Department of Work and Pensions 2004).

In response to the problems with education, employment and training, government agencies are focusing on the availability of support services as a key factor in facilitating access. For example, the Valuing People Support Team (2005: 40) argues that, 'there needs to be more support to get people into work if they want to'. However, more support may not facilitate access if is it more of the same, as the effectiveness of formal support systems, such as employment services (Beyer et al 2004) and sheltered workshop projects (Gosling and Cotterill 2000) has been variable. Concerns over the quality of support have led key agencies to conclude that formal services need to be reorganised with a particular emphasis on developing joined-up working between different support agencies in order to create seamless services as well as person-centred planning (Department for Education & Schools, Department of Heath, and Department of Work and Pensions 2007; Department of Health 2007; Learning Skills Council 2006). However, this prescription has been made many times with little evidence of improvement. In 2001 only around 10 per cent of people with learning difficulties were in paid employment (Department of Health 2001) and this rose to just 11 per cent by 2005 (Valuing People Support Team 2005). Despite agreement between government and people with learning difficulties that access to education, employment and training really matters, and despite various initiatives, multiple and inter-connected barriers continue to exist. These in turn present barriers to full social inclusion and full adult status (Department of Health 2007; Riddell *et al* 2001).

Access to leisure activities represents another dimension of social inclusion. 'Social, work and leisure roles that provide sources of self-esteem, choice, stimulation and support' are 'intrinsic to a "normal life"' (Reynolds 2002: 63). There is less government interest in leisure but it is another area of access that people with learning difficulties experience difficulty with. Research has identified the many barriers at work here; Beart *et al* (2001), in reviewing previous studies highlights lack of opportunity, living in large institutions, negative public perceptions and resource restrictions as playing a major part. Lack of money and transport are identified time and again as major barriers to leisure outside of the home (Beart *et al* 2001; Reynolds 2002; Russell 1995). What is significant though is that understanding the barriers to access, while helpful up to a point, does not lead to sufficient understanding of access and of how access works to make it happen.

Access as a slippery notion

If we can't make access happen in practice can we at least understand it as a concept? In theoretical terms access is not out there to be discovered, it is instead a social construct; as Devas (2003: 235) sees it, 'a product of disability theory and the disabled rights movement'. This does not make access and accessibility any less slippery as concepts or any less difficult to define and measure (Church and Marston 2003). It just means that we bring other particular constructs to use in the task.

One can try to pin down the concept of access by considering what it is not. The UK government, for example, assert that 'access to services is not just about installing ramps and widening doorways for wheelchair users'.[1,2] In lifting access beyond the physical or technical, they go on, 'it is about making services easier to use for all disabled people'. Nonetheless, envisioning this is tricky as the illustrations given of reasonable adjustments in relation to the Disability Discrimination Act (1995/2005) and Disability Equality Duty bring us back to ramps and induction loops.

If access is about making services easier to use then what does this mean? Government examples relevant to people with learning difficulties are limited to easy-to-read versions of information and disability awareness training. The former places the challenge of access in the domain of literacy and the latter in the domain of attitudes. In policy terms there are access barriers and access solutions, so placing access conceptually as a simple case of a solution to a problem.

In the research literature, access is increasingly being understood as a process, rather than a state or a one-off event. This might be, as Emmanuel and Ackroyd (1996) position it, a process of addressing all barriers; physical, structural, environmental, emotional and psychological. Or it might be, as Rummery *et al* (1999) understand it, a process of negotiation. Ribot and Peluso (2003) discuss access in terms of getting to somewhere, being part of something and, importantly, being able to derive benefit from things. This takes the concept beyond the simplistic notion of merely getting through the door to somewhere or something, and into the realm of what happens thereafter. This kind of complex definition of access is similarly adopted by Higginbotham *et al* (2007: 244) in their analysis of augmentative and alternative communication in which they see access as:

> The right, means, or opportunity to:
> - use or benefit from something (e.g. operate a communication device);
> - approach or see someone (e.g. converse with a person);
> - obtain or retrieve information from a person, the environment or an artifact (e.g. read from a communication device); and
> - provide use or benefit from something or someone (e.g. assist someone to communicate using AAC technology) (McKean 2005).

For Nind and Hewett (2005: 84) the important thing about access to communication is that it is a reciprocal, transactional process. 'Accessing' is not just about reaching the other person but about 'doing sensitive things to make ourselves available to access from the person with learning difficulties'. From this perspective people need to access each other; making access is a mutual endeavour that can be rapid or that can involve slow, painstaking work. Moreover, one can get involved in virtuous cycles (see also Ware 1996), where access facilitates access, which in turn facilitates more access. Of course vicious cycles can happen too. This makes access something that is fluid and dynamic with the potential to be robust or vulnerable.

Adding to the slippery nature of the concept, access is described in terms of being an absolute or relative concept. Church and Marston (2003), for example, argue that absolutist notions of accessibility in physical/geographical terms mean that there is either compliance or not. This, they argue however, lacks sensitivity to what people might want, such as more than one prescribed route to a destination. Thus something may be accessible according to the letter of the law, but not in the spirit of the law. Relativist concepts of accessibility take better account of the effort and time involved for the person and the impact on their daily lives. While for Church and Marston (2003) this is primarily related to physical/sensory impairments and the urban environment we can see the application of these ideas to people with learning difficulties and the social environment.

Access and overlapping concepts

One can see from the above discussion the parallels and overlaps with other concepts. In being more than just getting through the door, access, like inclusion, is more than about place. It has a quality of experience dimension. It is more ambitious than the old integration notion of being allowed in (as long as one fits and behaves). It carries connotations of rightful and active participation. Thus there are overlaps with inclusion, community and self-advocacy. Similarly, access and inclusion are not just concepts for academics, politicians and practitioners. These concepts are understood by young people too, and often in more subtle and nuanced ways. Allan (2005: 239) relates how inclusion and exclusion were understood by the secondary school students in her study as 'unstable processes, occurring in "moments" and often switching them from being included and excluded'. The people with learning difficulties in our seminar series certainly echoed this lack of stability in their experiences of access.

Devas (2003) helps us to place access and inclusion as concepts in relation to each other; inclusion is what happens when society is accessible. Using the social model of disability and the way it has positioned society as disabling, Devas (2003: 234) argues that 'although it is the individual who makes choices, it is down to society to create access'. For her then, another overlapping concept is choice; accessible environments must be conducive to people with learning difficulties understanding the available options and working with them.

Making choices and voicing them are inherent in both self-advocacy and achieving access. Much of the discussion about access in our series of seminars centred on issues of people taking control of their lives, taking risks, and taking responsibility. Real access, like real self-advocacy (Aspis 1997), brings with it difficult questions about the transfer of power and about whose interests are being served. Real access involves participating in the leisure activity you want to, rather than the one to which you might be steered by your support worker. Many of the chapters gathered here show how access, advocacy and social inclusion are interwoven.

Access as multidimensional, layered and meaningful

One of the outcomes of the seminar series and the emergent shared understanding of access was a multidimensional model of access in which we try to capture the different processes and elements involved. We outline this in our *Disability & Society* paper (Nind and Seale 2009) but reiterate and develop it with this book. The model is shown in Figure 1.1.

Dimension	Description	Role	Relationship
Physical access	Entering or approaching	Necessary but not sufficient for access	Physical access can be the first of many hurdles
Knowledge	Finding out about things	'information is empowering' (Thurman 2005: 83)	May be a prerequisite even to entering, approaching, taking a chance or making choices about future steps (Tarleton and Ward 2005)
Power	Ability to make things happen	Necessary to influence people and situations and so achieve and sustain access; 'information on its own has no power or value without an ability to act on it; either by ourselves or through the support of others' (Thurman 2005: 83).	Early and ongoing
Relationships and Communication	Using social networks and interpersonal interaction	Mediation and negotiation, support	Underpinning the whole process of access
Advocacy	Taking control and speaking up	Bringing together knowledge and power in personal action	Linked to power, 'self-determination is integral to access' (Devas 2003: 234)
Participation	Active involvement	Making access more than getting over the threshold or spectatorship from the edge	Both a process and product of access
Quality of life	Physical, material, social productive emotional and civic well-being (Felce 1997)	Belonging, enjoying, benefiting	Interwoven with access and resulting from it; 'barrier removal is not an end in itself. It is a means to an end. The aim of barrier removal is to facilitate the participation and improve the quality of life of people with impairment' (Shakespeare 2006: 50)

Figure 1.1 A multidimensional model of access

The danger in recognising the multiple dimensions is that access as a concept becomes so broad as to lose meaning. It is important therefore to pull this together in a tighter but encompassing construct. Our working concept, from having engaged in some intensive thinking and talking, is that access is rarely a one-off event of getting over the threshold and more a process of rallying various support mechanisms in negotiating a myriad of obstacles to meaningfully participate and derive benefit from something. Thus access happens in the minutiae of interactions in which new words are explained, practices are modelled, social episodes are opened up, small problems are solved and so on.

This conceptualisation of access helps to clarify some of differences between access as it is frequently described or assumed when little thought or research has gone into it and access as it is understood in our model, talked about by our seminar participants and described by the contributors in this book. These are in some respects distinctions between simplistic access and real world or lived access.

The first distinction is that simplistic access is linear; it involves a series of steps or breaking down a series of barriers. One might use the metaphor of going through a series of doors to a destination. But in lived access, getting through one door does not automatically provide the key to the next. Not only are the doors of different shapes and sizes with different types of locks but they can suddenly appear from nowhere and they can shut behind you, closing down your options. We suggest that if a linear model is retained, it is more useful to think of barriers to access as existing layer upon thick layer. But, just as Harris (2003) argues in relation to choice-making, we need to replace notions of idealized sequences of activity with pictures of real processes understood in relation to social practices.

Linear models underplay the complexity and multidirectional nature of the challenge and the sheer embedded-ness of the barriers to access. Alternatively, and more messily, wading through treacle might better encapsulate the sense of the effort people have to put into their repeated struggles. Some people may be better equipped for this but some may never get through. Using our earlier example of access to leisure, availability of opportunity, plus transport, plus support, does not always equal access. Staff supporting people with learning difficulties need to know them well enough to interpret their possible leisure interests and be willing to take risks in trying different or more creative activities (Reynolds 2002). The obstacles to choice and control lie in the life histories of people with learning difficulties in which often choices have been restricted, awareness of choices denied, and information and communication support have been poor, culminating in little experience of choosing (Harris 2003) and accessing. Obstacles similarly lie deep in the culture and working practices of poorly trained and poorly paid staff (Finlay *et al* 2008; McConkey and Collins, this volume). Hall *et al* (2006: 82) describe the experience of enabling access to mainstream mental health services for people with learning difficulties as involving 'somewhat tortuous and unpredictable processes'. Addressing deep cultural and attitudinal issues in access requires pervasive rather than sequential change.

The second distinction is that in simplistic models of access, access is driven either by the individual or by some formal mechanism or person in a formal role. In the first scenario we find the individual and her or his impairment blamed for failure to access. In the second we find apparently sophisticated calls for joined-up services and person-centred planning to pull the formal support together and fit it to the individual. In contrast, what we can see from the research and from individual accounts is that lived access happens at a local level of fine interaction and is frequently negotiated using informal support networks. In access to employment for example, informal support is provided by parents and carers (McConkey and Mezza 2001; Pierini *et al* 2001) and natural supports such as co-workers (Reid and Bray 1998; Wilson 2003) and peers (Gosling and Cotterill 2000). Ginny Aird and her co-authors (this volume) show the ongoing role of their parents in facilitating access to holidays and good health and also how much they gain from each other. Hall *et al* (2006: 83) argue that services that do not understand the 'complex social networks on which people with learning disabilities often rely' fail to facilitate access. The activity of social networks of informal supporters tends to be under-researched and not well understood because often people's knowledge is tacit and approach intuitive. Goodley (2000) found that in advocacy work interactions were influenced by a range of factors including the model of disability held and the social capital, knowledge, attitudes, values, expectations and assumptions of the advocacy worker. These are likely to be influential in access work too, both formal and informal.

A common theme emerging from the chapters that follow is that the quality of support makes all the difference to lived access. Yet to achieve quality support, formal measures are not enough. Quality support is embedded in the values and ethos of a service or community, which develop in interaction with the values and attitudes of key individuals. Quality support, like the empowerment discussed by Finlay *et al* (2008: 350):

> is about what happens between people moment by moment, in the mundane details of everyday interaction [and about] the way people talk to each other, in what utterances are taken up and what are ignored, in how and what options are offered, in how information is presented, how spaces are opened up for people to express preferences and how spaces are shut down. (Jenkinson 1993)

Moreover, the quality of support acts influences (and is influenced by) the personal attitudes and motivation of individuals with learning difficulties (see for example Flynn *et al* 2002). This is about the agency of individuals noted by Shakespeare (2006) as being much neglected in the social model of disability but intrinsic to an interactional model of how lives are actually improved.

Our third distinction is that in simplistic models there are access problems and access solutions. At the most simplistic end of the continuum these solutions are of the 'one size fits all' variety so that, for example, the problem of communicating information is solved by a simplified version of a text with pictures. However, simplifying text does not necessarily address the imbalance of power between information givers and receivers and does not always imply people with learning difficulties have been consulted in selecting the information needing to be communicated (Ward and Townsley 2005). Jan Walmsley's chapter illustrates how much more complex the challenge of making ideas accessible really is. Similarly, in simplistic terms technology may be seen as providing the way forward, whereas in reality often low-tech solutions are more effective (see Chris Abbott and Cate Detheridge's chapter). The lived experience of access is that both problems and solutions are more complex. This contrasts with what Thurman (2005: 85) argues is 'the commonly held aspiration that it is possible to make information accessible for everyone' with accompanying oversimplified 'well meaning but misguided tokenism'. Problems with access may emerge from, or be exacerbated by, other people's good intentions as much as bad. Access solutions may not be quick or cheap. Often the way forward involves a mixture of technological and human support, with sensitive communication and extra time for people (staff/family as well as those with learning difficulties) to absorb the idea or practise the skill needed for access to happen. In augmentative and alternative communication, access is no longer viewed just as a problem of matching the communication device to the person, but as a complex mix of technological, physical, cognitive, linguistic and social interaction factors (Higginbotham *et al* 2007). Sometimes fundamental changes would prevent access problems from arising and solutions from being needed.

In addition to contrasting simplistic notions of access with lived access, developing conceptual understanding of access can be aided by contrasting lived access and ideal access. In this the distinction becomes between how things are (often meaning that access is experienced as a struggle) and how they should be (see Nind and Seale 2009). Seminar participants repeatedly described their experiences of access as:

- involving a special effort to get ordinary things to which access should be standard;
- temporary, one-off or even fleeting, requiring resilience for continual renegotiation, when ideally access should be sustained and progressive;
- patchy, available to some but not all people with learning difficulties, whereas access should be equitable and inclusive of all;
- at the mercy of others, be it people's good will, additional effort or simply the transport turning up, rather than within the control of people with learning difficulties;
- offered via uniform strategies making for partial access, rather than via personalised strategies or flexible ways of working making for meaningful access;

- fragmented rather than holistic, thus requiring more effort to bring aspects of access together; and
- tokenistic, when it should be genuine and authentic.

There are echoes of the tensions listed here across the chapters in this book.

Access stories

Finally in this introductory chapter we want to consider the importance of narratives of access; for what we shared in the seminar series and what we share in this edited collection, are access stories. Smith and Sparkes (2008: 18) argue that, 'We organise our experiences into narratives and assign meaning to them through storytelling. Narratives thereby help constitute and construct our realities and modes of being.' Furthermore, narratives help, they go on to say, to give 'substance, artfulness and texture to people's lives'. Campbell and McNamara (2007: 99) state the obvious but important in their opening claim that 'a great deal of human learning occurs through storytelling'. Telling stories about access is one of the key ways in which we have been able to make accessible to each other both abstract ideas and concrete experiences. Storytelling has a social dimension (Elliot 2005) and the power of narratives is that there are characters we can identify with, journeys we can imagine sharing, and contexts that enable us to understand more deeply and thereby draw out our own connections to the story. Storytelling brings together insight and empathy and connects the private and public worlds (Goodley 1996).

This book provides a space for a range of people to tell their access stories. In doing so it demonstrates that each individual story illuminates a wider picture. One important note is that the voices of people with more profound learning difficulties are missing; no kind of access enables them to be heard directly in a book using symbolic language/written media. Sometimes in discussion of the key issues the relevance for this group of individuals is very much felt. At other times they appear absent. We echo some of the challenges made with regard to voice in qualitative research (see e.g. Jackson and Mazzei 2009) when we argue that we must hear silences too. In this spirit we would encourage readers to read and listen to our access stories in a way that 'will encourage [them/us] to invite the voices present in the silences rather than avoiding them' (Mazzei 2009: 51). Reflecting on the non-verbal interactions we have with people with profound and multiple impairments in light of the chapters will help in beginning to know more than just that which is 'readily discernible, knowable and transparent' (Mazzei 2009: 50).

We have chosen to organise the chapters thematically, integrating chapters by authors with contrasting backgrounds within sections so that, by reading access stories told from different perspectives alongside each other, we can cross disciplinary and professional boundaries without falling into the crevasses between. In each section we can hear people's voices directly and we can hear echoes of those voices through the resonating themes. As Goodley (1996: 336) argues, 'stories not only present the subjective definition of a situation, as accounted for by their tellers, but they also highlight the social constraints upon each individual'. Nonetheless, on their own, the stories of the people with learning difficulties in this book (Chapters 5, 8 and 11) could be reduced by the reader to sound-bites (see Goodley 1996) but, by locating them within the overall discussions of access structures and processes, they become an integral part of the theoretical project. Bringing together story upon story builds a picture of access that is informed by experience and research; that is detailed, subtle and nuanced. Thus, collectively these access stories highlight the human dimension of seeking better conceptual understanding of access, enriching our understandings such that we might both build theory and improve practice.

Notes

1 DirectGov 'Everyday Life and Leisure'
   (www.direct.gov.uk/en/DisabledPeople/Everydaylifeandaccess)
2 DirectGov 'Support and School'
   (www.direct.gov.uk/en/DisabledPeople/EducationandTraining/Schools)

References

Affleck, J. Q., Edgar, E., Levine, P. and Kortering, L. (1990) Post-school status of pupils classified as mildly mentally retarded, learning disabled, or non-handicapped: Does it get better over time?, *Education and Training in Mental Retardation*, **25**, 315–24.

Aird, R. (2001) *The Education and Care of Children with Severe, Profound and Multiple Learning Difficulties*, London: David Fulton.

Allan. J. (2005) Inclusive learning experiences: learning from children and young people, in M. Nind, J. Rix, K. Sheehy and K. Simmons (eds) *Curriculum and Pedagogy in Inclusive Education: Values into practice*, London: Routledge.

Aspis, S. (1997) Self-advocacy for people with learning difficulties: does it have a future?, *Disability & Society*, **12**, 647–54.

Aston, J., Dewson, S., Dukas, G. and Dyson, A. (2005) *Post-16 Transitions: A longitudinal study of young people with special educational needs – wave three*, DfES Research Report RR685.

Beart, S., Hawkins, D., Stenfert Kroese, B., Smithson, P. and Tolosa, I. (2001) Barriers to accessing leisure opportunities for people with learning disabilities, *British Journal of Learning Disabilities*, **29**, 4, 133–8.

Benjamin, S. (2002) 'Valuing diversity': a cliché for the 21st century?, *International Journal of Inclusive Education*, **6**, 4, 309–23.

Beyer, S., Grove, B., Schneider, J., Simon, K., Williams, V., Heyman, A., Swift, P. and Krijnen-Kemp, E. (2004) *Working Lives: The role of day centres in supporting people with learning disabilities into employment*, London: Department for Work and Pensions.

Campbell, A. and McNamara, O. (2007) Ways of telling: the use of practitioners' stories, in A. Campbell and S. Groundwater-Smith (eds) *An Ethical Approach to Practitioner Research*, London: Routledge.

Caton, S. and Kagan, C. (2006) Tracing post-school destinations of young people with mild intellectual disabilities: the problem of attrition, *Journal of Applied Research in Intellectual Disabilities*, 19, 143–52.

Church, R. L. and Marston, J. R. (2003) Measuring accessibility for people with a disability, *Geographical Analysis*, **35,** 1, 83–96.

Clough, P. (2000) Routes to inclusion, in P. Clough and J. Corbett (eds) *Theories of Inclusive Education*, London: Paul Chapman.

Department of Health (2001) *Valuing People: A new strategy for learning disability in the 21st century*, London: The Stationery Office.

Department of Health (2007) *Valuing People Now: From progress to transformation*, London: The Stationery Office.

Department for Education & Schools, Department of Health and Department of Work and Pensions (2007) *Progression Through Partnership*, London: HM Government.

Department for Work and Pensions (2004) *Building on New Deal: Local solutions meeting individual needs,* London: DWP, Online (http://www.dwp.gov.uk/publications/dwp/2004/buildingonnewdeal/mainreport.pdf) (accessed 10 December 2008).

Devas, M. (2003) Support and access in sports and leisure provision, *Disability & Society*, **18,** 2, 231–45.

Dewson, S., Aston, J., Bates, P., Ritchie, H and Dyson, A (2004) *Post-16 Transitions: A longitudinal study of young people with special educational needs – wave two*, DfES Research Report RR582.

Elliott, J. (2005) *Using Narrative in Social Research: Qualitative and quantitative approaches*, London: Sage.

Emmanuel, J., and Ackroyd, D. (1996) Breaking down barriers, in C. Barnes, and G. Mercer (eds) *Exploring the Divide: Illness and disability*, Leeds: Leeds Disability Press.

Eng, T. R., Maxfield, A., Patrick, K., Deering, M. J., Ratzan, S. C. and Gustafson, D. H. (1998) Access to health information and support – a public highway or a private road?, *Journal of the American Medical Association*, **280,** 15, 1371–5.

Felce, D. (1997) Defining and applying the concept of *quality of life, Journal of Intellectual Disability Research*, **41,** 2, 126–35.

Further Education Development Agency (1997) *A Real Job with Prospects: Supported employment opportunities for adults with learning difficulties and disabilities*, Bristol: FEDA.

Finlay, W. M. L., Walton, C. and Ataki, C. (2008) Promoting choice and control in residential services for people with learning disabilities, *Disability and Society*, **23,** 4, 349–60.

Florian, L., Maudslay, L., Dee, L. and Byers, R. (2000) What happens when schooling ends? Further education opportunities for pupils with profound and complex learning difficulties, *Skill Journal*, **67,** 16–23.

Flynn, M., Hollins, S. and Perez, W. (2002) Being seen… to be healthy: accessing healthcare, supporting healthy lifestyles, in S. Carnaby (ed.) *Learning Disability Today*, Brighton: Pavilion.

Goodley, D. (1996) Tales of hidden lives: a critical examination of life history research with people who have learning difficulties, *Disability and Society*, **11,** 3, 333–48.

Goodley, D. (2000) *Self-advocacy in the Lives of People with Learning Difficulties: The Politics of Resilience*, Buckingham: Open University Press.

Goodley, D. (2005) Empowerment, self-advocacy and resilience, *Journal of Intellectual Disabilities*, **9,** 4, 333–43.

Gosling, V. and Cotterill, L. (2000) An employment project as a route to social inclusion for people with learning difficulties?, *Disability & Society*, **15,** 7, 1001–18.

Hall, I., Higgins, A., Parkes, C., Hassiotis, A. and Samuels, S. (2006) The development of a new integrated mental health service for people with learning disabilities, *British Journal of Learning Disabilities*, **34**, 82–7.

Harris, J. (2003) Time to make up your mind: why choosing is difficult, *British Journal of Learning Disabilities*, **31**, 1, 3–8.

Her Majesty's Stationery Office (1995) *Disability Discrimination Act*, Online (http://www.legislation.hmso.gov.uk/acts/acts1995/Ukpga_19950050_en_1.htm) (accessed 10 December 2008).

Her Majesty's Stationery Office. (2001) *The Special Educational Needs and Disability Act*, Online (http://www.legislation.hmso.gov.uk/acts/acts2001/20010010.htm) (accessed 10 December 2008).

Higginbotham, D. J., Shane, H., Russell, S. and Caves, K. (2007) Access to AAC: present, past, and future, *Augmentative and Alternative Communication*, **23**, 3, 243–57.

Jackson, A.Y. and Mazzei, L. A. (2009) *Voice in Qualitative Inquiry: Challenging conventional, interpretive and critical conceptions in qualitative research*, Abingdon and New York: Routledge.

Jenkinson, J. C. (1993) Who shall decide? The relevance of theory and research to decision-making by people with an intellectual disability, *Disability, Handicap & Society*, **8**, 361–75.

Johnson, R. and Hegarty, J. R. (2003) Websites as educational motivators for adults with learning disabilities, *British Journal of Educational Technology*, **34**, 4, 479–86.

Learning Skills Council (2006) *Learning for Living and Work: Improving education and training*, Coventry: Learning Skills Council.

McConkey, R. and Mezza, F. (2001) Employment aspirations of people with learning disabilities attending day centres, *Journal of Learning Disabilities*, **5**, 4, 309–18.

McKean, E. (2005) *New Oxford American Dictionary* (2nd edn), New York: Oxford University Press.

Mazzei, L. A. (2009) An impossibly full voice, in A.Y. Jackson and L. A. Mazzei (eds) *Voice in Qualitative Inquiry: Challenging conventional, interpretive and critical conceptions in qualitative research*, Abingdon and New York: Routledge.

Mittler, P. (2000) *Working Towards Inclusive Education: Social contexts*, London: David Fulton.

Nind, M. and Hewett, D. (2005) (2nd edn) *Access to Communication: Developing the basics of communication with people with severe learning difficulties through intensive interaction*, London: David Fulton.

Nind, M. and Seale, J. (2008) The hard work of access: lessons for education from a seminar series on concepts of access, *The SLD Experience*, **51**, 11–18.

Nind, M. and Seale, J. (2009) Concepts of access for people with learning difficulties: towards a shared understanding, *Disability & Society*, in press.

Office for Disability Issues (2006) *Disability Equality: A priority for all*, London: Office for Disability Issues.

Peter, M. (1992) A curriculum for all: a hard task for some, in T. Booth, W. Swann, M. Masterton and P. Potts (eds) *Policies for Diversity in Education*, London: Routledge.

Pierini, J., Pearson, V. and Wong, Y. (2001) Glorious work: employment of adults with a learning disability in Guangzhou from the perspective of their parents, *Disability & Society*, **16**, 2, 255–72.

Redley, M. (2008) Citizens with learning disabilities and the right to vote, *Disability and Society*, **23**, 4, 375–84.

Reid, P. M. and Bray, A. (1998) Real jobs: the perspectives of workers with learning difficulties, *Disability & Society*, **13**, 2, 229–39.

Ribot, J. C. and Peluso, N. L. (2003) A theory of access, *Rural Sociology*, **68**, 2, 153–81.

Reynolds, F. (2002) An exploratory survey of barriers and opportunities to creative leisure activity for people with learning disabilities, *British Journal of Learning Disability*, **30**, 63–7.

Riddell, S., Wilson, A. and Baron, S. (1999) Captured customers: people with learning difficulties in the social market, *British Educational Research Journal*, **25**, 4, 445–61.

Riddell, S., Wilson, A. and Baron, S. (2001) Gender, social capital and lifelong learning for people with learning difficulties, *International Studies in Sociology of Education*, **11**, 1, 3–24.

Rummery, K., Ellis, K. and Davis, A. (1999) Negotiating access to community care assessments: perspectives of front-line workers, people with disabilities and carers, *Health and Social Care in the Community*, **7**, 4, 296–300.

Russell, J. (1995) Leisure and recreation services, in: N. Malin (ed.) *Services for People with Learning Disabilities*, London: Routledge.

Shakespeare, T. (2006) *Disability Rights and Wrongs*, London: Routledge.

Singer, J. (1999) 'Why can't you be normal for once in your life?' From 'a problem with no name' to the emergence of a new category of difference, in M. Corker and S. French (eds) *Disability Discourse*, Buckingham: Open University Press.

Smith, B. and Sparkes, A. C. (2008) *Narrative and its Potential Contribution to Disability Studies*, London: Routledge.

Social Exclusion Unit (1999) *Bridging the Gap: New opportunities for 16–18 year olds not in education, employment or training*, Cm. 4405. London: The Stationery Office.

Tarleton, B. and Ward, L. (2005) Changes and choices: finding out what information young people with learning disabilities, their parents and supporters need at transition, *British Journal of Learning Disabilities*, **33**, 70–76.

Taylor, B. J., McGilloway, S. and Donnelly, M. (2004) Preparing young adults with a disability for employment, *Health and Social Care in the Community*, **12**, 2, 93–101.

Terlizzi, M. (1997) Talking about work: I used to talk about nothing else, I was excited and it got a bit too much for my parents, *Disability & Society*, **12**, 4, 501–11.

Thomas, G. and Loxley, A. (2007) (2nd edn) *Deconstructing Special Education and Constructing Inclusion*, Maidenhead: Open University Press.

Thomas, G. and O'Hanlon, C. (2001) Series editors' preface, Thomas, G. and Loxley, A., *Deconstructing Special Education and Constructing Inclusion*, Buckingham: Open University Press.

Thurman, S. (2005) Without words – meaningful information for people with high individual communication needs, *British Journal of Learning Disabilities*, **33**, 83–9.

Valuing People Support Team (2005) *The Story so Far. Valuing People. A new strategy for learning disability for the 21st century*, London: Department of Health.

Walmsley, J. and Johnson, K. (2001) *Inclusive Research with People with Learning Disabilities: Past, present and futures*, London: Jessica Kingsley.

Ward, L. and Townsley, R. (2005) 'It's about a dialogue…' Working with people with learning difficulties to develop accessible information, *British Journal of Learning Disabilities*, **33**, 59 –64.

Ware, J. (1996) *Creating a Responsive Environment*, London: David Fulton.

Wilson, A. (2003) Real jobs, learning difficulties and supported employment, *Disability & Society*, **182**, 99–115.

Wistow, R. and Schneider, J. (2003) Users' views on supported employment and social inclusion: a qualitative study of 30 people in work, *British Journal of Learning Disabilities*, **31**, 166–74.

Part 2

Access to and through information

Access in mind

A review of approaches to accessible information for people with learning disabilities

Jan Walmsley

Introduction

This chapter reviews approaches to accessible information for people with learning disabilities, with a particular emphasis on making abstract ideas accessible. It is a story that spans approximately 20 years at the time of writing (2008). There is a long history of attempts to promote literacy amongst people whose intellectual and social functioning is limited, through special education, adult education and other initiatives (Hurt, 1988; Read and Walmsley, 2006). But it was only in the late 1980s that the onus began to be put on the producers of information, rather than its recipients, to promote access. I can personally date this to circa 1986, at a time when I was part of an Open University team that had launched *Mental Handicap: Patterns for living,* a pack of learning materials that aimed to improve communication and understanding between service providers and family members. Very soon after launch, we began to be challenged by advocacy organisations, led by the Camden Society for Mentally Handicapped People, to adapt this package to enable people with learning disabilities to study (Walmsley, 1997). The result was *Patterns for Living: Working together,* a learning package that featured audio dramas of the leading characters in *Patterns for Living* and gave access to some quite complex ideas via a 'soap opera' format. This was claimed to be the first ever University course produced for people with learning disabilities, and it was part of the beginning of a movement for accessible information that has to date embraced government bodies, researchers, local and health authorities and voluntary organisations, and has arguably contributed to an acceptance that it is the duty of producers of information to make their products accessible.

The move to create accessible information is amenable to a technical review of different approaches. It also raises some quite fundamental questions about the nature of learning disability. Is learning disability, as normalisation theory has it, the result of labelling, creating a cycle of stigma and devaluation, to be remedied by the promotion of 'valued social roles' including author, adviser and consumer of accessible information? How far does accessible information go to remedy the real disadvantages experienced by people with learning disabilities and do the outcomes repay the effort and resources required? How far can the environment be manipulated, barriers reduced, to solve the limitations learning disability impose? I will touch on these questions in the conclusion to this chapter. In this chapter I will consider why accessible information has become such an important issue, review a range of approaches to producing accessible information during the past 20 years and seek to assess the extent to which accessible information reduces barriers to the participation of people with learning disabilities in society as equal citizens.

Accessible information: understanding the context

This review suggests a quite startling change in assumptions about where the responsibility for ensuring that people with learning disabilities can understand information should lie. Understanding why this shift occurred requires a knowledge of the impact of theories, in particular the social model of disability, on thinking about disability. In brief, the social model regards disability as the creation of society, rather than caused by individual impairment. It is barriers in society that exclude, not people's deficits (Oliver, 1990). Hence we see physical changes to reduce barriers such as ramps on public buildings, hearing loops, audible announcements on trains and buses, large print and Braille versions of key documents, access guidance for the internet, and legislation, such as the UK's Disability Discrimination Act, aiming to reduce these barriers. Accessible information for people with learning disabilities is part of this movement to remove barriers. Accessible information cannot be taken in isolation. It is part of a rights movement that asserts 'nothing about us without us' (Aspis, 2000: 84). This has affected assumptions about the degree to which people with learning disabilities are involved in activities that impact on their lives. I include here a brief overview of key developments, focusing on four issues: speaking out, policymaking, access to services, and research.

Speaking out

Part of the shift in philosophy is attributable to the growth of the user movement in learning disability (Bersani 1998; Buchanan and Walmsley 2006; Crawley 1988). There are very few instances of 'speaking out' before the late 20th century, given the low literacy levels amongst people with learning disabilities, and an assumption that they could not express views and opinions. One rare instance was located by the author in a letter in the papers of the Bedfordshire Hospital, Bromham:

> Dear madame or sir
> I wonder if you would in any way do me a great favour. All I want to ask you is could you by any means help me to get discharge from the care and

control. As this is my 21 years I done under your care and control. I am 36 years old. This is the first time I have written to you. Nothing like sticking up for yourself.

Ruth Gammon, 1943

Other than isolated instances like this one, user voices are unheard until the late 20th century when self-advocacy including life stories and oral histories came into vogue (Atkinson 2005). This had its beginnings in participation workshops run in the 1970s by the Campaign for People with Mental Handicaps. At these events, people with learning disabilities spoke publicly about what had happened to them in the past (Williams and Schoulz 1979). These were followed, in the 1980s, by the formation of self-advocacy groups, People First organisations and groups/committees in day and residential services (Crawley 1988). Around the late 1980s a number of established organisations began to take self-advocacy seriously. The London-based Kings Fund, led by David Towell and Andrea Whittaker, made a major contribution to its gaining a firm footing in influential circles (Towell 1988; Whittaker 1991).

The self-advocacy movement is now well established as part of the policy-making fabric. Following *Valuing People* (Department of Health 2001) the English Government funded the development of advocacy, specifically self-advocacy organisations, and a system of consultation that aims to have broad representation from people with learning difficulties; the National Forum and Regional Forums. This commitment comes with obligations in the shape of targets and prescribed outcomes (Department of Health 2004; 2007). These have the effect of assimilating advocacy, including self-advocacy, into the service structure. For people with learning difficulties engagement is primarily through Partnership Boards, which operate at a local level bringing together local stake-holders as a means of improving services and developing strategies to enhance the lives of people with learning difficulties. This involvement puts a premium on accessible information; without it, the involvement of people is largely symbolic (Buchanan and Walmsley 2006; Fyson *et al* 2004). The development of 'speaking up' boosted accessible means of communicating. Not only were people needing to understand what other people say, they also needed to have means of expression for their own voices. I will consider examples of how this has been achieved in a review of technical approaches, later in this chapter.

Policymaking

There has been a fundamental shift in the role of people with learning diffi-culties in policymaking. This can be shown with reference to the two major White Papers, *Better Service for the Mentally Handicapped* (Department of Health and Social Security 1971) and *Valuing People* (Department of Health 2001). The 1971 White Paper sought to 'speak' only to policymakers and senior profes-sionals. Its language was formal, its format, an A5 booklet with no illustrations, was sober and uninviting. By 2001 when the next English White Paper to be concerned with learning disability, *Valuing People,* was published, it was produced in a separate accessible format, accompanied by an audio tape (see Figure 2.1). It was also informed by extensive consultation with groups representing people with learning difficulties and their families (Welshman and Walmsley 2006). Its successor, *Valuing People Now* (Department of Health 2007), has continued this approach, and its effectiveness as a mechanism is reviewed in the next section.

Access to services

It is a similar story about access to services. In 1971, top-down planning characterised the *Better Services* White Paper. The White Paper advocated provision of more community-based residential and day care services, and projected the numbers required for the population. There was no discussion of choice for consumers, of cultural suitability, or of including the people who would use the services in discussions about what was required. There was an unstated assumption that professionals and civil servants were the arbiters of what was

Figure 2.1 Picture of front cover of the accessible version of *Valuing People* (Department of Health 2001)

needed. By 2001, the White Paper advocated choice, independence, improved information for service users and carers, access to high quality mainstream healthcare, jobs, support for carers and the like. Policies like 'Direct Payments' and 'In Control Budgets' seek to transfer control of decision making by giving the budget for service provision to service users and/or their families and advocates. In 2007, a new consultation, *Valuing People Now* was launched on the priorities for the next three years (Department of Health 2007) This sought views from a wide range of people about priorities (see Figure 2.2).

Do you agree that the 4 big priorities are the most important things that Valuing People Now should work on?

People having more choice and control over their lives and services (Personalisation)

(tick one of the boxes)   ✓

Yes, I agree   No, I don't agree

What people do in the days and evenings – including getting a paid job

(tick one of the boxes)   ✓

Yes, I agree   No, I don't agree

People being healthy and getting a good service from the NHS

(tick one of the boxes)   ✓

Yes, I agree   No, I don't agree

Figure 2.2 Extract from accessible questionnaire contained within *Valuing People Now* (Department of Health 2007: 3)

Figure 2.2 illustrates that the principle that people should have choices over the types of services they want is well enshrined in policy: the 'personalisation' agenda. Accessible information, as in the questionnaire extract, is one key to the achievement of this.

Research

Researchers have been influenced by, and sometimes led, the move to inclusion. Other than some celebrated biographies, such as by Joey Deacon (1974), this began in the 1980s, initially in the US (Bogdan and Taylor 1982). Researchers began to find ways to 'give voice' to people's experiences. Early UK examples include a publication of life stories by Yorkshire Arts Circus (Ward 1989), Potts and Fido's oral history of a mental handicap hospital: *A Fit Person to be Removed* (Potts and Fido 1991) and Atkinson and Williams edited anthology, *Know Me as I am* (Atkinson and Williams 1990). Whilst these did not foreground accessibility to people with learning difficulties, the use of illustrations, photos and direct quotations began to create ways in. Subsequently autobiographies, biographies, life stories and accounts of experiences within services have been produced using a range of formats (Walmsley and Johnson 2003).

Not only has there been this shift to including people in research in various ways, academics have begun to accept that they have an obligation to improve access to research in learning disability. The Learning Disability Research Initiative, for example, funded in the wake of *Valuing People,* produced reports with parallel texts (see Figure 2.3).

The Norah Fry Research Centre produces 'Plain Facts' summaries of research, funded by the Joseph Rowntree Foundation, on tape and in print and available online.[1] In 2006 the leading British journal, *The British Journal of Learning Disabilities,* introduced a requirement that accessible extracts be included with published papers. The paradigm shift can be graphically illustrated with a 'then' and 'now' comparison:

Then (pre-1980s):
researchers decided on the questions to ask, and the methods;
people with learning difficulties were the objects of research;
reports not accessible.
Now:
people with learning difficulties help decide the questions, and methods;
people with learning difficulties do research;
accessible reports are required for research that involves learning disability topics.

Of course, this can be exaggerated. There are still many instances of research and publications that are not accessible. But much ingenuity has been used to create research methods and publications that go some way to genuine inclusion of the

Newsletter issue 1 September 2003

the learning disability research initiative

People with Learning Disabilities Services, Inclusion and Partnership

❖❖❖Editorial

We are delighted to be sending out this first newsletter about research funded by the Department of Health in relation to people with learning disabilities. Ken Simons, a lead researcher on one of the funded research projects passed away suddenly earlier this year. Ken committed his working life to people with learning disabilities, to supporting people with learning disabilities and to making research meaningful to them. We are therefore particularly proud to be presenting this newsletter in plain as well as technical language.

Valuing People:

For many people research is not easy to understand. It is not easy to see when it is relevant or useful. We have been employed as co-ordinators of the Learning Disability Research Initiative by the Department of Health and, as part of our role, have been asked to inform people about the research projects and their findings. This will last until all the projects are completed in three years time.

❖❖❖So, what is the Learning Disability Research Initiative?

Valuing People (para 10.15) committed £2m to research aimed at providing an evidence base to inform the planning, management and delivery of new services designed to improve the lives of people with learning disabilities and their families. The Research and Development Division at the Department of Health has managed the resultant research programme titled, People with Learning Disabilities: Services, Inclusion and Partnership and funding has been directed through the Policy Research Programme.

❖❖❖How were projects chosen?

A Commissioning Group made up of people from the RDD, policy divisions of the Department of Health and government departments relating to education and transport, academics, people with learning disabilities and their supporters helped to decide: the most important areas for research; how to send out invitations for researchers to apply to undertake research; how each proposal was to be assessed including external assessment by people with learning disabilities; and what research proposals would be selected. There were 144 proposals altogether! Ten of these have been funded to date. In a follow up bid relating to health needs and to assessing the impact of Valuing People two more projects have been funded and another on participation in research is planned. More news of these will appear on the LDRI web site shortly.

We expect that initial findings will very soon begin to emerge from the projects and it should not therefore be long before the findings are being converted to practice. To provide advice on how this might be handled a new Reference Group has been set up with a composition reflecting government, service provider, academic and service user interests.

Gordon Grant and Paul Ramcharan, Co-ordinators of the Learning Disability Research Initiative. Contact: g.grant@sheffield.ac.uk or p.ramcharan@sheffield.ac.uk or Tel: 0114 2266840.

1

Figure 2.3 Example of newsletter produced by the Learning Disability Research Initiative

views, skills and experiences people with learning difficulties have to offer. This has contributed significantly to thinking and techniques of access.

In summary, then, there has been a huge shift in thinking about the rights of people with learning disabilities to be included in many activities such as poli-cymaking, research and choice of services, and this has been accompanied by recognition that user groups, such as self-advocacy groups, have a key role to play. Accessible information both produced for and produced by people with learning disabilities has been an integral part of these developments. I will now review different ways this has been attempted.

A review of accessible information techniques

It would be impossible to cover the full range of approaches to accessible information in this chapter. I have, instead, selected examples from the following fields to analyse in some depth: policy documents, education, research, reports and consultations, and research by people with learning difficulties. The focus is on making *ideas* accessible, as this is probably the most challenging aspect. The review covers the following approaches to making information accessible:

- parallel texts: easy to read summaries of full report;
- easy to read text sometimes with line drawings or photos;
- story so far and summaries;
- short plain language summaries of longer reports and chapters;
- video, audio, DVD;
- IT: internet, websites.

Policy

The approach taken in the major policy initiatives associated with learning disability in England has been to produce a full report, and to accompany this with an easy to read summary; what I have termed 'parallel texts'. I have taken as my example the *Valuing People* (Department of Health 2001) White Paper as this has been the central document in England since its publication. The White Paper was published at the same time as an accessible version, illustrated with cartoon type drawings (see Figure 2.1). The 'translation' of quite complex abstract ideas about rights, a central theme of the White Paper, is the area I focus on here. The accessible version says of rights: 'Having Legal and Civil Rights: People with learning disabilities are citizens too' (http://www.publications.doh.gov.uk/ learningdisabilities/access/intro3.htm). The full version is:

> Legal and Civil Rights: The Government is committed to enforceable civil rights for disabled people in order to eradicate discrimination in society. People with learning disabilities have the right to a decent education, to grow up to vote, to marry and have a family, and to express their opinions, with help and support to do so where necessary. The Government is committed to providing comprehensive guidance for electoral administrators on helping disabled people, including those with learning disabilities, through the whole electoral process – from registering to vote until polling day itself. All public services will treat people

with learning disabilities as individuals with respect for their dignity, and challenge discrimination on all grounds including disability. People with learning disabilities will also receive the full protection of the law when necessary. (Department of Health 2001: 23)

Whereas the accessible version is so brief as to be almost a headline, the full version gives a great deal more detail. The term 'citizen', used in the accessible version, does not appear in the full version which instead spells out the types of rights it is referring to. I would argue that the accessible version is almost misleading in its attempt to be simple. 'Citizen' is not a simple concept, and has little meaning unless attached to more detailed exposition of the rights associated with it. There is a danger that in the drive to be accessible, full meaning is lost. It may be that making ideas on rights accessible to people with learning difficulties requires more words, not less, and is more than one document can achieve in isolation.

Reports and consultations

Since *Valuing People* (Department of Health 2001) there has been more consistent application of some of the principles of making information accessible in Government reports and consultations. The use of photographs has replaced the somewhat childish line drawings that were in vogue when *Valuing People* was produced. I have selected an extract from the Health Care Commission's investigation into the service for people with learning disabilities provided by Sutton and Merton Primary Care Trust (Health Care Commission 2007). There is an accessible version of its methods and findings, an extract from which is reproduced in Figure 2.4.

Photos have replaced the cartoons used in *Valuing People*. There is a commendable attempt at summarizing what was found to be wrong, though the photos do not enhance this reader's ability to understand the text. The language used is simple but requires a reasonable level of literacy, probably higher than that demanded by tabloid newspapers. In practice, this type of report should make it possible for a supporter to help people with learning difficulties with reasonable communication skills to understand the findings. It is unlikely to be usable directly by any but the most mildly learning disabled people.

The consultation associated with *Valuing People Now* also uses photos and a carefully designed layout to facilitate comment from a wide range of people (see Figure 2.2). It is designed to be used in association with the 'easier to read' version of *Valuing People Now,* which is similar in format to the Healthcare Commission's report cited above. Again, this can be seen as an aid to supporters to help people make informed comment. However, the tick box agree/don't agree format, while pretty accessible, also restricts what people can contribute to agreeing, or otherwise, to proposals formulated by others.

What we found when we looked at the services

- there were some good services, for example Osborne House and the day centre at Orchard Hill Hospital
- we found that people were looked after in a way that was easy for the staff but that was not always what was best for the people living there
- people did not have a lot to do and sometimes only had four hours a week of doing activities such as learning new things, painting or listening to music. Most of these activities were at the hospital

- most of the houses were not suitable because it was difficult for people who use wheelchairs to get around
- we found that sometimes people were not given the privacy they need because there was not enough space
- sometimes people were not treated in a respectful way such as not being told what was happening or why something was happening
- many people did not get the chance to see staff who have special training and are good at understanding what help people need such as help with feelings and behaviours, and help with eating and drinking

Figure 2.4 An extract from an accessible version of a report by the Healthcare Commission (2007) *Investigation into the service for people with learning disabilities provided by Sutton and Merton Primary Care Trust* © Commission for Healthcare Audit & Inspection 2007

Education

The example I have selected to illustrate approaches in education comes from *Working as Equal People,* an inclusive package from the Open University, produced in partnership with a People First organisation (Open University 1996) The process by which this was achieved is described in Walmsley (1997). The approach used in *Equal People* was to introduce each topic with a four-page highly illustrated accessible version, including activities based on audio visual components, both documentary and drama. This was followed by a less accessible, more detailed chapter, with summaries, called 'Story So Far' boxes, to enable supporters to help people with learning disabilities understand the fuller text. An example is produced from the topic called 'Working Together for Welcoming Communities' (see Figure 2.5).

As an author I can testify that it was an important discipline to have to summarise in relatively simple language at regular intervals. However, providing access to the ideas in *Equal People* proved to be demanding and highly skilled

Box 9.1 Story So Far

We've been thinking about communities

Sometimes building communities means helping people joining in with their local community through sharing leisure and work opportunities

Sometime it means helping people get a sense of themselves as a separate community

Sometimes it means getting together to decide what a particular community wants for itself

Figure 2.5 Example of a 'Story So Far' box used in *Learning Disability: Working as equal people* (Open University 1996: 59)

work for supporters. The written summaries are just tools for people to use. In themselves, except for people with quite mild disabilities, they are but tools. Undoubtedly, if such a package were to be produced today, greater use could be made of interactive technology, the internet, memory boxes, etc., which I will consider later.

Research: short summaries of longer reports

There are numerous instances of research reports that summarise longer reports. Plain Facts, the Norah Fry Research Centre's long-running initiative is one such example, which uses audio recordings and printed illustrated summaries. It covers diverse topics including housing, education and parenting. Like many examples of accessible summaries, the approach is to bullet point the key points and use illustrations (in this case line drawings) to support the message. A recent example is shown in Figure 2.6, taken from The Plain Facts summary of Beth Tarleton and Joyce Howarth's research into parents with learning difficulties (Tarleton and Howarth 2006). As with all the illustrations cited so far in this Chapter, the illustrations appear to function better to break up the text, and make the reports appear inviting, rather than illuminate the meanings.

An alternative approach is to provide accessible abstracts in print only. This is the approach adopted by the *British Journal of Learning Disabilities* since 2006. Authors of original papers are required to provide a plain language summary of their work. One example, taken from a recent issue, is from 'How we developed a multi disciplinary screening project for people with Down's Syndrome given the increased prevalence of early onset dementia' by Nicola Jervis and Linda Prinsloo (2008: 13). The accessible summary reads:

> People with Down's Syndrome are more likely to develop dementia than the general population and at an earlier age.
> Researchers and clinicians who have looked into this have said that all people with Down's Syndrome should be assessed once in early adulthood so that people know what their skill level is in case changes occur later on. This article talks about how we did this in Manchester.

Parents with learning difficulties

More people with learning difficulties are becoming parents. People with learning difficulties can be good parents if they are given the right support.

Sometimes people think that people with learning difficulties can't be good parents.

The government says that parents with learning difficulties should be given support to help them be good parents.

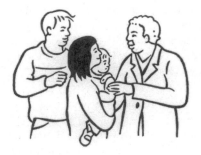

Some services around the country are supporting adults with learning difficulties to be good parents.

Figure 2.6 Extract from Plain Facts 47: 'Being good parents', May 2006

It will be noted that some of the language: 'dementia', 'clinicians' is unlikely to be readily understood without further explanation; that some concepts such as 'general population' and 'early adulthood' may be problematic; and that there is no information about the bulk of the paper, namely how this was undertaken in Manchester. In common with many such accessible summaries, it is perhaps enough to whet the appetite, but by itself it does not convey the richness of the article. One might suggest that this could be improved by adding bullet points on what was found, and its implications. But this runs the risk of creating a long list, which can be off-putting for people who read only a little.

It is difficult to escape the conclusion that accessible summaries represent headlines that fail to convey the complexity of research reports, and that some authors lack the skills to unpack technical language. In reflecting upon one of my own efforts to summarise a chapter I wrote on caring (Walmsley 2000), I note that while I conveyed a reasonable impression of the life stories on which I had based the chapter in order to concretise an abstract argument, I did not manage to communicate the rather subtle argument that was the main thread, that women with learning disabilities have a complex relationship with 'caring', as both cared for and carers, and that sometimes are denied the opportunities to care afforded to other women.

Research by people with learning disabilities

The final category in this section is to consider how research by people with learning difficulties is communicated. Researchers have gone to enormous lengths to include people in a whole range of ways, comprehensively reviewed by Walmsley and Johnson (2003). There have been developments since. Anita Young and Rosemary Chesson for example, developed a careful technique to enable people with learning disabilities and carers to decide what are the priority areas for research to help people with learning disabilities be healthy (Young and Chesson 2008). My focus here is on how such research is reported. Much of this type of work has been reported in accessible illustrated summaries such as used in Plain Facts, including a number of Plain Facts summaries. For example Plain Facts 48 was conducted by a group of young people from North Somerset People First on what people need to know about growing up. As this approach has been considered earlier in this chapter, I will consider here some more text-based approaches. One example is of a chapter I co-authored with Jackie Downer, a self-advocate, in 1997. It involved audio-taped interviews with Jackie, in which my contribution was scribe and interpreter. The chapter, 'Shouting the loudest' is a classic academic text with no 'accessible' features. It seeks to represent Jackie's views, but the context is provided by me as academic author (Walmsley and Downer 1997).

The second example is of the National Survey of Adults with Learning Difficulties in England and Wales, 2003/4 (Emerson *et al* 2005), conducted in the wake of *Valuing People* by the University of Lancaster, BRMB, and Central

England People First, an advocacy organisation controlled by people with learning difficulties. Central England People First contributed to the research design, the training of the research team, and the final report, which is available online with an audio commentary.[2] The research team developed a comprehensive set of tools to access the views of people with quite limited communication abilities, for example show cards to ask questions (see Figure 2.7).

The Report is unusual in that it was only produced in an accessible version. It used the familiar device of reporting in plain language with line drawings, but also included a commentary from the self-advocates involved (see Figure 2.8). Because it is available on the web, those with the technology can also listen to the findings.

Use of the internet, with its capabilities for using visual and audio technologies combined with print, opens up channels of opportunity for self-representation, access to information, social networks, friendships etc. (Seale 2007). There has, however, been a somewhat uncritical acceptance of its potential. Morris in an as yet unpublished paper claims, 'People with learning difficulties face a significant risk of being further socially excluded through not having access to digital technology' and argues that the barriers people experience have been little researched. Seale (2007) reviewed the home pages of people with Down Syndrome with a view to considering the value of online publishing as a vehicle for self-advocacy. She concluded that although several authors had or claimed the technical skills to author their pages, the evidence was that authors were supported by family members in writing their narratives. She concluded that this potentially compromised online publishing as a vehicle for self-advocacy.

My final example is of an imaginative use of photographs in a Heritage Lottery-funded project to tell the history of Day Centres in Croydon, an outer London Borough where, in common with many other areas, there was a Day Centre closure programme. The project worker located old photos and artefacts, and visited the buildings with current and former users. These were a way to prompt reminiscence. Helen Graham, the project worker, recorded people's commentaries, and used them in combination in the final report (see Figure 2.9).

How happy do you feel about your life at the moment?

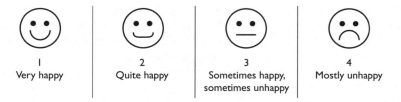

Figure 2.7 Example of show cards used by research team as part of a National Survey of Adults with Learning Difficulties in England and Wales, conducted in 2003/4 (Emerson *et al* 2005)

A Place to Live

We think too few people (less than one in seven) live on their own or with a partner. Too many young people still live with their parents and too many older people live in supported accommodation. Living independently makes many choices possible but, just like everyone else, people with learning difficulties worry about safety in the area they live in. We don't think this should stop people living independently. They should have the choice of being independent <u>and</u> safe.

We were not surprised that so many people's privacy was not respected and that most people in supported accommodation did not have a choice about who they lived with and where. As people with learning difficulties the right to have choice about a place to live and to privacy are very important.

Ian Davies & Karen Spencer

We asked people about where they lived and who they lived with.

Just over two in three people (69%) were living in private households. This means that they were living alone, with a partner or with their parents or other relatives. Just under one in three people (31%) were living in some form of supported accommodation.

Of the people living in private households:

○ nearly three out of four people (73%) were living with their parent(s)
○ one in six (17%) were living with other relatives

27

Figure 2.8 Example of commentary on research findings by research advocates included as part of report on the National Survey of Adults with Learning Difficulties in England and Wales, conducted in 2003/4 (Emerson *et al* 2005:27)

In my view, this use of specific photographs, rather than generalised photos (as in the Healthcare Commission report) or line drawings, makes the illustrations of greater value to the non-reader. Technology prevents me from illustrating the voice boxes that people were able to activate at the project exhibition, another highly accessible technique.

Figure 2.9 Example of how real photographs can facilitate production and reporting of accessible information (Helen Graham and the Croydon History of Day Centres Project 2008)

Discussion and conclusion

In discussing approaches to making research by people with learning disabilities accessible, I have covered only a fraction of the work in the public domain. It falls into two categories. The first is the illustrated summary report. It has the drawback of oversimplifying and, unless the illustrations are very carefully selected (which is rare), using pictures to do little more than break up the text. The second is to write standard reports, articles, books and chapters, but to ensure people with learning difficulties are represented in ways which they choose. It does not directly promote access by people with intellectual disabilities; it does promote access to the complexities of people's experiences by others. One advantage it has is that it does not lose the complexity of meaning that seems almost unavoidable when the summary approach is used. Although digital technology has the technical potential to transform this field of endeavour, challenges of access, capability, skills and confidence may preclude this potential from being used.

The extent to which the many and commendable efforts to improve access to ideas reduce and remove barriers is debatable. This is important. However, as Redley (2008) notes in relation to the 'Right to Vote Information Pack',[3] there is a tendency to equate learning disability with low levels of literacy. This is but one manifestation of a much more complex impairment that inhibits understanding of abstract ideas and, in some cases, Redley (2008: 283) argues, there is a lack of capacity:

Commitment to the normalizing goals of Valuing People, equal rights, independence, choice and inclusion should not preclude discussion of the fact that some citizens are unable to exert their right to vote, are dependent upon others making choices for them and are consequently excluded from important public events like elections.

This rather bleak view brings us back to the questions I posed in the introduction. Is learning disability, as normalisation theory has it, the result of labelling, creating a cycle of stigma and devaluation, to be remedied by the promotion of 'valued social roles' including author, adviser and consumer of accessible information? Promoting access is an important element of developing 'valued social roles'. Producing accessible versions of policy, consultations, reports and research sends a clear message that people should be included, that efforts should be made to enable understanding. Furthermore, producing accessible documents offers work opportunities for people with learning disabilities, to author, advise and indeed to critique accessible versions. Organisations like CHANGE in the UK[4] offer people real jobs, some of which specialise in accessible information. This does not, however, demonstrate conclusively that stigma is the only or even major cause of devaluation. Valued social roles can go some way to reducing devaluation, but as I suggest below, other difficulties remain.

How far does accessible information go to remedy the real disadvantages experienced by people with learning disabilities? Do the outcomes repay the effort and resources required? In this chapter I have sought to present a balanced view of the benefits of the drive to accessible information, while acknowledging that it is often as much symbolic as practical. It is resource-intensive to produce good quality accessible information. Although human ingenuity can overcome many challenges, the extent to which the many and commendable efforts to improve access to ideas reduce and remove barriers is debatable.

How far can the environment be manipulated, barriers reduced, to solve the limitations learning disability impose? It is not proven that accessible approaches to information taken alone do more than reduce these barriers for some people, those who are already literate. However, unlike Redley, I am optimistic, and would argue that accessible information is a tool to be used *with* people with learning disabilities by skilled supporters. As Jane Seale put it, we should 'recognise the *resilience* that might be created through interdependent collaboration with support workers' (Seale 2007: 185).

In conclusion, there has been a significant movement in a number of important areas to develop accessible information for people with learning disabilities. There has also been a burgeoning of ways in which people's views and experiences can be communicated to others. This is of major symbolic and political significance. However, it is hard to find evidence that these approaches have made a major difference to people's understanding of complex ideas, or ability to convey them. Most of the approaches illustrated in this chapter can serve as aids for supporters to work alongside people with learning difficulties, to help them gain this important access. Few, if any, can be used in isolation. At the present state of our knowledge, there appears to be no real substitute for independent and skilled human support. This is the message people should take away from this chapter.

Notes

1 Norah Fry Plain Facts (http://www.bristol.ac.uk/Depts/NorahFry/PlainFacts/ NewPlainFacts/html/List.html).
2 Department of Health Survey of Adults with Learning Difficulties in England 2003/04 Online report with audio commentary (http://www.dh.gov.uk/en/ Publicationsandstatistics/Publications/PublicationsStatistics/DH_4120033).
3 Disability Rights Commission (2005) Rights to vote information pack (http://www. equalityhumanrights.com/Documents/Disability/Services/Right_to_vote_pack.doc).
4 CHANGE (http://www.changepeople.co.uk/).

References

Aspis, S. (2000) Researching our history: who is in charge?, in L. Brigham, D. Atkinson, M. Jackson, S. Rolph and J. Walmsley (eds) *Crossing Boundaries: Change and continuity in the history of learning disability,* Kidderminster: BILD.

Atkinson, D. (2005) Narratives and people with learning disability, in G. Grant, P. Goward, M. Richardson and P. Ramcharan (eds) *Learning Disability: A life cycle approach to valuing people,* Buckingham: Open University Press.

Atkinson, D. and Williams J. F. (eds) (1990) *Know Me as I am,* London: Hodder and Stoughton.

Bersani, H. J. (1998) From social clubs to social movement: landmarks in the development of the international self-advocacy movement, in L. Ward (ed.) *Innovations in Advocacy and Empowerment for People with Intellectual Disabilities,* Chorley: Lisieux Hall.

Bogdan, R. and Taylor, S .J. (1982) *Inside Out: The meaning of mental retardation,* Toronto: University of Toronto Press.

Buchanan, I. and Walmsley, J. (2006) Self-advocacy in historical perspective, *British Journal of Learning Disabilities,* **34,** 133–8.

Crawley, B. (1988) *The Growing Voice: A survey of self advocacy groups in adult training centres and hospitals in Britain,* London: Values into Action.

Deacon, J. (1974) *Tongue Tied,* London: National Society for Mentally Handicapped Children and Adults.

Department of Health and Social Security (1971) *Better Services for the Mentally Handicapped,* London: Her Majesty's Stationery Office.

Department of Health (2001) *Valuing People: A new strategy for learning disability for the 21st century,* London: Department of Health.

Department of Health (2004) *Annual Report on Learning Disability,* Cm 5086, London: Stationery Office.

Department of Health (2007) *Valuing People Now,* London: Stationery Office.

Disability Rights Commission (2005) *Right to Vote Information Pack,* Online (http://www. equalityhumanrights.com/Documents/Disability/Services/Right_to_vote_pack.doc) (accessed 10 December 2008).

Emerson, E., Malam, S., Davies, I. and Spencer, K. (2005) *Adults with Learning Difficulties in England 2003/4*, London: Office of National Statistics.

Fyson, R., McBride, G. and Myers, B. (2004) Progress or participation? Self-advocate involvement in learning disability partnership boards, *Learning Disability Review*, **9**, 3, 27–36.

Graham, H and the Croydon History of Day Centres Project (2008) *Stories of Cherry Orchard, Heavers Farm, and Waylands*, Milton Keynes: The Open University, Online (http://www.open.ac.uk/hsc/__assets/qbw0zopgkfu74nu62n.pdf) (accessed 1 December 2008).

Healthcare Commission (2007) *Investigation into the Service for People with Learning Disabilities Provided by Sutton and Merton Primary Care Trust*, London: Healthcare Commission. Online (http://www.positive-options.com/news/downloads/Commision_for_Healthcare_ Audit_and_Inspection_-_Investigation_-_Sutton_and_Merton_PCT_-_2007.pdf) (accessed 11 December 2008).

Hunt, N. (1967) *The World of Nigel Hunt,* Beaconsfield: Darwen Finlayson.

Hurt, J. (1988) *Outside the Mainstream: A history of special education*, London: Batsford.

Jervis, N. and Prinsloo, L. (2008) How we developed a multi-disciplinary screening project for people with Down's Syndrome given the increased prevalence of early onset dementia, *British Journal of Learning Disabilities*, **36**, 13–21.

Morris, N. (2008) Digital Divide and People with Learning Difficulties, Milton Keynes, unpublished paper.

Oliver, M. (1990) *The Politics of Disablement,* London: Macmillan.

Open University (1996) *Learning Disability: Working as equal people,* Milton Keynes: Open University.

Potts, M. and Fido, R. (1991) *A Fit Person to be Removed,* Plymouth: Northcote House.

Read, J. and Walmsley, J. (2006) Historical perspectives on special education, 1890–1970, *Disability & Society,* **21**, 5, 455–70.

Redley, M. (2008) Citizens with learning disabilities and the right to vote, *Disability & Society*, **23**, 4, 375–84.

Seale, J. (2007) Strategies for supporting the online publishing activities of adults with learning difficulties, *Disability & Society*, **22**, 2, 173–86.

Tarleton, B. and Howarth, J. (2006) *Being Good Parents.* Plain Facts 47, May, Bristol: Norah Fry Research Centre.

Towell, D. (1988) *An Ordinary Life in Practice: Developing community-based comprehensive services for people with learning disabilities*, London: King's Fund.

Walmsley, J. (1997) Including people with learning disabilities: theory and practice, in: L. Barton (ed.) *Disability Studies Past Present and Future*, Leeds: Disability Press.

Walmsley, J. (2000) Caring: a place in the world?, in M. Janicki and E. Ansello (eds) *Community Supports for Aging Adults with Lifelong Disabilities,* Baltimore, Maryland: Paul H. Brookes Publishing Co.

Walmsley, J. and Downer, J. (1997) Shouting the loudest: self-advocacy, power and diversity, in P. Ramcharan, G. Roberts, G. Grant and J. Borland (eds) *Empowerment in Everyday Life: Learning disability,* London: Jessica Kingsley.

Walmsley, J. and Johnson, K. (2003) *Inclusive Research in Learning Disability: Past present and futures*, London: Jessica Kingsley.

Ward, J. (ed.) (1989) *Secret Lives,* Castleford: Yorkshire Arts Circus.

Welshman, J. and Walmsley, J. (eds) (2006) *Community Care in Perspective,* London: Palgrave.

Whittaker, A. (1991) *Supporting Self-advocacy: A report of two conferences held in June and September 1989 at the King's Fund Centre*, London: King's Fund.

Williams, P. and Schoulz, B. (1979) *We Can Speak for Ourselves,* London: Souvenir Press.

Young, A. and Chesson, R. (2008) Determining research questions on health risks by people with learning disabilities, carers and co-workers, *British Journal of Learning Disabilities*, **36,** 22–31.

Chapter 3

Creativity, choice and control

The use of multimedia life story work as a tool to facilitate access

Ann Aspinall

Introduction

Life stories can be traced back to narratives of people with a learning disability on leaving long-stay institutions in the latter half of the 20th century. Initially, life stories tended to be sequential accounts of people's lives within a particular social or historical content. More recently, life stories have been expanded to include elements such as the authors' hopes and aspirations for the future. Evidence does point to the fact that completing a life story can promote personal growth within these individuals (Hussain and Raczka 1997; Walmsley 1995). Life stories can give people with a learning disability the opportunity to tell their own version of their life, perhaps for the first time.

There have been extensive reviews (Edgerton 1967, 1988; Thompson 1988) on life story work with other groups, for example Jewish women in London, and these suggest a methodology of approach, influenced by the principles of the feminist movement, which has been adapted for use with people with a learning disability (Bogdan and Taylor 1982; Walmsley 1995). A variety of reasons for this type of work have been proposed; Walmsley wanted to discover the experiences people with a learning disability have had in caring and being cared for and her rationale was that such experiences are related to their biographies. A different reason was given by Hussain and Raczka (1997) who found that, as with other groups, the experiences of those with a learning disability influence their ability to become independent and to function autonomously within the community setting. Their study showed that by giving people with a learning disability a sense of who they are and an expression of their feelings through life story work, they were empowered and transition from long-stay hospitals to community residential homes was made easier. Hussain and Raczka state the two main objectives of their life story work are to enable the person to develop a sense of present day security where previously life events were too unstable to achieve this, and to enable the person to develop a sense of identity by talking about his or her ideas, thoughts and feelings about life.

The most common way for life story work or material to be captured has been through a face-to-face interview with the person with a learning disability, using tape recordings or notes, and then written up to be shared in a textual format. The participation by the person with a learning disability in the compilation of material and choice of content makes the story very personal and more meaningful for him or her as an individual. They are empowered to disclose information or retain it, being, in this work, the expert imparting knowledge to the interviewer, a role that is often unfamiliar to people with a learning disability. Those people with a learning disability who have written their own life stories have commented on the feelings they have experienced, for example Mabel Cooper (1997) who has a learning disability, recorded her life story onto tape, which was then transcribed. She hoped this would encourage others with a learning disability to do the same.

For many people with a learning disability it is not possible to 'tell' their life story in the way that Mabel Cooper and others have done. Those with little or no verbal communication do not have the capability to express their feelings through the media of interview or audiotape. Brandon (1989) emphasises that we need to explore and experiment with different levels and types of communication to overcome clients' difficulties with expression or comprehension by really listening, especially when someone's speech is slow and indistinct, and by enabling people to talk and relate. The more disabled our clients are the more we will have to use methods that do not rely primarily on verbal content. In order to allow people with learning disabilities to tell their life story it is often necessary to be creative both in the way that the story is told and in the medium used. One possible way of being creative is through the use of computer technology. In this chapter I will use real examples from my work at The Home Farm Trust Ltd (HFT) to describe how technology can be used as a medium to facilitate access to life story work. To provide a context for this specific use of technology I will start by giving a general overview of how technology can be used by people with learning disabilities.

Access and inclusion: a role for technology

The emergence of computers and ICT (Information and Communications Technology) in the early 1990s was seized upon as an opportunity to give access to communication for people with a learning disability. ICT had been recognised as having an important range of uses for children and adults who, because of physical, sensory or intellectual disabilities, have special needs. These uses include face-to-face and written communication, education, employment, environmental control and recreation (Hegarty 1991; Hegarty and Whittaker 1993; Nisbet and Poon 1998). Between 1989 and 1996 HFT, a national charity supporting more than 800 adults with a learning disability, implemented an organisation-wide project to install approximately 135 computers into day services and people's homes. The benefits of ICT for the service users of HFT have been well documented (Aspinall and Hegarty 2001; Hegarty and Aspinall 2006).

When multimedia capabilities became a normal feature of the modern personal computer they became a very powerful tool for inclusion and the uses were only limited by the skills, enthusiasm and creativity of the staff supporting people with a learning disability. Being able to import graphics and using symbols to support text opened new communication channels for HFT's service users. With staff support, service users were able to produce their own multimedia newsletters. These were distributed on CD and contained audio, recorded by service users themselves, where appropriate. The newsletters soon contained stories written by service users about their daily lives, places they had visited, hobbies and work. The computers became important in allowing people to make choices, especially when moving from large residential homes into smaller houses in the community. They could research the facilities of the areas they chose to live in using the internet; they could even use software to design the layout of their own living space; they could, using displays of digital photos, choose who they wanted to live with and, importantly, who they did not want to live with. The choices were endless and creative use of software and images (downloaded from the internet or taken using a digital camera) could enable them to communicate their choices and aspirations in an accessible way. This met with the government's strategy of the time and the beliefs of *Valuing People* (Department of Health 2001). The use of photographs and symbols in agendas, meeting notes and other documentation enabled service users from HFT to play an active role in participatory research (Porter *et al* 2005).

Multimedia life stories

It was soon realised that multimedia gave more opportunities for inclusion. Support staff, who received training in the use of computers, were able to create individualised programs using mainstream applications where no 'special needs' software existed. For one lady in her early 40s, Annie, this was her introduction to using a computer that was to give her many experiences of inclusion in her community. Annie elected to attend weekly computer sessions as part of her day care. She would patiently await her turn on the computer but stubbornly refused to look at the screen. By chance the tutor learnt that Annie had, in her teens, taken part in a school production of 'Peter and the Wolf' and decided to try to encourage Annie by creating a multimedia version of this famous musical story. Using a mainstream authoring tool, she created an onscreen book format, importing pictures and musical clips and recording the narrative of the story, page by page. To personalise the program, the tutor included a separate area (accessed through the main menu) with a few photos of Annie and her home. Clicking on these photos made them fill the screen. Annie's reaction was one of great enthusiasm. She smiled as soon as she heard the music and hummed the familiar tunes. She looked at the pictures onscreen and really enjoyed seeing her own photos. With her limited vocabulary she was able to tell other people about her home. Annie was given a copy of the CD and she took it with her to local college classes. She soon learnt how to operate the program and where to click to get the desired result.

Having seen the benefits for Annie, Annie's tutor decided to create a multi-media life story for another person with a learning disability: James. This time James would take more control over what was included in the personal record of his life experiences and achievements. Help and support were sought from his circle of friends, family and staff who gave input by providing photographs and other resources. His mother was able to provide drawings that James had created in his school days and which had remained in a box in her attic for more than 30 years. She was really delighted that these were included, saying that no-one had ever shown the interest in James's school work that was shown for the achievements of his very able brothers. His mother also brought in all the old family photos and James was able to look through them and choose which he wanted to be included in the 'past' section of his multimedia life story. It was at this point that his mother tried to influence the process. Some years earlier she and James's father had gone through a fairly acrimonious divorce and although this had left them with a bitter relationship, they had both worked hard to conceal this from James. His mother, however, found it difficult when James chose to include several photos of his father in his life story. This required the life story facilitator to be sensitive but firm in explaining that this was James's life story and the photos to be included were his choice. James also chose to include his favourite places in the 'present' section. The facilitator walked round his local area with him supporting him to take photos. He chose to include both of the pubs in the village as his favourite places; again frowned upon by his mother. James got great pleasure from showing his completed life story to staff and telling them about his school days.

Using multimedia life stories to promote control and choice

Life stories can be created in a variety of media including a textual report, a photo-album, an audio account, a video report or even in a 'memory box', which uses physical things to represent memories. With the exception of the tactile experience of the memory box contents, multimedia can bring all of the other media together and create a very powerful arrangement of those memories that are most important to the subject of the life story. But why create a life story at all? Even those people with a learning disability who are able to communicate verbally often find it difficult to tell others about themselves, their past and present life, their aspirations, their likes and dislikes – all the things that make them the person they are. Many people with a learning disability have limited or no verbal communication and so they frequently rely on others to speak for them. However, when they have worked with a facilitator to create their life story, they can be in control by simply pressing keys on the computer keyboard (or any number of alternative input devices).

Choosing to share the past, present or future

Creating life stories is a good starting point to developing a person-centred plan for an individual. It illustrates the person's past, gives a description of where he or she is currently and can really show the individual's dreams and aspirations. The staff who support Phillip know that he has a dream of owning his own house but it was not until they worked with him to find pictures to import into his life story that he was able to show them that his dream is more than this. He wants a beautiful garden with his own gate and the front door painted blue. Whilst this may not be entirely within the realms of possibility the staff are now working with Phillip to research the possibilities of his moving to a supported living environment and, using the internet as a starting point, they can research localities and the amenities on offer, all the time including Phillip and asking him his preferences.

The content of the life story should always reflect the choice of the storyteller but sometimes careful consideration has to be taken by the facilitator. The intimacy created through working with the person whose life is being 'illustrated' can sometimes cross professional boundaries, especially when the facilitator is told very personal things, some of which can be disturbing both for the facilitator and the person he or she is working with. For example, at a life story workshop run by the British Institute for Learning Disabilities in 2005, I learnt that life stories have been used by counsellors to work with prisoners who have low levels of literacy. The reason for working with prisoners was partly to discover whether any events in their lives had led them to their criminal activities. It was discovered that many of them had suffered abuse as children. The counsellors had set up a system of support should any of the process remind them of unpleasant memories. It is important to have this facility in place when working with people with a learning disability too. It was Natalie's choice not to include the 'past' section in her life story. For her this was a very disturbing time with many unpleasant memories. Her life story began in a time when her circumstances were happier and she felt comfortable with including her dreams for the future.

Choosing the style

People with a learning disability often find it difficult to put their life events into a chronological order. An organised life story can help them to do this. For some this may not be the approach they want, choosing instead to randomise events, giving priority to those that are more important to them rather than the order in which they occurred. If they are facilitated properly, the personality of the author of the life story will become apparent from the presentation. Suzannah, for instance, chose a very formal, methodical style to her life story with events clearly organised into separate areas: school days, family holidays, family events etc., whereas Phillip's life story is in complete contrast, with a riot of colour and many comical animations demonstrating his sense of humour.

Choosing the topic

These days, with digital cameras being readily available, getting photos is not likely to be a problem but it must be remembered that the author of the life story must be given the choice of which photos are included; most of us have photos which we would rather not show publicly. Old photos, from pre-digital times, can be scanned and imported as can other documents, for example the school work kept by James's mother. Francis had kept several newspaper reports and photos of his successes in the Special Olympics. His horse riding is a big part of his life and he is very proud of his medals. It isn't always appropriate for him to take his newspaper cuttings with him to job interviews but having them included in his life story enables him to proudly display his trophies in a very acceptable way to interviewers, and the pictures act as an aide memoir so that Francis can tell them about his considerable equine achievements and the job roles he has held in the riding stables.

There are many ways to make the life story personal; staff working with Melanie included a multimedia weekly activities calendar in hers. They realised that this was so useful that they extended this to a monthly calendar. They were able to use photos of activities with people and places familiar to Melanie for each special day. For Christmas they imported a Christmas song so that when Melanie clicked on 25 December, illustrated with a Christmas stocking and presents, a familiar tune played. Birthdays of family and friends were illustrated in a similar way. Melanie soon learnt that by clicking on the photo of herself with the birthday cake and candles she would hear her friends singing 'Happy Birthday' to her.

Some people have even recorded a full narrative to their life story. This is a simple process when using PowerPoint, making it activate when a certain screen/slide is selected. It cannot be stressed just how empowering this is for people with a learning disability. This feature enables them to choose the words of their narrative and practise it until they are satisfied with it; the voice-over for the slide is their own and not someone telling their story for them. This worked really well for Michael who could tell his own story when with his usual support worker but would become nervous and stutter when trying to relate to new or relief staff.

Choosing the media

Sound is very important to most of us and being able to include music and sounds in a multimedia life story can make it a more animated and more personal experience. Music can invoke nostalgia, recalling happy events, for example Peter and the Wolf for Annie. Ensuring that the sound of seagulls plays when a seaside holiday snap is shown onscreen can bring the scene alive and it becomes more meaningful. Sometimes people choose to add narration to their life story. They are able to choose who records the narration and it is very empowering if they are able to do this themselves. Even those people who cannot read or who have no verbal communication can make a contribution. David does not speak and has never heard his own voice recorded but when he was creating his life story he was asked what his favourite film was and he hummed the theme tune to James Bond. The facilitator recorded David's humming and this played automatically when the photo of James Bond was on screen. David's reaction is to grin broadly at his own achievement every time he hears this. It is usually the first 'page' of his life story he chooses to show to people. David has a very limited concentration span and rarely chooses to attend meetings, even ones that affect his future, but he was so keen to show his family members and professionals his life story that he attended his care review meeting. Once the computer was switched on and the life story selected he was able to control the computer himself, selecting the hot-spots to take him to the screens he wanted to show; there is no prize for guessing which he chose first!

Being in control

The principle of life stories can also be used with a group of people to put them in control. For example, a facilitator worked with a group of people with autism and the staff who support them. Because of the high support needs of the residents of the house there was a high turnover of staff. None of the group was able to physically show prospective staff around the house or to tell them about themselves, so they produced a multimedia life story of the house that would be used during interviews for new staff. Through being involved with the process from the beginning, the residents were familiar with the life story and could control it by interacting through a touch screen. The first screen was a photo of the house, and by touching the front door, the user 'entered' the house and was taken to a screen showing the hallway with the bedroom doors. Each door had a photo of the resident, and by selecting a door the user 'entered' the bedroom. This took the user to the life story of the individual. Each individual chose what he or she wanted the interview candidate to know about them. This process allowed more interaction between the residents and the staff who were employed to support them.

Supporting multimedia life story work

The benefits of a multimedia life story for individuals with a learning disability will not be maximised unless the staff that support them realise these benefits and understand that the life story should be created in collaboration with the individual, allowing him or her the choice of what it contains and how it is presented. In addition, support staff must have the ICT skills necessary to develop the life story. HFT ensures that all of its support staff have the opportunity to attend a two-day course to introduce them to the ethos of life story work and to give them the skills they require to support their service users. For some staff this is their first formal ICT training, for others it extends their skills, but for all it is an enjoyable experience that is aimed at showing how empowering the end result can be for the people they support. The course has evolved over several years and its success is attributed to the fact that the course participants are asked to bring with them some of their own favourite photos. They learn the ICT skills through creating their own life story. At the end of the course each participant shows his or her life story to the other participants. There is always a huge range of styles and content and they soon realise that the life stories not only show factual information but also reveal the personality, sense of humour etc. of each individual. Almost without exception they reflect that this has been an enjoyable experience and the highlight is showing their work to others who are all eager to watch and listen. If this is so exciting for people who are able to communicate their feelings, emotions and wishes, then how much more empowering is it for those people with learning disabilities who cannot articulate their views, opinions, hopes and wishes and whose stories are rarely listened to with interest.

Susan's story

Susan has shared her residential home with two other people for more than 20 years. She has mild learning disabilities and has some literacy and numeracy skills. When she joined the computer group she really enjoyed the sessions and soon learnt to use the life-skills program, 'Out and About: The living community'. The class tutor offered to show Susan how to send and receive emails. The tutor identified each step in the process and created a task analysis sheet for Susan to follow. Each step was written as a simple instruction supported by a photograph, for example of the power switch, or a 'screen print' showing which icon to click on. Susan was given her own email address and soon understood the difficult concept of sending and receiving emails. At each computer session the tutor sat next to Susan and supported her through the process of sending an email to the tutor's email address. However, Susan did not have the confidence to follow the instructions on her own, always looking to her tutor for support and encouragement at every step. Imagine the tutor's surprise when she returned from her summer holiday to find an email that Susan had sent completely on her own initiative, following the steps herself! Her father is a competent computer user and Susan and he were soon exchanging emails. Then her father gave the tutor the email addresses of other family members and friends to add to Susan's contact list. The family is extensive and live in many different parts of the world, all keeping in touch through email. Soon she was emailing people in Australia, Brazil and Sweden as well as the UK. She could not instigate the emails but she could reply to emails in her in-box. Her family members were so pleased to be able to contact Susan directly and not go through her parents, and were excellent correspondents, most of them attaching photographs to their emails. Susan learnt to print out the photos and she kept them in a folder next to her computer.

Having learnt these new skills and showing a keen interest to extend her computer knowledge, Susan was really delighted when she was asked if she would like to create her own multimedia life story. The tutor discussed this with Susan's parents who were both very supportive and keen to be involved wherever they could. The tutor asked Susan's mother to provide a written outline of Susan's life; she also asked Susan to write down anything she wished to be included and as much about her childhood as she could remember. Susan was also asked to bring in some photos that she would like to include. A meeting was arranged between Susan and the facilitator, at this time no-one else was invited to the meetings. Susan arrived at the appointed time clutching a carrier bag full of photos. The facilitator sat down to discuss the photos and to plan the life story; she asked Susan to choose which photos she wanted to include and was not surprised when the answer was 'All of them!' There were 152 photos and Susan did not have the skills to scan them into the computer. The facilitator, not wanting to delay the process or lose the motivation, took on the task of scanning in each photo. This can be a long, tedious process and it requires a certain amount of ICT and organisational skills. This is also true of the technical skills when using PowerPoint. However, the facilitator used the life story sessions to develop Susan's ICT skills, encouraging her determination to learn more and to contribute as much as she could to the whole process.

The first stage was to decide how to organise Susan's life events and personal information. The facilitator worked with Susan to produce a storyboard, a graphical representation of each PowerPoint slide. Susan wanted a very formal, structured look to her life story. After the introduction screen the user is offered a choice of three areas to view: past, present and future. Susan wanted to work on the 'past' first using her notes (and those of her mother) and her photos. This area was again sub-divided into various sections including such titles as school and holidays. In her notes Susan had written about the things in her past that were most important to her; she had repeated time and again that she enjoyed riding her bike. Her mother threw light on this by saying that when she rode her bike in the street where she lived as a young girl she was totally accepted by her peers in the village and this was an activity that she was able to share and join in on equal terms. Susan was adamant that the photo of her riding her bike with her friends was to be included. She also wanted to include the photo of herself riding alongside her father, emphasising the importance she placed on this activity, which she can no longer undertake.

One interesting conversation between Susan and the facilitator during the construction of the life story centred around one photo taken on a family holiday in Germany. To the viewer it is a typical holiday snap taken many years ago showing Susan smiling at the photographer whilst paddling in a lake on a warm summer's day. Susan was keen that this photo was given a prominent position on the screen. She talked animatedly about the holiday and it occurred to the facilitator that, as with anyone else's holiday or family snaps, the photo meant more to Susan than to the casual viewer: when she looked at the photo she recalled the whole experience of the holiday, the happy family time spent with her parents and siblings. The same could not be said of the photo that showed Susan in a very smart school uniform. She told the facilitator that she had not been happy at that school but she wanted the photo included anyway. Her mother explained that it was her decision to take Susan away from the special school she attended and send her to the private school so that Susan would receive a better education. However, her mother saw how unhappy Susan was because she could not keep up with her peers and eventually the headmaster of the special school agreed to Susan returning to that school.

Working through the storyboard and creating the multimedia life story proved to be a very rewarding experience for Susan. She learnt new skills and made many decisions about the look of the life story, such as the background colour, the positioning of the photos, any text that was included and even recorded her own narration to some of the photos. She included her hobbies as a section. This showed some photos of watercolour paintings she had created when on holiday with an artist, a family friend. These had never been seen by the staff who supported her, and when they were shown to others they began to see Susan in a new positive light, acknowledging her skills rather than her deficits. She also had an impressive array of photos of herself with celebrities, which would stimulate conversation when shown. People with a learning disability often find it difficult to start a conversation or understand the nuances of 'small talk', so this encouragement is really significant.

Susan was invited to show her life story at a very prestigious event, the opening of an ICT Centre. She did this with great enthusiasm and was able to manoeuvre her way around the life story because she had been involved in the process from the beginning. Interestingly, during 'rehearsals' she always chose the same photos. After the event had finished Susan was interviewed for the BBC News. This interview was recorded and included in her life story. The idea of a life story is that it evolves, changes and grows as the person wishes. Susan was given a copy to keep. This is another advantage of a multimedia life story: it is very portable on a CD or memory stick. Susan showed this to her family and friends, and when doing this she was able to take control. Her life story has now become part of her life and Susan has become a champion and advocate for life stories amongst her peers, showing how empowering they can be.

Summary

In this chapter I have tried to address four key questions:

1   Why create a life story?
2   How should the life story be created?
3   What should the life story contain?
4   Who should be involved in the creation of a life story?

I will now summarise the key points I have made in this chapter that help to address each of these questions.

1. Why create a life story?

People with a learning disability find it difficult to put events in their life into context and often cannot organise events chronologically. A life story can help them to do this. The life story can jog their memory about special events, things they like to do, experiences they have had and then they are in control of telling people – family, friends, professionals, prospective employers – about the things that are important to them. Creating a life story can teach new transferable skills and will produce a lasting end product that can be added to but it is also fun!

2. How should the life story be created?

A life story can be created in one or more of several media, for example a photo album, a scrapbook or a memory box. Multimedia is a very powerful medium and lends itself to the creation of a life story. But whatever medium is used it should be the choice of the individual who is the central character. The design, presentation and content of a life story can demonstrate the personality of the creator and it is important that the individual is allowed to make all of the choices.

3. What should the life story contain?

This is definitely the choice of the individual, but people can be assisted to make their choices by using a checklist of areas they might want to include such as past, present, future. Within the timeline the areas covered could include family, friends, holidays, about my home, work, school days, college etc.

4. Who should be involved in the creation of a life story?

Family and friends can provide a wealth of information and resources that can be used to make the life story more interesting but the individual should be involved at all times, with the possible exception of the technical aspects of using the computer program, e.g. PowerPoint. The technicalities, for example scanning in photographs, can take longer than the individual may be capable of concentrating.

References

Aspinall, A. and Hegarty, J. R. (2001) ICT for adults with learning disabilities: an organisation-wide audit, *British Journal of Educational Technology*, **32**, 365–72.

Bogdan, R. and Taylor, S. J. (1982) *Inside Out: The meaning of mental retardation*, Toronto: University of Toronto Press.

Brandon, D. (1989) The power to heal?, in D. Brandon (ed.) *Mutual Respect: Therapeutic approaches to working with people who have learning disabilities,* Surbiton: Good Impressions Publishing.

Cooper, M. (1997) Mabel Cooper's life story, in D. Atkinson, M. Jackson and J. Walmsley (eds) *Forgotten Lives – Exploring the history of learning disability,* Kidderminster: BILD.

Department of Health (2001) *Valuing People,* London: HMSO.

Edgerton, R.B. (1967) *The Cloak of Competence: Stigma in the lives of the mentally retarded,* Berkeley: University of California Press.

Edgerton, R.B. (1988) Ageing in the community: a matter of choice, *American Journal of Mental Retardation,* **92,** 4, 331–5.

Hegarty, J. R. (1991) *Into the 1990s: The present and future of microcomputers for people with learning difficulties,* Market Drayton: Change Publications.

Hegarty, J. R. and Aspinall, A. (2006) The use of personal computers with adults who have developmental disability: outcomes of an organisation-wide initiative, *The British Journal of Developmental Disabilities,* **2,** 2, 137–54.

Hegarty, J. R. and Whittaker, M. (1993) Computers for people with severe learning difficulties, *International Journal of Computers in Adult Training,* **3,** 1, 41–51.

Hussain, F. and Raczka, R. (1997) Life story work for people with learning disabilities, *British Journal of Learning Disabilities,* 25, 2, 73–6.

Nisbet, P. and Poon, P. (1998) *Special Access Technology,* Edinburgh: Call Centre.

Porter, J., Aspinall, A., Parsons, S., Simmonds, L., Wood, M., Culley, G. and Holroyd, A. (2005) Time to listen, *Disability and Society* 20, 5, 575–85.

Thompson, P. (1988) *The Voice of the Past,* Oxford: Oxford University Press.

Walmsley, J. (1995) Life history interviews with people with learning disabilities, *Oral History,* Spring, 71–7.

Part 3

Access all areas

Chapter 4

Access all areas

The use of symbols in public spaces

Chris Abbott and Cate Detheridge

Introduction

The public space, whether it is a library, supermarket, swimming pool or even a town square, is a little more accessible than it used to be for many citizens today. Welcome attention has been paid to the need to build ramps for those with physical disability, to provide audio prompts in addition to visual material and to offer large print versions of information cards or timetables. The picture is very uneven, with some countries, and indeed some areas within countries, having made much more progress than others; but the process has begun. For people with learning disabilities, the process is at a much earlier stage and they are often subject to many and varied forms of social exclusion (Armstrong 2003; Billington 2000; Riddell and Watson 2003).

Accessibility issues that affect people with learning disabilities are little discussed and often misunderstood. The issue is not just related to plain text or simplified versions of English; there is also a need to consider navigation routes that do not contribute to cognitive load and to offer information in a symbolic or pictorial form. The use of graphic symbols for communication has been widespread within the Augmentative and Alternative Communication (AAC) community for many years, but their use for literacy and accessibility has a much shorter history (Abbott 2000, 2002; Abbott *et al* 2006; Detheridge and Detheridge 2002). There are, however, increasing numbers of examples of well-designed uses of symbols within public spaces (Pampoulou and Detheridge 2007), together with some limited data on current symbol use, awareness and potential (Abbott and Lucey 2005; Jones *et al* 2007) and it is on this practice that our chapter will concentrate.

Public transport systems have been among the pioneers in the use of image-based information, although often with the needs of travellers using other languages rather than those with learning disabilities. Airports have been fertile breeding grounds for symbols, with many now having progressed to animated images. It is debatable, of course, whether the image of a moving blob on a stylised conveyor belt is as explicable as a well-defined image of a bag; and with the vagaries of modern baggage-handling systems it is probably also giving an overconfident impression of reality.

Other types of transport have been slower to adopt the use of symbols, except in multilingual countries or those where literacy rates are low. There are a few exceptions to this general picture. In Sweden, for example, the train timetables are as complex as in any other country, but each express train has a symbol; perhaps a parrot or a deer. This symbol appears in the timetable, on the platform display board and on the train itself; a great help to travellers from other countries as well as indigenous passengers with learning difficulties. In other countries, attention has been paid to the need for culturally-appropriate symbols rather than adopting a single international standard. In South Africa, for example, work with the Zulu community as part of a study into iconicity showed the need for different symbols than those used by the majority community (Haupt and Alant 2003).

In public spaces other than transport systems, the picture is much less hopeful. Very little use of symbols or any alternatives to text can be noted in large numbers of public spaces such as leisure centres, shopping malls and public libraries. In multilingual countries, many of these public spaces now offer alternate language versions of information, but symbol-based texts are the exception rather than the rule. Where they do exist, they tend to feature more often on websites associated with public spaces rather than inside those spaces themselves. For the tourism industry, lack of accessible environments represents not just a failure of recognition but a considerable loss of opportunity, as has been explained in recent research into the potential for this area (Pühretmair and Miesenberger 2006).

How can symbols help? Some case studies

Visitor centres

Symbols, if used wisely, can help make some public places more accessible. The Sensory Trust worked with Widgit to develop signage and education packs for the Eden Project, an international visitor destination in Cornwall. The Eden Project focuses on the relationship between people and plants, and it was therefore entirely appropriate that the decision was taken to make the work of the project accessible to the widest possible audience. Indeed, the first ever *Rough Guide to Accessible Britain* placed the Eden Project as the number one visitor attraction in the Parks and Gardens category for visitors with disabilities in the UK.

The first phase of the project, which began some years ago, was to develop a range of signs using simple text and symbol information (see Figure 4.1). More recently, alternative formats of the education packs have been developed jointly by Widgit and the Sensory Trust. The Eden Project already had standard education packs, available at the project or downloadable from its website, but the new packs are available in two versions: fully symbolised or with some symbols supporting key text (the packs are also available in Braille, Plain English, large print, and French, German and Japanese). Each section of the packs is supported with flash cards for vocabulary practice and games. Funding for such

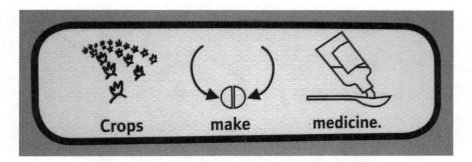

Figure 4.1 Example of a symbolised sign at The Eden Project

projects can be difficult to come by, but the work at the Eden Project was supported by the ReDiscover Fund, a joint venture between the Millennium Commission, the Wellcome Foundation and the Wolfson Trust. The Sensory Trust explains on its website the thinking behind the resources it has developed:

> The Sensory Trust was involved in all the aspects of the project although our main focus was to develop the diversity packs. It was written into the bid that Eden would develop educational packs which would focus on the two main project themes, GM crops and Intellectual property rights. The educational packs will make provision for teacher-lead tours at Eden, and also provide links to resources that can be used within schools without requiring a visit. Eden also felt that this resource should be available for all visitors to the site and so developed the diversity packs.
>
> The diversity packs are there to inform the visitor of all the new developments that have recently taken place such as the new educational building – The Core, and the exhibits produced through ReDiscover along with information on partnership projects. Often the subjects covered by Eden are new to people or complicated; well communicated information in a range of formats allows the visitor to gain a deeper understanding of the issues. (Sensory Trust 2008a)

Another successful case has been that of Exmoor Zoo. It has developed a simple graphical map to assist wayfinding, with the main routes picked out in animal patterns, along with animal symbols to guide visitors through exhibits. On the back of the map is an identification activity sheet, with symbols of some of the animals to tick off or name as they are spotted. The map is supported by symbolised fact sheets containing key information about the animals by each of the main exhibits. It is important to give visitors the full experience, not just how to find their way round, and this is one way of beginning to achieve that aim (see Figure 4.2). These symbolised fact sheets will also be available as a guide book from the zoo's website for follow-up work.

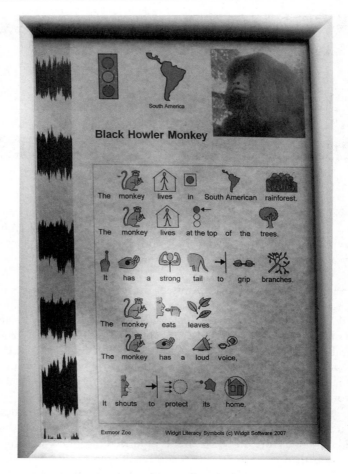

Figure 4.2 Example of a symbolised sign at Exmoor Zoo

It is disappointing that more such visitor centres have not seen fit to develop accessible resources in this way. The Eden Project was one of two case studies in a recent UK government report on signage and wayfinding, but the supportive comments there come with warnings about the need to involve users and to ensure maintenance of the facility that is developed:

> It was ... clear that symbols and signage were only part of the wayfinding process that people with learning difficulties use. The methodology behind both case studies included a focus on, and a high level of involvement with, people with learning difficulties whilst developing the signage ... It was also shown that an increased awareness in the reasons behind, and the use of, such systems are necessary to ensure that they are

not altered and remain consistent after installation. (Office of the Deputy Prime Minister 2006: 22)

Green spaces

An example of the type of resource that has been developed at the Eden Project is the PLANTS project, developed with European Union funding. PLANTS was a three-year project designed to investigate the use of technology to gather all kinds of data about growing organisms. When it came to developing an exhibit that would explain this work to visitors, the decision was taken to work with the Sensory Trust and use Widgit symbols and Braille to make the display as accessible as possible. The display is interactive and uses audio as well as text, with visitors prompted to respond to questions.

The Sensory Trust is also working with Widgit, Mencap, the Eden Project and Disability Cornwall, this time funded by the Lloyds TSB Foundation, on the Connect project, which aims to help older disabled people and people with learning disabilities to become better connected with public green spaces. The Connect project is a three-year study. Year one involved gathering evidence on the factors that stop this group from accessing green space; year two was focused on implementing and experimenting with ideas to redress the issues; and year three on writing guidance for green space managers on ways they can improve accessibility. An explanation of the project is available at the Sensory Trust website:

> It is widely understood that public green spaces can make an enormous contribution to people's quality of life and wellbeing. The benefits go far beyond providing something attractive to look at. Research studies have shown that spending time in outdoor spaces can lower blood pressure, reduce stress, help motivate people to take exercise, to look forward to things and offer the chance to take responsibility for the care of something living ... By dealing with some of the barriers that prevent older disabled people and people with learning disabilities from enjoying public open space we will enable more people to spend time in public open space and therefore engage more fully with the whole of their community. ... such people often find themselves excluded from enjoying local parks, gardens or woodlands because of a range of physical, social and intellectual barriers. ... some of these barriers result from poor design and management but many are linked to more complex issues. ... This project is designed to address these issues and to work with older disabled people and people with learning disabilities to identify realistic and effective changes and opportunities. (Sensory Trust 2008b)

The Sensory Trust and Widgit worked together again on a seasonal trail for the National Trust garden at Stourhead (Widgit 2008a). Working with local potential users from the Swindon Coalition for the Disabled and North Somerset People First, the team developed a range of resources to support the seasonal trail. The aim throughout was to make use of all five senses: sight, hearing, touch, smell and taste. For example, visitors are encouraged to feel the stone pillars of the Temple of Flora, to smell the leaves of cedars, to listen to natural spring water in the Grotto and to touch the rough trunk of the Tulip Tree. Although the National Trust owns many properties all over the country, this was the first time such a trail had been created. Heather Smith, the National Trust Head of Access for All, has welcomed the opening of the Stourhead seasonal trail and hoped that the project would make a real difference to visitors with a wide range of disabilities and so become a template for other National Trust gardens.

Public buildings

In some countries it is routine to see symbolised information and Braille in public buildings such as leisure centres, but this is still the exception rather than the rule in the UK. One such exception is the South Woodham Ferrers Leisure Centre in Chelmsford, Essex. The Centre asked Widgit to help with symbolised information and it was soon realised that this was not just a matter of putting the standard symbol next to a word. For example, the two gymnasia at the centre were always used for different activities, so an appropriate symbol was selected for each, even though the accompanying word was the same. Although the initial impulse for this development was a particular group of users from one centre, it seems likely from the comment below that the effect could be more wide-ranging:

> The requirements of the DDA coupled with our own accessibility and equality policies allowed us to take an innovative approach to the design of the signage around our new leisure centre. Feedback from customers, colleagues and external partners has been very positive, with several enquiries about them. When the signage at our other facilities is reviewed we will almost certainly use this design and concept again, which is now felt to be good practice. (Mark Owers, Sport and Recreation Officer, Chelmsford Borough Council, quoted on Widgit 2008b)

Of course, not everything goes as smoothly where large organisations like local authorities are concerned. Although the eventual outcome was pleasing to all concerned, the process by which symbols were added to signage in Surrey was not simple (Widgit 2008c). The aim was to make specific sites more accessible to users with dementia and learning difficulties by adding familiar symbols. However, like many organisations, Surrey County Council has a corporate identity policy, and in this case the rule was that only the county's oak leaf logo could appear alongside text. However, the matter was resolved after further explanation, and the signs in question now have symbolised as well as textual content. It is good to see that Surrey now has a really good leaflet with practical advice on accessible information (Surrey County Council 2008).

Whether it be a large national organisation like the National Trust or a small but important development like a new school, attention to the needs of users with learning disabilities at the planning stage is always beneficial. As part of the Symbols Inclusion Project in Warwickshire, Rose Marie Scott, the Headteacher of the newly built Oak Wood Primary and Secondary School was helped in her planning of symbol use around the school. Workers from the Symbols Inclusion Project showed the Headteacher the programme 'Communicate: In Print' and went through some of the symbols that would be needed. It was agreed that some new symbols would have to be drawn by the Graphic Designer at the Widgit Development Office. There was also discussion about how big the signs on doors should be, and what colour borders they should have. Back at the Widgit office, the new symbols were drawn and the Headteacher was sent paper copies of them for approval. Widgit then sent the symbols in the appropriate format to the signage company that was making the signs.

It is good to see such one-off examples of good practice but the need is for routine attention to be paid to the needs of people with learning disabilities as they access green and public spaces.

Key aspects to using symbols in public spaces: understanding the process

A recent English Heritage report (English Heritage 2005) calls for accessible information that will enable users to make informed choices, and goes on to provide clear guidance:

> Leaflets should contain a map with indications of distances, gradients, position of seats and any obstacles or hazards. Symbols, names of features and other information should be mirrored in the site's signage... It may be best to produce leaflets for general use in an easily readable print size. The Royal National Institute of the Blind (RNIB) recommends a 'clear print' standard of 12 point, and enlarging the text to 14 point or larger in versions that can be printed off as needed for people with impaired vision... Incorporation of information as graphics can be valuable for people who do not speak English, or have learning difficulties. (English Heritage 2005)

As is clear from the case studies outlined earlier, an essential element in bringing symbols to public places is the involvement of users. However, the first requirement is an awareness of the issue, and it is encouraging to note the beginnings of an awareness of the needs of symbol users on the part of heritage sites (see Chapter 6). Signage and waymarking alone are welcome but not sufficient; public sites and spaces need to be made accessible through inclusive interpretation as well as directions. By inclusive interpretation, we mean to indicate the artefacts and publications by which the site transmits information: notice-boards, booklets and other resources. It is also essential that organisations, which may be new to this area, are helped to find ways of building such accessibility into their organisational structures. We will now use an example of the Stourhead Trail Project to illustrate key aspects in the process of using symbols in public spaces.

One of the aims of the Stourhead Trail Project, mentioned earlier, was to enable the National Trust to develop a methodology that could be replicated elsewhere, and it is worth considering in more detail how this was done. The process is explained very fully on the Sensory Trust website (Sensory Trust 2008c). The aim of the project was to improve access physically, intellectually and culturally, to enable all visitors to explore and enjoy National Trust gardens. The project had two objectives: to produce a seasonal trail, and to create a process that could be repeated across other National Trust sites. The project took place over 18 months to ensure time for the development of ideas, comparative consultation sessions, and research into the provisions of information and inclusive techniques.

The criteria for the trail project were:

- it should be inclusive;
- it should make allowances for the seasonal aspects of the sites;
- it should be portable to minimise the impact of additional interpretation in the landscape;
- it should be written in plain language;
- the process should be consultation-led;
- the process should be transferable to other sites.

The beneficiaries of the project were identified as:

- people with learning difficulties;
- people with sensory impairments;
- older people;
- people with impaired mobility;
- children;
- family groups;
- non-English speakers.

The process of creating the trail was broken down into several different activity areas:

- consulting with people;
- identifying the highlights of the site;
- overcoming barriers to access;
- working out what information to include;
- identifying useful formats.

The process involved many representatives of the beneficiary groups during the development stage. They worked together, adapting and making changes as they went along. It was a fundamental part of the project that those involved should work together with users to create something appropriate and useful, and not simply get a stamp of approval on a draft design. It was important therefore to begin with very few preconceptions of how the trail would develop and allow it to be shaped by the different consultation sessions.

The consultation work took place on site at key stages of the design process. Local groups with various disabilities and impairments of all ages were invited to take part in structured consultation sessions. Tools such as Sensory Mapping were used to identify sensory highlights that would form the stopping points on the trail. Users discussed the design and content of the information and tested its effectiveness and usability when visiting the site. The feedback from these sessions was crucial to the development of the designs, and gave everyone involved a real understanding of what was needed in providing information for a wide range of users. The groups involved were also pleased to see the effect of their opinions in later adaptations of the designs.

The project involved many people from different disciplines both within the National Trust and others; this was a key factor in making the project a success. It was important to talk to everyone involved in the process, from people on the ground who can inform on the content and the highlights of a site, the people putting the information together, the people within the organisation that will be responsible for budgets, promotion and staff awareness, and the people giving out the information; right through to those using the information. By taking in all the aspects of a project the team ensured that they were providing something people needed and wanted, and that there was a sustainable system in place to continue to provide for that need.

The final trail was made available in Plain English, Widgit Literacy symbols, Braille and audio. The paper version was produced in A5 format to make it easy to carry, and the design was in black and white so that the trail could be printed with an ordinary office printer. Illustrations were used throughout to support the identification of stops along the trail and these were line drawings that were designed to provide maximum contrast.

The benefits for the National Trust included a broadening of the audience for Stourhead, spreading of seasonal interest, encouraging repeat visits, enhancing visitor experience, fulfilling legislative responsibilities and greater staff and volunteer satisfaction.

Meeting user needs: some practical guidance

Aware of the need for more and clearer guidance for those responsible for public spaces, we now offer some practical guidance on meeting user needs for accessibility, together with indications of where this can be seen in practice:[1]

- Wayfinding images on signage are best provided as single but relevant images. Colour coding of routes and consistency of signage is very important.
- Symbol summaries on information boards can be very helpful. Eden used short sentences of three to five symbols on information boards to give a summary of the content, not just a single symbol as a title. This single title for a whole section of information use is often seen as insulting, since none of the real information is given. A very short summary, however, can be a huge help, giving the reader the opportunity to independently learn, then further information can be mediated. (The Eden Project)
- All main text information should be supported for non-readers (Exmoor signs). This information should also be available on site and through the web as extra resources.
- Image/symbol keys to experiences are very helpful, for example the sensory keys used on plant signs alongside English and Latin names. (Stourhead)
- Simplified maps will also assist in wayfinding. (Exmoor and Stourhead)
- Timetables can be made more accessible if symbols next to event times tie up with images at the event site and wayfinding to get there.
- It is important to support information packs at appropriate levels. For example, it is important that some people on the autistic spectrum have a notion of what they are going to experience before they do so.
- Some people may not be familiar with symbols, especially if there are new ones designed for the project, so new symbol and vocabulary glossaries, games and flash cards can be useful.
- Pre-information is helpful to someone when deciding where to go, and this should say what access there is on site for learning as well as physical disabilities. Many sites have good support but do not advertise the fact.
- Tactile and interactive displays improve accessibility for many users. (The Eden Project)

The way forward: increasing accessibility of public spaces

It is essential to involve people with learning disabilities in these developments, but not in a tokenistic or illusory way. Real involvement of and attention to the needs of people with learning difficulties is complex, demanding and often frustrating; but it is vital to the success of the enterprise. The work of the Heritage Forum as described in Chapter 6 of this volume offers a workable and worthwhile model as a way forward.

There are many examples of good practice, which are fully accessible to people with learning disabilities. But these examples are not the norm. To really increase accessibility there needs to be better and higher profile guidance for public spaces. This is one of the aims of the Connect Project:[2] to give advice and guidance for accessible green spaces. Guidelines also increase public awareness and a better understanding of the needs of people with learning disabilities.

Difficulties remain, however, such as the varying understandings of the nature of accessibility needs themselves:

> The lack of any standard definitions or 'groupings' of levels of ability for people with learning difficulties means that it is very difficult to compare or contrast the results from different research projects or case studies. As such, most 'stand alone' as individual pieces of work and it is not possible to extrapolate data about which style or system of symbols is most effective. (Office of the Deputy Prime Minister 2006: 34)

We still need more pressure from government and through application of the Disability Discrimination Act to ensure that what is currently seen as isolated but exemplary practice becomes mainstream and expected. The DDA may focus mainly on jobs and facilities and not explicitly mention leisure sites, but this does not mean they should be seen as outside the legislation:

> Museums, galleries, exhibitions and other places of interest are improving accessibility all the time. This includes the way that exhibits and buildings are presented. Visitors can benefit from supported tours and information in simple formats – for example, symbols and pictures alongside text. (Directgov 2008)

Leisure places increase quality of life and this needs to be understood. Most managers when creating a public space are aware that they need to consider physical disabilities, but they do not recognise the need to support people who have learning disabilities, or find difficulty accessing text. We are only at the beginning of understanding the many and varied ways that we can support all users of public places; we urgently need more research to fully explore the strategies and devices that can be employed. Projects are vital, since they put pressure on government and policymakers to ensure that legal protection is implemented and applied, but the aim must be not the isolated project but a change in popular thinking to ensure that thinking about people with learning difficulties is the rule and not the exception.

Notes

1 More information on meeting user needs for accessible information in public spaces can be found online (http://www.widgit.com/accessibleinformation/projects/).
2 The Connect Project (http://www.sensorytrust.org.uk/projects/reports/lloyds.html).

References

Abbott, C. (2000) *Symbols Now*, Leamington Spa: Widgit.
Abbott, C. (2002) Writing the visual: the use of graphic symbols in onscreen texts, in I. Snyder (ed.) *Silicon Literacies: Communication, innovation and education in the electronic age*, London: Routledge.

Abbott, C., Detheridge, T. and Detheridge, C. (2006) *Symbols, Literacy and Social Justice*, Leamington: Widgit.

Abbott, C. and Lucey, H. (2005) Symbol communication in special schools in England: the current position and some key issues, *British Journal of Special Education, 32,* 4, 196–201.

Armstrong, D. (2003) *Experiences of Special Education: Re-evaluating policy and practice through life stories,* London: RoutledgeFalmer.

Billington, T. (2000) *Separating, Losing and Excluding Children: Narratives of difference,* London: RoutledgeFalmer.

Detheridge, M. and Detheridge, T. (2002) *Literacy through Symbols: Improving access for children and adults* (2nd edn), London: David Fulton Publishers.

Directgov (2008) *Visitors with a Learning Disability*, Online (http://www.direct.gov.uk/en/DisabledPeople/Everydaylifeandaccess/VisitingPlacesOfInterest/DG_4018602) (accessed 27 August 2008).

English Heritage (2005) *Easy Access to Historic Landscapes*, Online (http://www.english-heritage.org.uk) (accessed 27 August 2008).

Haupt, L. and Alant, E. (2003) The iconicity of picture communication symbols for rural Zulu children, *South African Journal of Communication Disorders, 49,* 40–49.

Jones, F.W., Long, K. and Finlay, W. M. L. (2007) Symbols can improve the reading comprehension of adults with learning disabilities, *Journal of Intellectual Disability Research, 51,* 7, 545–50.

Office of the Deputy Prime Minister (2006) *Final Report for Signing and Wayfinding for People with Learning Difficulties,* Online (http://www.communities.gove.uk/documents/planningandbuilding/pdf/144248.pdf) (accessed 27 August 2008).

Pampoulou, E. and Detheridge, C. (2007) The role of symbols in the mainstream to access literacy, *Journal of Assistive Technologies, 1,* 1, 15–21.

Pühretmair, F. and Miesenberger, K. (2006) Accessible information space to promote accessible tourism, Paper presented at ICCHP 2006, Vienna.

Riddell, S. and Watson, N. (2003) *Disability, Culture and Identity*, Harlow: Pearson Prentice Hall.

Sensory Trust (2008a) *Discover Eden Project Report,* Online (http://www.sensorytrust.org.uk/projects/eden/rediscover.html) (accessed 30 June 2008).

Sensory Trust (2008b) *Connect*, Online (http://www.sensorytrust.org.uk/projects/reports/lloyds.html) (accessed 30 June 2008).

Sensory Trust (2008c) *Stourhead Seasonal Trail,* Online (http://www.sensorytrust.org.uk/projects/stourhead/index.html) (accessed 1 July 2008).

Surrey County Council (2008) *How to Make Your Information More Accessible*, Online (http://www.surreypb.org.uk/section3/communication/Information%20leaflet%20web%20version.pdf) (accessed 1 December 2008).

Widgit (2008a) *Signage in a Leisure Centre*, Online (http://www.widgit.com/accessibleinformation/projects/sportssignage.htm) (accessed 30 June 2008).

Widgit (2008b) *National Trust*, Online (http://www.widgit.com/accessibleinformation/projects/nationaltrust.htm) (accessed 1 July 2008).

Widgit (2008c) *Street Signs in Surrey,* Online (http://www.widgit.com/accessibleinformation/projects/surrey.htm) (accessed 1 July 2008).

Chapter 5

Access all areas

We are VIPs

Ginny Aird, Alan Dale, Sarah Edgecombe, Louisa Jones, Trevor Rowden, Mark Sabine, Amy Tyler, Mary Waight and Sara Wornham

Introduction

Before we tell you about what we think about different types of access, we would like to tell you a little bit about ourselves and how we went about writing this chapter. We all come from Bracknell, but we have different roles or jobs:

Ginny Aird	Member of Be Heard in Bracknell self-advocacy group (a group for people with learning disabilities)
Alan Dale	Member of Be Heard in Bracknell self-advocacy group
Sarah Edgecombe	Ginny's support worker
Louisa Jones	Member of Be Heard in Bracknell self-advocacy group
Trevor Rowden	Member of Be Heard in Bracknell self-advocacy group
Mark Sabine	Self-advocate
Amy Tyler	Occupational Therapist in the CTPLD (Community Team for People with Learning Disabilities)
Mary Waight	Occupational Therapist in the CTPLD
Sara Wornham	Member of Be Heard in Bracknell, self-advocacy group

We volunteered to write a chapter for this book on access after going to the seminars at Southampton University.

Mary sent out invites to all the people who had been to the seminars to come to a meeting to talk about our chapter. Ginny, Alan and Mark all came. Sarah came with Ginny because she is Ginny's support worker.

We decided to meet for six weeks and talk about different types of access. We talked about things that had happened to us in our lives to do with leisure, employment, health and education. Everything we talked about we taped on a tape recorder and Amy typed up what we said.

One week Sara and Louisa joined us. Trevor could not come to the meetings because he was busy when we met. Mary went and talked with Trevor. He told her some things that had happened to him.

Amy showed us what she had taped. Jane Seale from Southampton University came to see us, to help us with our chapter. We decided what to put in our chapter. Mary and Amy typed it up and Alan helped.

Our chapter is about what we think access is. It is about access in general and then what we said about the different topics. It ends with what we think is important about access for people with learning disabilities.

Leisure

When we talked about leisure, we talked about getting out and about and having fun.

Getting out and about

We talked about getting out and about in our local town, Bracknell. Sometimes it costs a lot to go out. Taxis can be too pricey. We said that buses are different, they are not expensive. You can get a free bus pass. Sometimes the buses can be late, even as much as 20 minutes. There are special taxis for wheelchairs, buses are also wheelchair accessible.

We have a new transport scheme in Bracknell that has just been set up by Day Services, you can travel anywhere in the town for £1 a journey; this scheme seems to be working quite well.

We talked about walking around the town and going out at night. We do not like using underpasses as we feel that we may be attacked, we also feel unsafe at night when walking around the town.

Having fun

We talked about different ways of spending our leisure time:

- going to the cinema;
- going swimming;
- doing different sports;
- watching sports especially football;
- watching television;
- listening to music.

We talked about having help to go to different places. It is good to have help, if you need it. It did not feel good that sometimes support staff might want to come with you because it meant that they could go to the cinema for free as a carer. This is not fair or right. It was alright if staff wanted to come as a friend and pay but it was wrong for them to use you to get into the cinema for free. We talked about this a lot because it was very important.

We talked about a new scheme in our town which is a special card which can be used to help you have cheap prices at the Sports centre. It is called an 'E-Plus

Card'. Mark said: 'To have one you need to take a photo, you need put name down, full name and date of birth – get it through the post – wait for post, sent to front door – Got it!' We feel that this is a good scheme as we get discounts and we've been able to get out and about more using the card. Ginny said 'You can use it in all these different places, you can use it at the Tea House, BB's you can get … and some at Greggs the bakers and sports centre and the library.'

Holidays

Mark told us of a good holiday he had been on. Mark had been down a coalmine with a group of friends and staff. They went down very slowly. The mine was empty. It used to be a working mine. It used to have horse and carts. There was a guide who told them all about what used to happen in the mines and it was very interesting. The mine had been flooded once. There was also a special shop to look around; you could look at pictures through glass.

Mark enjoys spending time at the local respite unit. He goes out with the support staff to visit old houses and castles, or he might go to the cinema.

Ginny had been on holiday with her mother and a friend of her mother's. They went to Devon. They had a nice cottage. Ginny described what she did on holiday: 'I went swimming in the Jacuzzi, went for a walk round; where we saw some animals; goats and things, pub lunch, went for some more walks … and best of all the weather was nice, I had the nice weather, everyone else had the grotty weather!'

Trevor also went on holiday with his family but they usually go to hot places like Greece.

Alan was planning his holiday. He was hoping to go to Cornwall to a hotel. He was going to travel there by train. His carer was going to travel with him and then return home. He would be met by people from the hotel when he arrived in Cornwall. He was looking forward to being by the seaside and going for long walks. In the past Alan had been on holidays abroad, he told us about his trip: 'I went by ferry. It was a long ship. Took a long time to get there, slept on the ship.' He then said: 'Went on a French bus. They had good food in France, it was nice.'

We thought that sometimes it was useful to have someone to travel with when going on holiday. All of us felt that it was essential to have someone to help us to plan our holidays, this might be a parent or support staff.

Our thoughts about getting out and about

Overall the most important reasons for getting out and about are:

- not being bored at home;
- keeping fit;
- keeping busy and occupied;
- being stimulated and keeping our minds active;

- making new friends;
- holidays are refreshing and a good opportunity to get away from Bracknell.

There can sometimes be barriers to getting out and about and accessing leisure activities; these are:

- difficulties in organising where to go and what to do;
- there are not enough buses – we feel there are not enough routes around Bracknell and that they do not run late enough;
- it can be expensive to do lots of activities;
- we are worried about our safety if we go out at night and sometimes during the day;
- we have personal responsibilities like pets to think about.

We feel that the solutions to the barriers could be:

- Having support when and if we need it to organise activities and to partic-ipate in them. This support might be from support staff family or friends.
- The E-Plus Card gives us discounts and is also a bus pass. The new transport system for £1 per journey is helpful and seems to be working well.
- We need accessible information about activities that is easy to understand.
- We also need good directions to help us find our way around Bracknell to different activities.

Health

When we talked about health, we talked about keeping healthy, going to the doctors and going to hospital.

Keeping healthy

We talked about health. We started by thinking about what helps us be healthy, such as eating fruit and vegetables and not too much chocolate or cake.

Mark had lost a lot of weight. He said he did it by eating Weight Watchers food. It was hard work to lose weight but he was glad that he did it.

Ginny has to watch what she eats because she is diabetic. She has to take tablets and watch her blood sugar because she does not want to get ill. Her mum helps her with her blood sugar level. If her blood is too high, she has to eat less. Mary asked what happens if it is too low. Ginny said: 'Even if I am very low, my mum always gives me an emergency bar of chocolate in my bag!' This is in case she feels a bit woozy.

Ginny has to go to a special diabetic clinic where she has a blood test and she sees the doctor. She also goes to special diabetic eye clinic as well as a normal optician. Ginny described what happens: 'They put in drops and you have to sit in the waiting room for 20 minutes, then they look at the big pupils in your eyes to see if you've either got cataracts or something wrong with your eyes and things like that.'

Ginny has to go every couple of months for a blood test and she has to fast for 12 hours. She feels hungry when she does this. She has to go to the special clinic once a year. Ginny's mum helps her make sure that the food she eats is suitable for diabetics.

Alan has to have a special diet as well. He cannot eat wheat. If he does, he gets ill. Ginny asked Alan about his diet:

> *Ginny* – So if you went to a birthday party, or Julie had a birthday cake and you've accidentally eaten the cake, does it affect you after?
> *Alan* – Yeah.
> *Mary* – How do you refuse cake, is it an easy thing to do?
> *Alan* – I do refuse.
> *Mary* – Is it easy to remember what has wheat in it and you can't eat it, or is it hard?
> *Alan* – I can't eat any cake, it is hard.

Alan has to remember to ask people not to give him food with wheat in it. When he is buying food he has to look at the labels on the food to make sure that the food does not have gluten in it. Alan checks the food himself.

We talked about having tests to make sure our health is good such as eye tests, when you have to read letters and the optician shines a light into your eyes. We talked about blood tests, which are not very nice. Mark does not like needles. He told us about having to have two injections in his stomach and hip. He was very brave.

Going to the doctors

Alan talked about what he does when he needs to see the doctor. He makes an appointment on his mobile phone with the receptionist who gives him a time and date to come in. Sometimes he has to wait a long time to get an appointment, even as long as a week. If his doctor is on holiday he is happy to see one of the other doctors as long as it is one of the nice ones. There is a doctor at the surgery who is not a very nice man. He doesn't care about people's illness. He just does paperwork. There are three good doctors and one bad doctor. Alan has to catch the bus or a taxi over to the surgery. He goes on his own. When he gets there, he walks inside and says 'I have made an appointment to see the doctor.' The receptionist looks up his name on the list. Then he goes upstairs when he is called. His doctor may write him a prescription. He gets his tablet in a special plastic box with the days on it, called a nomad pack. This helps him to remember when to take his tablets.

Ginny talked about her doctor. Sometimes she makes an appointment and sometimes her mum makes one for her. It depends upon how she is feeling. Her mum takes her to the doctors in the car. Ginny said: 'My mum comes in with me, because if there's something wrong with me, he always talks to me and my mum if I can't understand what he's saying.' Mary asked if the doctor will check with her first if it is alright to talk with her mum, Ginny answered, 'Yes, he checks with me first if it is alright, if he talks with mum first and then...'.

Ginny then talked about making an appointment: 'Yes, and I don't have a problem making an appointment, I can ring at 8 o'clock in the morning and they just give one, if they're fully booked I have to ring up the next morning and see if there's a space and they usually fit me in.'

Her doctor writes her prescriptions out and her mum always allows her to go and get her medication as they're in town at work. She goes up to the Superdrug in town and she gets it herself. She uses the boxes that come from the chemist for her medication and takes it herself. Sometimes she forgets and her mum has to remind her :'Sometimes I forget and mum says "Have you had your tablets?" and I say "No", she reminds me.'

Doctors may give you different tests, such as thyroid tests or smear tests. Doctors can also give injections like flu jabs to stop you having flu. Mark, Ginny and Sarah have to have flu jabs every year because of their health needs.

Sometimes people need to have special treatments. Mark told us about having to have oxygen. Every night in bed he has oxygen, one at home and one at the respite unit. If he runs out of the oxygen he or his mum phones up the company.

Going to hospital

Mark told us about how he had been very ill about a year ago. He had been shaking and sweating. His mum saw that he was very ill and called the doctor who said: 'Phone ambulance quick!' The ambulance came. He had to be put on a special bed or trolley to take him to the ambulance from his house. He went to hospital. The ambulance had its sirens going!

Alan told us about when he had been in hospital. He had had a DVT or deep vein thrombosis, which is a clot in his leg which stops the blood in his vein and is very painful. He had to go in an ambulance to the hospital. The paramedics used a special chair to help him down the stairs at the flat where he lives. He went to a local hospital and stayed there for five days. When he first went in he had to wait on the bed until they got him to a ward. They put him on a trolley and they looked at him. When he was on the ward he had some problems about his diet because the staff did not listen to him when he told them that he cannot eat wheat: 'I said to them, they didn't take any notice.' Eventually they gave him the right food.

Trevor said that when he is in hospital it is difficult to find his way around because he has a poor memory and it takes him a long time to remember things. If he is staying in hospital he can forget where his bed is. His mum and dad help him with his appointments at hospital. They take him there and help him to find the right place. If he needs an operation the doctors explain it, but his mum helps him to understand what is going to happen. He once had pressure sores when in hospital and his mum had to make a fuss about what had happened.

Our thoughts about health

Overall the most important reasons for staying healthy are:

- We need to keep well so that we can enjoy our lives to the full.
- We need to eat well and have a good diet to keep healthy.
- We need to be able to exercise and keep fit to be happy and healthy.
- We need to be fit and healthy to be independent, so we do not have to rely on others for help.
- We need to be healthy because we all have responsibilities in life.

We thought the following might be barriers to keeping healthy:

- Not having enough understanding about our health conditions, e.g. diabetes or coeliacs disease.
- Not having good accessible information about our health.
- Specialist food is not always available from shops, in restaurants or in hospital.
- Labelling on foods is often unclear, too small, and difficult to understand. Labelling also changes in different shops.
- Staff in supermarkets and shops are not always helpful.
- Some people may need help to access sport/keep fit activities: support is not always available.
- Some activities can be expensive.
- Not everyone can do exercise: they may need specialist classes.
- Hospitals can be frightening and scary places: some people have had bad experiences when in hospital.
- GPs do not always listen to what we have to say or explain things clearly to us. We may avoid going to the doctors if we don't like them.
- Some people may need help to arrange and/or attend medical appointments or may need reminding about appointments, e.g. opticians, podiatry.
- Not everyone is able to communicate how they are feeling health-wise. This may mean that important health issues are missed.

We feel that the solutions to the barriers could be:

- Educating health providers including GPs, hospitals and community services about the needs of people with learning disabilities.
- To have a choice of which GP you would like to see: male or female.
- To have clear, easy to understand information about our health conditions in different formats, e.g. written, spoken or DVD.

- To have access to community nurses within the CTPLD for advice and support about our health.
- Liaising with supermarkets about the labelling on food and the availability of specialist food.
- Speaking to local supermarkets if we feel that the staff are rude or unhelpful.
- Having support when and if we need it to arrange and attend health appointments.
- Having support to communicate our health needs through a variety of different methods.

Education

We talked about the different college courses people had been on:

Life skills	Maths
English	Computers
Work preparation	A 'Moving On' course about getting a job
City & Guilds in Food Hygiene	Running a coffee shop
Cookery	Citizenship
Communication in the work place	Childcare

Louisa and Ginny talked about Louisa's course in running a coffee shop:

Louisa – Yeah, as soon as we get in registration and everything then we have a little bit of time of talking, going over the rules and then we wash our hands and we got certain aprons to wear when we're standing behind the counters and we set up the chairs and that, then we're ready by 11 o'clock for first break. Then we serve teas, coffees – we either do hot food, sausages, bacon, scones and then in the afternoon as well, we do like cakes, crisps, coffee, fruit salads and stuff like that.

Ginny – What do you have at lunchtime then?

Louisa – Then we shut the coffee shop for a break cos we're entitled to have a break as well. So we go off and have our lunch break and once we have had our lunch break we come back. Once we come back, the tutor has to go over the rules and we have a go at cooking up some other stuff as well as doing some other cooking.

Louisa said that sometimes she finds it hard to remember what she has to do. The tutor will ask her to do something and she finds it difficult to remember what she was asked the first time around. Louisa would ask again and she'd go away and think what was she meant to be doing, and then she would ask the tutor again if she still wasn't sure. After a while the tutor would ignore her and Louisa would think 'Oh, that's what I'm meant to be doing!' She does listen, but she is not very good at taking it all in. Her memory is not very good.

We talked about cookery courses because many of the group had done cookery (some of them with Mary and Amy). You have to prepare before cooking, wash hands, and tie back hair and sort out the room.

Applying for and attending courses

The group said that it can be easy to apply for a course but sometimes you have to wait; there is no guarantee that you'd be on the course.

Sometimes they said it is good to do the same course twice or three times as it helps to remember what was being taught and you always learn something new or more.

Attending courses is important. If you didn't turn up every week or you're not well or you're on holiday and you couldn't be bothered to go to college they kick you off of the course. Sara talked about her experience: 'They'd say to you, "We haven't seen you for the last three weeks, are you coming in or do we have to rethink and kick you off the course"— but not in that such words.' Everyone felt this was fair if someone hadn't been attending college.

Trevor talked about his course at Learn Direct. He uses computers at the local library. He has someone who helps him if he does not understand what he needs to do. The computer asks questions through earphones and he has to follow the instructions. Most of the work he does is reading and sums. He has a two hour session but he has a break in the middle. He felt that Learn Direct was better than college because it was quieter.

Our thoughts about education

We all thought of different ways to help us learn when on courses:

- To have clear instructions.
- Give people time to understand what they need to do and check they've understood.
- Make sure that instructions are not confusing and that there is too many given all at once.
- Treat students as adults.
- Help people with hearing impairments by looking at them when you're speaking.
- Repeat what is being said.
- Explain clearly.
- Support what is said with written instructions and pictures or symbols.
- Have big writing.
- Use practical exercises like role play.
- Use television, videos and DVDs.
- Make sure that the environment is right, e.g. quiet enough.

Employment

We talked about our different experiences of employment.

Alan's job is voluntary. He is chairperson of Service Users Forum for the company who provide his support workers. This is his main job. He has to chair the meetings, make sure they listen to what he says and that they are on time. Lots of people go to the meetings, staff and other people who use the service. The forum is held at a big office in another town and Alan has to take a taxi to get there. He pays for the taxi, but he is able to claim the money back. He was chosen to be on the committee and the people on the committee elected him to be chair. He has done the job five times. There are due to be elections soon and he hoped to be elected again.

Alan would like to have a job at the supermarket in town. He would be bag packing and stacking shelves. His job coach is helping him with this.

The job coaches come from an agency called 'Breakthrough', which has been set up to help people find jobs. Job coaches go to the Job Centre and help them find a job at the Job Centre, they then ring up to get an appointment for their interview. They help with the interviews. Everyone felt that you could just turn up at the agency in the town centre and they would help them to find a job. Often a care manager would have to set this up for you. When you first go to the agency they would ask you questions and take your details to put you on their records. Then you go and find a job at the Job Centre. You need to get a CV done which tells employers about your education, skills and work experience; Breakthrough helps you to write this. They have a list of jobs. They can help you to get a CRB (Criminal Records Bureau) check done if you need one for your job. Ginny told us what a CRB check is: 'It's to see if you have a criminal record. Just to make sure that you haven't done anything naughty. That's why I had to have a CRB before I came here (CTPLD). Before I got paid here I had to have a CRB check. It took a long time!'

Alan has had various jobs:

- He litter-picked at a local school and leisure centre but he left that job as it hurt his back.
- He worked at a corner shop helping people with their shopping – he stopped that job because he went to school.
- He worked at a supermarket for 10 years but left because one of the managers had a go at him and was picking on him. She said that he could not leave his rucksack on the counter but there was nowhere else safe where he could leave it because they did not give him a locker.
- He worked as a gardener for the respite unit.

He was paid for working in the shops and the leisure centre but not for gardening, which was voluntary.

Trevor had had a job at the Leisure and Sports Centre. He used to work in the swimming pool checking that people had brought their tickets to go swimming. If they had not paid he had to send them back to the front desk. If there was any trouble he had to radio to the poolside for help. It was usually kids who had not paid. He was found the job when he was at college. He did it one day a week for seven years. Towards the end of his job he was paid because his mum persuaded the leisure centre to pay him. The money went into his bank account. Unfortunately he lost his job and was replaced with a computer. He hasn't had a job since. He would like a job at a local primary school helping the children.

You might find a job through the newspaper or the internet and the local employment agency would help you.

Mark talked about the jobs he would like to have. He would like to work in the local market having a stall selling uniforms for security guards and the police or school uniforms. Or he would like to work at the local volunteer café as the boss. If he had that job he would make sure that the staff wore uniforms. He felt that it was important that people with jobs wore uniforms and had ID so that you knew who was doing the job.

Ginny talked about her job. She works in the CTPLD office. She likes it because she doesn't have to wear a uniform and she likes doing paperwork. In her job she does timesheets, shredding paper, photocopying, getting the milk, taking the post to the respite unit and doing other things like that.

Our thoughts about employment

We decided that the good aspects of having a job were:

- It gets you out of the day services.
- You get to see different people and meet new people.
- You can make friends and have a laugh.
- There is a routine.
- You get paid; and one day we may be rich!
- It is something to do.

There can be some barriers to finding a job:

- Getting a job can be a very long process.
- There are waiting lists at Breakthrough.
- We do not always get the right kind of support.
- There is often lots of red tape and bureaucracy.
- It can be hard to find the right job.
- Our benefits affect how much we can be paid; there are limits on hours and money.
- We may have to do voluntary work before we get paid.

The solutions to some of these barriers might be:

- To have good support networks.
- We need access to good job coaches. Bracknell needs more job coaches.
- We need the right training to help us learn about jobs.
- There needs to be lots of job opportunities.
- There needs to be good information about how to get a job, which is easy to read and understand.

Conclusion

We decided that these are the main things that access is about:

- access is to go to places;
- access is to go out more;
- access is if someone is in a wheelchair, they need special help such as lifts or ramps, they need easy access to get up the stairs;
- access is getting out and about;
- access is about having the right help to get out and about; it might be information or it could be someone who would help, e.g. support worker;
- access is about good information, understanding what is happening and being about to make choices;
- access is good information which helps us find our way around new or strange places;
- access is when people spend time to explain to you what is happening;
- access is when people pay you attention and listen and answer your questions properly;
- access is being able to go out in ways we can afford;
- access is having help (if we need it) to plan going out or holidays.

Most importantly, we feel that access is about treating us like VIPs (Very Important People). We have all enjoyed talking about access and we've found it very useful.

Chapter 6

It's my heritage too

Developing participatory methods for promoting access to heritage sites

Jonathan Rix with the Heritage Forum

Background

The members of the Heritage Forum, who contributed to the project that this chapter describes and discusses, include members from the Royal School for the Blind; Liverpool 8 Resource Centre; Parthenon House; Halewood Resource Centre and Old Swan/Dovecot Day Centre (see Table 6.1).

Funding and support for the Access to Heritage project were received from the Liverpool Capital of Culture Company, Liverpool People First, the Mersey Partnership, Liverpool CC, Knowsley MBC, the NW Disability Arts Forum, Merseytravel, National Museums Liverpool, Royal MENCAP Society, MENCAP Liverpool and Libertas, the RTR Foundation, Liverpool LDDF, Knowsley LDDF and the Arts Council.

The following heritage sites were visited around Liverpool and Merseyside: the World Museum, the Walker Art Gallery, the Maritime Museum, the National Wildflower Centre, Speke Hall, the Williamson tunnels, Metropolitan Cathedral, the Anglican Cathedral, the Conservation Centre, Lady Lever, Staircase House, Stockport, St George's Hall and the Tate Gallery.

Introduction

Over recent years there has been a growing appreciation that people with learning difficulties should be involved in assessing heritage site provision (Economou 1999; Rayner 1998; Rix 2005; Ruiz 2004). Figure 6.1 outlines in symbolised format a range of different activities or opportunities that can be offered by heritage sites. It has been recognised that heritage sites can be a valued resource for those individuals who face barriers in relation to structuring thought, remembering and communicating, and for the practitioners who work alongside them (Clarke *et al* 2002). Despite this recognition there is still a lack of resources to make it easier for this diverse audience to visit heritage sites and express their views on the experience (see Figure 6.2).

The Access to Heritage Project, which began in autumn 2005, hoped to fill this gap. It had three clear aims:

Table 6.1 Members of the Heritage Forum

Royal School for the Blind	Liverpool 8 Resource Centre	Parthenon House	Halewood Resource Centre	Old Swan/Dovecot Day Centre	Project Workers	Project Supporters
Matthew Heard	Tina O'Connor	Donald Birchall	Tom Barton	Antony Doran	Project Leader: Alan Griffiths	Jimmy Cullen
Daniel Harwood	Philip Foxley	Lesley Marshall	Eddie Barton	Linda Sullivan		Eileen Willshaw
Christopher Bingham	Lila Wilson		Barry Francis	Dawn Newby	Project Coordinator: Ticky Lowe	Kate Rodenhurst
Mark Anderson	Sheila Cosgrove		Suzanne Faulkner	Angela Green		Jonathan Rix
Ricky Bemtham	Brenda Walker		June Jenkins	Sheila Letts		
Robert Stirrup	Liz Gouirah		Geraldine Regan			
Lynda Hogan						
Nichola McGorrin						

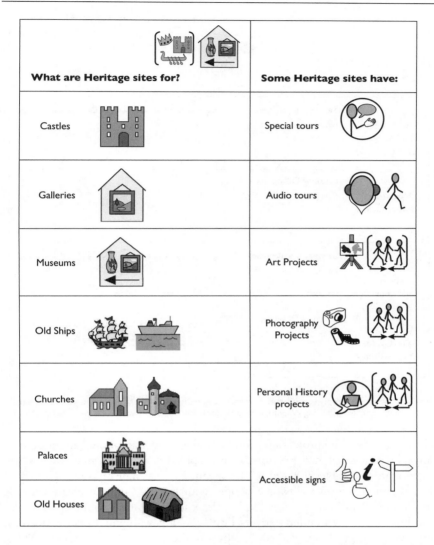

Figure 6.1 Symbolised information about heritage sites using Widgit Literacy Symbols © Widgit Software 2008 (www.widgit.com)

1   To assist and encourage people with learning difficulties to access Merseyside's culture and heritage sites, as is their right.
2   To enable heritage sites to learn from people with learning difficulties about how best to make themselves accessible to people with learning difficulties and therefore benefit everyone.
3   To create intellectual access guidance that can be used in heritage sites everywhere.

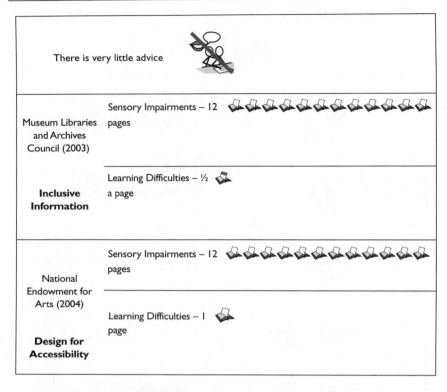

Figure 6.2 Symbolised representation of how little advice there is for heritage sites about how to make sites accessible using Widgit Literacy Symbols © Widgit Software 2008 (www.widgit.com)

The members of the project's Forum have identified and focused attention on a range of issues that had previously been spread across a number of research documents (see Tables 6.2 and 6.3 for a summary of their findings). They have shown that the need to involve people with learning difficulties in assessing provision within heritage sites can be met effectively if it is built upon a relationship across an extended period of time. They have highlighted the need for improved signage (Lines *et al* 2003; Office of the Deputy Prime Minister 2006; Rayner 1998), emphasised the importance of the senses (Blewitt 2004) and demonstrated the role food plays in effective social activities (Bohata and Reynolds 2002), even in a research project! The Forum has identified that sites need to produce accessible information including marketing, pre-visit information and on-site interpretation, and that they should challenge and enhance the personal attitudes and awareness of their staff (Goodall *et al* 2003; MENCAP 2003; Rix 2005; Whittaker *et al* 2005). Perhaps most important of all, the Forum has provided guidance about the process of consultation. Its work demonstrates the comparative ease of an inclusive approach and its manageable outcomes. It

Table 6.2 Findings and recommendations of the Heritage Forum: Working with Heritage Access Consultants

Venue attitudes and ethos	• A consultation process should be undertaken whenever new interpretation is designed and made for heritage sites. • Settings need to identify individuals responsible for initiating and responding to communication with this community of users. • Contacting sites about issues of access should not be drawn out process. • Staff in settings often promise that they will accompany a group or join them for a discussion but do not turn up. This seems like bad manners, suggests that the people with learning difficulties are not important, and is very demotivating. Arrangements should be kept to; or false promises not made. • Sites should build up a range of staff with experience of working with these users. • When involving these users in an access consultation, time scales need to be realistically planned. Most people with learning difficulties cannot be rushed. • People enjoy having their work recognised and showcased. • These users should be supported to produce work of high quality.
Effective visits	• All visit arrangements must be flexible to the individuals and/or their groups. • It is appropriate to focus on one contained aspect of a heritage site during each visit. • Attention tends to be kept for a maximum of one hour. • A break for food is important as a social and refocusing opportunity. • Starting a visit before I I am can cause problems with transport. • Transport issues will often cause problems for those attending. • A good pattern for a site visit is: one hour visit/workshop; short recall activity ; lunch (with discussion); longer recall activity. • Discussions about a visit can take place within a site's Café and still be effective. • At least one member of staff should attend the post visit recall meeting.
Uncertainties about working with people with learning difficulties	• People in all walks of life find that their views of effective practice are transformed by their involvement with people with learning difficulties. • When building a relationship with other organisations, such as funders, the involvement of people with learning difficulties breaks down barriers and motivates further engagement. • Many people working in heritage sites have no experience of people with learning difficulties and are uncertain about what to expect and what to do. Only first hand experience can teach staff that they have to do very little that is different or difficult. • Heritage site staff can be enthused about an upcoming visit by discussions with an advocate prior to the visit.
Involving supporters	• Having consistent supporter presence and engagement is a key factor in the continued involvement of people with learning difficulties. • Supporters can easily dominate proceedings, despite having the best of intentions. • Providing supporters with a questionnaire allows them to raise issues based on their experience as advocates, issues sometimes not initially identified by the person with a learning disability. • By providing supporters with a voice it reduces the incentive to incorporate their views into the participant's questionnaires/feedback. • Supporters often wish/need to leave at set times (eg: straight after lunch) to fit in with other activities.

Table 6.2 continued

How should Heritage sites involve people with learning difficulties	• It takes up to 10 visits for people to develop heritage site literacy. • These users have found it best to work in short bursts across a longer period of time. An ongoing relationship of regular visits across a period of several months is appropriate. • Users intending to carry out access audit projects need to be strong self-advocates and/or to have an independent individual to facilitate their advocacy. • Priorities should be set by the people with learning difficulties. • Advocates should not be seen as the 'access expert' who can speak on behalf of the people with learning difficulties. • Strong personal relationships need to be built between group members. Trust needs to be established across a period of time. • If others are arranging finances for the project or advising in any other way, they should attend meetings with the people with learning difficulties. • The enthusiasm of people with learning difficulties for new experiences, and the pace at which they work, means that supporters/staff can easily direct a process with their own ideas, ways of working and/or ambitions without being aware of it. • Supporters/staff must always constantly reflect on whether the people with learning difficulties are directing the process or whether they are being required to follow. • Having a social element to projects is beneficial for all involved. • Heritage sites need to provide individuals with the opportunity to assess proposed changes before they are finally implemented.
Information Gathering	• People should be encouraged to explore different ways of communicating; through pictures, symbols, signing, speech, written word, recorded word, audio, video, hands-on. • Views of individuals should be gathered in a variety of ways: visual questionnaires, observation, discussion in the moment, discussion retrospectively, drawing pictures and writing labels, brainstorming activities, taking photographs, recording with video, using postcards of artefacts, bring artefacts to individuals, workshops, regular meetings, discussion/interviews/questionnaires with supporters. • Digital cameras effectively allow for rapid recall and discussion. However, they present technical challenges, and raise issues of ownership. • Accompanying (but not leading) people with learning difficulties as they visit a heritage site provides invaluable insights and opportunities to explore their perspective. • It is valuable to involve a wide range of individuals with learning difficulties so as to get a fuller picture of access challenges and opportunities.

Table 6.3 Findings and recommendations of the Heritage Forum: Making Settings Accessible

General factors
- People with learning difficulties do not usually have wide experience of heritage sites, and do not know what is available at venues to use them to their full potential.
- It often needs lots of shorter visits for people with learning difficulties to get the most out of a venue.
- Information is best delivered when it is given lots of times in small chunks.
- There is often an overlap in approaches to access that means a solution designed for some is also solution for many others.

Providing additional opportunities for communication
- Sites are most effective when more senses are being used.
- There should be more use of sound, but it is important that the sound is not muffled and that there are not too many sounds going on at once.
- Audio text at the press of a button is well received.
- Videos and music create a sense of place and reduce reliance upon reading text to access information.
- Interactive computer games are popular.
- Hands on exhibits create a very accessible space, but opportunities are currently limited.
- Exhibits need to have strong contrast in colour and texture to be accessible to all.

Making people welcome
- On arrival people with learning difficulties need to be made to feel welcome.
- Disability awareness training is needed for staff. This training should involve people with learning difficulties.
- There needs to be plenty of seating available throughout a site.

Strategies to attract people
- Heritage Sites need to tell people with a learning disability, and their supporters, about what specific services are available at their site, such as workshops.
- Sites need to proactively engage with this area of the community, encouraging involvement in mainstream activities.
- Pre-visit information would benefit these users.

Strategies for effective signage
- There is a lack of symbols in use in interpretation and where there is use it is often of an inconsistent nature.
- Most sites have unclear way finding.
- There needs to be clear, large, symbol-based signs.
- There needs to be signs to make clear what can be done in different spaces (e.g. what can be touched and what can be sat on).
- The use of colour coding for directions is helpful. Contrasting colours on floors and walls help to define a space.
- Signs need to be clearly visible. The artefacts they relate to need to be evident.
- Signs should not be crowded, and should use large strongly contrasted fonts.
- A simplified text identifying key information should be used with supporting symbols/pictures

People as effective resources
- The most effective access facilitator is a tour guide who engages with people and builds on their current understanding.
- The use of costumes brings a space to life.
- Providing simplified materials for guides within rooms would help both staff and visitors in discussing a site and its artefacts.

underlines that a decision to supply resources equitably within the mainstream provision (Goodall *et al* 2003; Whittaker *et al* 2005) should be greeted as a reasonable, affordable and valuable opportunity that can be to the advantage of all users. Upon reading their work, heritage sites should feel encouraged to provide access to their sites through a diversity of communication channels.

Working with the Forum has also underlined for all involved that the individuality of people with learning difficulties is far greater than their label might lead heritage sites to believe. If the views of this diverse population are to be effectively captured then a wide range of individuals who have this label applied to them need to be canvassed to get a fuller picture of access challenges and opportunities. However, the research process that has been undergone also provides evidence that heritage sites can work with these users in ways with which they will feel comfortable, because they involve approaches with which they are already familiar. For example, as part of its work, the Forum has supported the development of provision at St George's Hall, Liverpool, making 18 visits to the hall, and advising site designers on signage and other presentation issues. The Forum also raised additional funds to develop a temporary multi-sensory exhibition for the Hall in conjunction with artists, and to employ a film maker to record their work both in carrying out access audits and creating the exhibition.

Setting up the Forum

Research, particularly academic research, tends to exclude people with learning difficulties through complex texts and theorised debate (Walmsley and Johnson 2003). The Access to Heritage project aimed to avoid this exclusionary outcome by practising three core principles of inclusive research:

1   that research must address issues that really matter to people with learning difficulties, and which ultimately leads to improved lives for them;
2   that it must access and represent their views and experience;
3   that people with learning difficulties need to be treated with respect by the research community (Walmsley and Johnson, 2003: 16).

Ongoing reflection has been key to ensuring that the project stuck to its inclusive principles. For example, the project was initiated in 2004 after a number of failed attempts to raise the interest of funders elsewhere in the UK. A project steering group raised initial funds to employ the project coordinator and establish the Forum. A small number of people with learning difficulties initially attended the steering group, but it soon became obvious that these meetings were dominated by others. Once the Forum was firmly established, therefore, the steering group disbanded and its members joined Forum meetings when required.

The 25 members of the Forum come from five key community groups operating out of day-service resource centres and a school. The project focused on identifying and recording their experiences so that the people with learning difficulties have control over them, and have access to the results. As much as possible, decisions were made at meetings of the Heritage Forum, which were held at different venues throughout the Liverpool and Merseyside area so as to make it easier for its members to attend.

The project recognised the need to provide administrative support to facilitate the work of the Forum. A volunteer project leader, Alan Griffiths, identified and managed links within the local administrative network and created funding partnerships with a range of funding bodies. A funded project coordinator, Ticky Lowe, facilitated meetings and visits as well as communication between participants, and helped maintain a momentum for the project and the Forum. Some gatekeeper personnel from heritage sites and local organisations also attended Forum meetings at different times, as did the first author of this chapter. A monthly update was circulated to keep everyone informed. From the outset it was recognised that trust and respect had to be established between all participants. With this in mind, the first few meetings encouraged people to find out about each other and their individual interests. Forum members created a personal profile in which they outlined things that they liked and disliked, noted their hobbies and interests, and identified which senses they found the most effective for communicating.

It soon became evident to the Forum that the majority of the members had minimal experience of heritage sites. Hardly surprisingly this meant that they were not sure what they could expect to find at sites and what they should do when they got there. It was important, therefore, that people made some visits to a number of sites so that they could familiarise themselves with heritage experiences before making final decisions about the form of the project.

Originally, the project was proposed by the lead author as an access to heritage project; however, after a number of funding setbacks some of the gatekeeper personnel in particular were eager for the Forum to focus on other outputs. It was recognised that the views of the project supporters should not direct the outcome of the decision, so there were a number of meetings at different venues at which the Forum members considered whether they would like to be involved in an arts-based project, an access project or an as yet undefined alternative. Forum members were in strong agreement that they wished to continue with an evaluative access project.

The Forum members decided that they wanted to examine the whole visitor experience at the heritage sites they visited. They wished to consider:

- how they found out about a venue;
- how they got there;
- what happens when they got there;
- whether they felt welcome;
- how they found their way around;
- whether they could understand what it was all about;
- whether it was aimed at them;
- whether it held their interest.

The arrangement of visits

The Forum made over 50 visits to 13 venues across Liverpool and Merseyside. The majority of these were unaccompanied, but the Forum also chose to attend some specific activities offered by heritage sites. The members joined a hands-on workshop led by museum education staff, accompanied guided tours at several venues, and used audio tours that were on offer.

Having decided to visit a particular site, the project coordinator made contact with the venue on behalf of the Forum. This allowed the sites to show that they were interested in the Forum and its aims, and for the Forum to respond to any questions the site might have about their research methods. During this initial contact, the Forum would invite a member of staff to meet with the group during the visit, and would offer to share insights that came out of the visits.

Generally, about four people with learning difficulties went on each visit, involving one or two of the groups that make up the Forum. On these visits they followed their favoured routine. They arrived at 11 o'clock, usually travelling by taxi, spent an hour going around the site (or often, part of the site), and then went to the site café to discuss the experience. If requested they would either feed back their findings straightaway or record them in an accessible written report.

Recording the experience

At all Forum sessions, visual images played a key communication role. Symbols, photographs and drawings were used alongside the written and spoken word to facilitate the sharing and recording of ideas. The project coordinator supported this process by supplying a wide range of images, objects and materials at meetings. A variety of tools were trialled by the Forum to assist in the visit debrief sessions too. Video footage was taken of some visits, but examining and using the material proved to be challenging. Additional expertise was sought to produce an accessible record of the Forum's findings, but it was not available during the initial evaluative process. There was also a trial of disposable and digital cameras. These provided a useful record of the experience, but the images from the disposable cameras were not available soon enough to help discuss visits, and though the digital cameras offered the opportunity of immediate images their value relied upon the availability of equipment and technical knowledge. Postcards of artefacts were used on occasion, too, and though they limited discussion to predetermined items, they were of some positive value.

The Forum also created a post-tour questionnaire that allowed them to record experiences, the ways they had used different senses, and what they had found enjoyable and not enjoyable. This was a useful discussion tool, allowing people to express their views through text and/or imagery alongside their peers and supporters. The Forum recognised, too, that the supporters had insights through their experience as advocates and as observers of the experience. They also recognised that supporters might feel a need to incorporate these views into those of people with learning difficulties if they did not have their own questionnaire. The supporters were therefore provided with separate questionnaires. These often raised issues that the Forum had not initially identified but went on to discuss.

The views of the project coordinator were also taken into consideration. As the only individual who attended all the visits, Ticky felt that she gained an insight into the perspectives of Forum members in a broader sense. She also reflected on the experience with members of the Forum, the project leader and the academic researcher. She used this insight to help the Forum compare and contrast perspectives during discussions. In addition, her observations, recorded as a participant-observer, reflected her involvement in site visits in which she noted and responded to the actions and interests of the Forum members while trying to avoid directing their focus. As a result of these observations she raised questions with the Forum during the debrief session.

The Forum used an ongoing, informal process of theoretical saturation (Strauss and Corbin 1998) to evaluate their data and generate their recommendations. They recorded findings in a particular category until they recognised that no new relationships, properties or dimensions were emerging and that they were repeating themselves. As the Forum would say, 'We've said that quite a few times now.' In addition, issues that lacked clarity were used as the basis for discussions and questions on subsequent visits. Individual members of the Forum and their supporters would also explore and discuss materials and experiences beyond the formal Forum meetings and would feed back their views at subsequent sessions. The Forum members took the opportunity, as well, to assess how effective some of their ideas would be in practice. They arranged one workshop to explore their view that notes on exhibits need to contain key information only and that simplified text and symbols could help with access to written descriptions of artefacts.

The Forum, relationships and ways of working

The Forum and its supporters' experience was that they needed up to 10 visits to develop heritage site literacy, and that they would have been helped with pre-visit information. Given that they were not aware of what was available to them, either free of charge or as part of the mainstream and programme-specific provision, it was evident that sites are not making links with people with learning difficulties and their service providers, and are not actively marketing what is already on offer.

This hesitancy to engage was not surprising to the Forum members, as they realised that many people working in heritage sites have minimal experience of people with learning difficulties and feel uncertain about what might be expected of them. Having to overcome these barriers is time-consuming and demotivating, however. For example, up to four hours were regularly spent on initially identifying an appropriate staff member to speak to at a site, and then there was often hesitancy and uncertainty about working with the Forum. It was often only after discussions with the project coordinator that site staff were enthusiastic about upcoming visits, but this enthusiasm rarely spread through the rest of the workforce, so that when Forum members arrived at sites they generally did not feel welcomed. This lack of engagement was also evident in the small number of sites that sent staff to discuss the Forum's experience of a visit. Only three sites asked for feedback. Worse still, it was commonplace for site staff to say they would meet up with the Forum but not turn up.

The Forum recognised that firsthand experience is the only way for people to learn that they have to do very little that is different or difficult when meeting people with learning difficulties. For this reason, the Forum recommended that Disability Awareness training, which involves people with learning difficulties, should be undertaken at all sites. This would allow heritage sites to establish a network of staff with experience of involvement with this part of the community. A key finding that underlines the importance of a positive human response is the Forum's recognition that access to a site is best supported neither by technology nor facilities, but by a tour guide who engages with people and builds on their current knowledge and experience. It is also important that a number of supporters, when reflecting on their involvement with the Forum, recognised that the people with learning difficulties had had a transformative effect, both on their own views of effective practice, and on their own enthusiasm and ability to engage with them as individuals.

One of the key factors that the Forum identified for successful working related to timescales. Partly this was as a result of being a collaborative and inclusive project, requiring the development of trust and strong social cohesion. Longer time schedules allowed this social element to be developed to the benefit of all. For example, time was allocated for a food break, providing not only a social opportunity but also a chance to refocus the group; as a result café meetings became key debriefing points.

The Forum preferred to work in short bursts across a longer period of time too, as it supported flexible arrangement for members of the Forum. It also fitted in with the manner in which people with learning difficulties are often supported by the wider community; for example transport issues mean that starting before 11am excludes many, whilst finishing late can interfere with supporters' wider working lives. Shorter activities across time also helped those who do not easily concentrate over extended periods and meant all involved could make sure that what had been communicated had been understood. It allowed people to provide information a number of times and in small chunks, and for the Forum to give a concentrated focus on individual aspects of a heritage site during each visit.

The desire for an ongoing relationship of regular visits across a period of several months did not always match up with the approach adopted by sites. For example, when working with the designers at St George's Hall, funders and heritage staff had created time constraints that work against an inclusive approach; so, for instance, suggestions could not be tested to see if they worked as the Forum intended.

It was recognised by the Forum that, on occasions, heritage sites preferred to communicate with an 'access expert' rather than directly with them. For example, the project coordinator was positioned as the sole representative invited to design meetings at St George's Hall. The Forum recognised the role that the project coordinator and other independent individuals played in supporting their advocacy; however, they felt strongly that priorities should be set by the people with learning difficulties, and that those arranging finances, advising the group or wishing to discuss their findings should attend meetings with the people with learning difficulties.

The relationship between individuals as self-advocates and those advocating on their behalf is a complex one. The attendance of Forum members was even affected by this, as without consistent supporter presence and engagement, few members could maintain involvement. At Forum meetings it was also clear that these supporters or other visitors could dominate proceedings with relative ease. A number of supporters highlighted the ongoing need to reflect on whether the people with learning difficulties were being encouraged to follow or lead.

There was also a need for ongoing reflection in relation to project aims. Without intending to, it is all too easy for supporters' interests and priorities to come to the fore, partly because of the mix of enthusiasm and uncertainty felt by people with learning difficulties for new experiences and partly because of the pace at which they tend to work. Both the project coordinator and the academic adviser recognised that their own interests could have had an overly influential impact on the foci of the project. As described earlier it was the academic adviser's original proposal that an access project should be under-taken, whilst the project coordinator was interested in the sorts of tactile art experiences that formed the basis for the Forum's multi-sensory art project at St George's Hall. Of course, the Forum clearly voiced their desire to carry out these projects, taking ownership of them and both gaining and contributing a great deal in the process; however, questions of agency are still raised.

As the external academic advising the Forum, the issue of agency was evident to me, in three key areas. First, many people with learning difficulties have a 'record of agentive encounters' (Bruner 1996: 36) related to the past and the future that teaches them that their view will rarely be sought and/or their voice will be misheard. Second, the hesitancy of people to engage with indi-viduals with learning difficulties means that they often require another indi-vidual to intercede on their behalf. Their agency is therefore frequently expressed through the agentive act of another. This too becomes part of their 'record of agentive encounters', and it can be all too easy to come to rely upon others' interventions, and for this to become an unchallenged part of one's identity. Third, as supporters intervening on behalf of another, it is a constant challenge to assure that we do not easily accept our agentive acts as being the agency of another. Part of the identity of supporters must be questioning their own 'record of agentive encounters' so they can come to understand how their self 'extends outwards to the things and activities and places with which we become "ego-involved"' (Bruner 1996: 36), and imposes its agency upon others. This requires openness and honesty, but can never fully resolve the dilemma. In supporting you may take control; in not supporting you may leave barriers in place.

The Forum views on accessible provision

Throughout their research the Forum members were struck by how provision that enhances their access will benefit many different people. An example of this broader value was their suggestion that heritage site staff within each room have access to simplified materials to assist them in talking to lots of people about artefacts and the site. The Forum recognised, too, that their desire for more seating at sites would be appreciated by plenty of other visitors.

The members were particularly struck by the inconsistent nature of symbols to support interpretation (when sites use them) and their general lack of use elsewhere. The complexity of this issue was not lost on the Forum, however. For example, the group had a long discussion about whether their final reports should use Widgit symbols (as used in Figure 6.1), those supplied by MENCAP (as used in Figure 6.3) or those from a number of other providers. What was clear was that most sites have confusing wayfinding. Signs are often not clearly visible and do not obviously link to their intended artefacts. The Forum felt colour coding for directions would be useful, and that contrasting colours on floors and walls would help define a space; however, too many colours and patterns would be counterproductive. The Forum found that clear, large, symbol-based signs were the most valuable. They were not happy with crowded signs, but liked fonts that were large and strongly contrasted. They valued simplified text that identified key information and used supporting symbols/pictures. They also valued signs that explained what people could do in different spaces (e.g. what can be sat on and what can be touched).

The Forum members were particularly keen when sites enabled them to use different senses. They valued the use of sound, including audio text at the press of a button, but recognised that it was problematic if there were too many sounds going on at once or if a sound was muffled. They identified strong contrast in colour and texture as making exhibits accessible, and that the use of people in costumes brought spaces to life, particularly if the people in the costumes responded positively to them. Similarly, the Forum members responded positively to hands-on exhibits, but noted that opportunities to touch things were limited in most settings. A number of supporters were surprised by how much pleasure people got from rummaging through drawers to explore the less 'fashionable' artefacts. Technology was also recognised as a way to minimise reliance upon written text, and the Forum enjoyed interactive computer games and felt that music and video created an inviting sense of place.

Our advice about access to heritage sites	
People with a learning difficulty:	
• Have not ususally visited many heritage sites • Like short visits • Like information in small chunks	• Want clear directions • Like to use all their senses • Don't enjoy lots of things happening at the same time
• Want heritage sites to tell them what is going on • Want to feel welcome • Like staff who are trained by people with a learning difficulty	• Enjoy videos, music and computers • Want hands-on exhibits • Enjoy the use of contrasting colours for directions • Enjoy the use of contrasting colours for exhibits
• Like signs with symbols • Like signs with simple language • Like signs that are easy to see and read	• Like people to explain the site • Enjoy costumes • Want somewhere to sit down

Figure 6.3 Advice from the Heritage Forum about access to heritage sites

Conclusion: keeping it going

The Forum believes that its research work has just begun. In settings across the UK and beyond there are numerous specific technical issues that are untested and which can only be answered by engaging with people with learning difficulties (Rix 2005). The Forum firmly believe that a consultation process can fill this gap, and should be undertaken whenever new interpretation is designed and made for heritage sites. However, one group of 25 people cannot do it all. Heritage sites have to consider how they can best attract the attention of this population, and convince them that their views are valued.

Throughout this project the Forum expressed its satisfaction at having its work identified, showcased and appreciated. It recognised the importance of being involved in a process based on trust, respect and a commitment to produce high quality work. Given that the work of people with learning difficulties is so often sidelined, this is hardly surprising, but it would have a positive impact on any researcher's motivation. The Forum has also shown that this research process is one that can be replicated in many different settings with relative ease: views can be gathered through visual questionnaires, observation, discussion in the moment, discussion retrospectively, drawing pictures and writing labels. The research has demonstrated the value of brainstorming activities, taking photographs, recording with video and using postcards of artefacts and bringing artefacts to individuals. As researchers, Forum members have attended workshops, held regular meetings, participated in discussions and interviews and completed questionnaires with supporters. They have demonstrated that the approaches that heritage sites are familiar with, work with them too.

The Heritage Forum in Liverpool and Merseyside wishes to continue its work. Each site and each exhibition present new challenges and opportunities that can usefully be assessed by people with learning difficulties. The Forum wants other groups to follow their example too, and begin evaluating provision where they live. Hopefully this simple but effective process can gain the interest of heritage sites and funders across the country; if it does, then many more individuals from this vital part of our community will see a place for themselves within our heritage provision and will come to believe that it represents a vital part of themselves.

References

Blewitt, J. (2004) The Eden Project – making a connection, *Museum and Society*, **2**, 3, 175–89.

Bohata, K. and Reynolds, S. (2002) *Engaging Communities in Learning*, Cardiff: Learning and Skills Development Agency for Wales.

Bruner, J. (1996) *The Culture of Education*, Cambridge, MA: Harvard University Press.

Clarke, A., Dodd, J., Hooper-Greenhill, E., O'Riain, H., Selfridge, L. and Swift, F. (2002) *Learning Through Culture. The DfES Museums and Galleries Education Programme: a guide to good practice*, Online (https://lra.le.ac.uk/bitstream/2381/27/1/learningthroughcult.pdf) (accessed 6 August 2007).

Economou, M. (1999) *Evaluation Strategy for the Redevelopment of the Displays and Visitor Facilities at the Museum and Art Gallery, Kelvingrove*, Online (http://www.hatii.arts.gla.ac.uk/research/KelvinEval/KelvEvStrategyFinal.PDF) (accessed 7 August 2007).

Goodall, B., Pottinger, G., Dixon, T. and Russell, H. (2003) Heritage property, tourism and the UK Disability Discrimination Act, *Property Management*, **22**, 5, 345–57.

Lines, A., Sims, D., Powell, R., Mann, P., Dartnall, L. and Spielhofer, T. (2003) *Bigger Pictures, Broader Horizons: Widening access to adult learning in the arts and cultural sectors*, National Foundation for Educational Research, Report 394, Slough: NFER.

MENCAP (2003) *'There's nothing that can't be done', Arts for All (UK)*, Online (www.mencap.org.uk/html/news/arts_for_all.htm) (accessed 15 December 2003).

Office of the Deputy Prime Minister (2006) *Final Report for Signage and Wayfinding for People with Learning Difficulties, Building Research Technical Report 6/2005*, London: Building Research Establishment for Office of the Deputy Prime Minister.

Rayner, A. (1998) *Access in Mind: Towards the inclusive museum*, Edinburgh: Intact (The Intellectual Access Trust).

Rix, J. (2005) Checking the list: can a model of Down Syndrome help us explore the intellectual accessibility of heritage sites?, *International Journal of Heritage Studies*, **11**, 4, 341–56.

Ruiz, J. (2004) *A Literature Review of the Evidence Base for Culture, the Arts and Sport Policy*, Scottish Executive Education Department, Edinburgh: The Stationery Office.

Strauss, A. and Corbin, J. (1998) *Basics of Qualitative Research: Techniques and procedures for developing grounded theory*, Thousand Oaks, CA: Sage Publications.

Walmsley, J. and Johnson, K. (2003) *Inclusive Research with People with Learning Difficulties: Past, present and future*, London: Jessica Kingsley.

Whitaker, S., Millar, S., Edmonstone, A. and Hartley, K. (2005) *Not in College, Unemployed and Not Much Fun: Barriers to further and higher education, employment and leisure and cultural opportunities, for people with communication impairment in Scotland and suggested solutions*, Royal College of Speech and Language Therapists, Submission to Scottish Parliament Equal Opportunities Disabilities Inquiry.

Part 4

Rights and responsibilities

Chapter 7

Promoting access to community and participation

What role can citizenship education play?

Hazel Lawson

Introduction

One of the aims of the school curriculum in England is to enable all young people 'to become *responsible citizens* who make a positive contribution to society' (Qualifications and Curriculum Authority 2008b, emphasis added). Over the past 20 years, citizenship education has been developed in most established democracies in Europe, North America and Australasia ostensibly to promote the more active engagement of citizens in their democracies (Osler and Starkey 2006; Print 2007). Indeed Print (2007: 330), drawing on Crick (1998) defines citizenship education as 'programmes in education for democratic citizenship, that is, learning about being a citizen in a democracy through educational programmes in schools'.

In this chapter I examine citizenship education in England and consider the role citizenship education might play in promoting meaningful access to community and participation for people with learning difficulties. I begin by briefly exploring the meaning of 'being a citizen' for people with learning difficulties for whom fixed and traditional notions of both citizenship and adulthood may not comfortably apply. I then consider the concept of citizenship in relation to childhood; children are, of course, the recipients of, and participants in, citizenship education. The background and context of citizenship education in England is explored with specific reference to children and young people with learning difficulties. Four key themes are then addressed in terms of how citizenship education can promote access: pedagogy, participation, choice and community. I argue that citizenship education needs to be regarded as more than a curriculum subject and enacted as a principled ethical approach so that children and young people are 'living citizenship'. This then has potential for 'living access' to community and participation.

Notions of citizenship: what does it mean to be a citizen?

One of the principles underlying the *Valuing People* (Department of Health 2001) government proposals to improve the lives of people with learning difficulties and their families and carers is recognition of their *rights as citizens* (the others being inclusion, choice and independence). Key roles of a citizen have been identified as: community member, consumer, family member, lifelong learner, taxpayer, voter and worker (Further Education Funding Council 2000), with social, consumer, domestic and work roles (Law 2000). 'Being an adult' carries connotations of productive activity, including economic self-sufficiency, non-dependent family roles and personal autonomy, having full responsibility for one's own life (Dee 2006; Griffiths 1994). However, conceptions of citizenship and adult status like these may exclude some people with learning difficulties for whom such roles and levels of autonomy may not all be possible in our society (Vorhaus 2005; 2006). The very language of this debate, for example 'economic self-sufficiency' or 'full personal autonomy', as Morris (2005) points out, frequently excludes people who have learning difficulties, amongst others.

Morris (2005) perceives two main perspectives on citizenship: an individualist approach, where the nature of citizenship is determined by an individual's capacity to make choices; and a structuralist approach, where social and economic factors are considered to have greater influence on individual action. People with learning difficulties may be disenfranchised from both these perspectives: their capacity to make choices may be limited without appropriate structures and support, and social and economic factors impinge upon opportunities and possibilities to be economically self-sufficient, to be in paid employment, to be viewed as political participants. As the Disability Rights Commission (now subsumed within the Equality and Human Rights Commission) affirms, 'Without appropriate support, it is difficult or impossible for many disabled people to participate in economic (or political or social) life and fulfil their obligations as citizens' (Disability Rights Commission 2005a: 28). Citizenship can therefore be a problematic concept in relation to people with learning difficulties.

Citizenship and childhood

Is citizenship an adult status for which we are preparing children and young people, or are children citizens in their own right too? Historically childhood has been viewed as a preparation stage for adulthood (Verhellen 2000) and consequent citizenship. Neale (2004: 7) describes two ways of viewing children: as 'welfare dependants' or as 'young citizens'. As welfare dependants, children are viewed as incompetent and vulnerable, as needing care, protection and guidance; their childhoods are determined by adults. Regarding children as young citizens, he argues, means children are viewed as people, with strengths and competencies, needing recognition, respect and participation, and influencing their own childhoods. This relates to the distinction made in the sociology of childhood between childhood as *becoming* or as *being*, as 'a preparatory status for adulthood' or as 'a status in its own right' (Arthur and Croll 2007: 233).

If citizenship is seen as 'an entitlement to recognition, respect and participation' as Neale (2004: 8) proposes, then this applies to children as much as
adults. Furthermore, citizenship rights have been extended to children under
the terms of the United Nations Convention on the Rights of the Child
(United Nations 1989), which provided rights to children of protection,
provision (access to health and education, for example) and participation
(Gilbert *et al* 2005). As Verhellen (2000: 35) comments, 'these participation rights
recognise children as meaning-makers and acknowledge their citizenship'.

There remains a confused position in the field of education, however. Whilst
the school curriculum aims for pupils *to become responsible citizens* (Qualifications
and Curriculum Authority 2008b), government guidance on listening to the
voices of young people states that pupil participation sends 'a powerful message
that children and young people of all ages *are citizens too'* (Department for
Children, Schools and Families 2008: p7, emphasis added) and the National
Curriculum in action website states that 'young people *are already citizens'*
(Qualifications and Curriculum Authority 2008a).

Citizenship is thus also a problematic concept in relation to childhood. All
children take part in citizenship education in schools yet the concept and interpretation of citizenship can be varied. Such differing understandings of citizenship may translate into different understandings of, and approaches to,
citizenship education in schools (Gearon 2003; Kerr and Cleaver 2004). This
may especially be the case for children with learning difficulties if the nature of
adult citizenship is also problematic for them. I suggest that this presents a dual
difficulty and complication in interpreting citizenship education for children
and young people with learning difficulties.

Citizenship education

In this section I will consider two key issues: citizenship as a curriculum subject
and education about citizenship, through citizenship and for citizenship.

Citizenship as a curriculum subject

Citizenship became a statutory National Curriculum foundation subject in
England from September 2002 for pupils aged 11–16 years. It is also part of a
non-statutory framework for Personal Social and Health Education (PSHE) and
Citizenship for the primary education phase where 'preparing to play an active
role as citizens' is one of four strands (Department for Education and
Employment/Qualifications and Curriculum Authority 1999). The importance
of citizenship education is described as follows:

> Citizenship equips pupils with the knowledge and skills needed for
> effective and democratic participation. It helps pupils to become
> informed, critical, active citizens who have the confidence and conviction

to work collaboratively, take action and try to make a difference in their communities and the wider world. (Qualifications and Curriculum Authority 2008c)

The organisation of citizenship education within the curriculum and school can take a number of forms (Fergusson and Lawson 2003; Kerr *et al* 2007): for example, dedicated discrete curriculum time for citizenship lessons; citizenship through other subjects and curriculum areas; involvement in the life of the school and community; extension activities and school events. All pupils, including those with learning difficulties, are entitled to a broad, balanced curriculum, which includes the National Curriculum and therefore citizenship. The Qualifications and Curriculum Authority (QCA) publishes schemes of work and guidance on the teaching and assessing of citizenship. These publications draw on the National Curriculum inclusion statement and go further than previously published guidance and schemes of work for other subjects in terms of relevance and meaningfulness for pupils with learning difficulties. However, they are not specifically designed for these pupils and often require much adaptation. The QCA series of booklets entitled *Planning, Teaching and Assessing the Curriculum for Pupils with Learning Difficulties,* though, were developed explicitly for staff working with pupils with learning difficulties and the PSHE and citizenship booklet (Qualifications and Curriculum Authority 2001) outlines the importance of those curriculum areas for pupils with learning difficulties:

> PSHE and citizenship offer pupils with learning difficulties opportunities to:
> * make decisions and choices;
> * develop personal autonomy by having a degree of responsibility and control over their lives;
> * make a difference or make changes by their individual or collective actions;
> * find out that there are different viewpoints which lead to a respect for the opinion of others. (Qualifications and Curriculum Authority 2001: 4)

It also develops the meaning of citizenship education for pupils with learning difficulties, particularly for those at the earliest levels of development:

> Knowledge and understanding of citizenship starts by pupils interacting with adults they know and other pupils in familiar one-to-one activities and small group situations, as well as taking part in the regular routines, roles and responsibilities of classroom and school life. Pupils learn about the right and wrong ways to behave through the boundaries set by others. Citizenship gives contexts in which all pupils, particularly those with learning difficulties, can move from a personal view of themselves and their immediate world, towards a much wider perspective. This helps them think about other people and ways in which they can make a difference to others

and the world around them. Pupils learn about the differences in people and how to value those differences. (Qualifications and Curriculum Authority 2001:5)

Pavey (2003) argues that this QCA guidance makes assumptions that more abstract notions are not accessible and she wonders whether citizenship education is watered down for pupils with learning difficulties. Her own research, for example, indicates that political awareness is a low priority for schools and colleges. The 2008/09 Citizenship programmes of study are based on three key concepts: democracy and justice, rights and responsibilities, and identities and diversity. Curriculum content includes political, legal and human rights; roles of the law and justice system; voting and elections; freedom of speech; public services; public money; diversity; and the world as a global community. It will be interesting to see how these are interpreted for teaching children and young people with learning difficulties, whether they are 'watered down', especially as these are areas to which people with learning difficulties have historically had little access.

Education about citizenship, through citizenship and for citizenship

We can take a fairly narrow view of curriculum as what is 'taught' in lessons, the subject knowledge elements of curriculum, but if we take the detail of curriculum content away it forces us to develop a view of fundamental principles. What is the essence of citizenship education for all children and young people? Is this any different for children and young people with learning difficulties? Kerr (2000) makes interesting distinctions between:

- education *about* citizenship: explicit curriculum knowledge and content;
- education *through* citizenship: active, participative, often implicit, experiences; and
- education *for* citizenship: equipping young people through the first two for adult citizen status and life.

We can see how these different interpretations may also translate into different approaches within schools.

The third of these, education *for* citizenship, relates back to the earlier point about children being citizens or becoming citizens. The Citizenship Foundation states that citizenship education is 'education *for* citizenship – that is, education which aims to help people learn how to become active, informed and responsible citizens ... to prepare them for life as citizens of a democracy' (The Citizenship Foundation, no date, emphasis added). There is a tension here between citizenship education as a set of learning outcomes and citizenship as an ongoing process (Arthur and Croll 2007). Are we preparing children to become citizens, education *for* citizenship now, or do we want them to be enacting citizenship as a member of a school community or other communities?

Kerr and Cleaver (2004), in their literature review of citizenship education one year on from its statutory introduction, noted that the majority of schools were focusing narrowly on citizenship education in the curriculum and had not fully considered the implications of the active citizenship dimension, thus focusing more on education *about* citizenship. We need to consider with honesty, sensitivity and realism that some aspects of the citizenship curriculum content may not be appropriate for some pupils with learning difficulties, and move from a concern about entitlement to specific content and accompanying concerns about 'watering down' (Pavey 2003) to a consideration of the fundamental nature of citizenship, active citizenship and education *through* citizenship (Lawson 2003a).

There are numerous calls for active citizenship by 'encouraging and providing opportunities for young people to engage and participate' (Kerr and Cleaver 2004: 33) and through students engaging with the 'practice of democracy' (Kennedy 2003: 65). A major perceived barrier to such active citizenship, it is argued, lies in prevailing cultures and institutional and social structures in schools (Alexander 2002; Faulks 2006), which are perceived as being 'largely hierarchical and undemocratic' (Kerr and Cleaver 2004: 33) and as not promoting student voice (Clarke 2002). Watts (2006: 88) goes as far as to say that the broad context of schooling in contemporary England actually 'militates against education in citizenship and democracy'.

The review by Ireland *et al* (2006: vi) of active citizenship noted that secondary school pupils had opportunities for, and experiences of, active citizenship, but that these tended to be confined to the school context and they were 'opportunities to *take part* rather than opportunities to effect *real change* by engaging with the decision-making process'. Additionally these experiences often only involved certain groups of students, 'the committed or enthusiastic', rather than all students, despite an invitation for all students to participate. In particular, Ireland *et al* (2006: 78) suggest, 'the less academically able, those who underachieve and the socially excluded' need to be more explicitly included. Despite legislation that enshrines children's rights, especially for children defined as having special educational needs, there are, Allan (2008: 40) notes, 'few opportunities to exercise these rights because schools are more concerned to ensure children are passive, under control and subject to discipline'. This might be particularly so for children and young people with learning difficulties who experience greater control and surveillance over their lives (Allan 1999).

There are enormous challenges here for citizenship education and for school communities. Yet it seems to me that it is primarily through the ethos and community of the school, the teaching approaches and attitudes adopted by the staff, the relationships between staff and pupils and the dignity and respect afforded to each other that recognition and practice of active citizenship occurs. What does it actually mean when we state that we respect and value pupils? Where are pupils experiencing democracy in action? What aspects of whole school ethos and individual class culture relate to citizenship? What do these actually look like in practice? Are they real and meaningful experiences? Can they have a real impact?

Four themes emerge here for further exploration in terms of their implications for promoting access through citizenship education: pedagogy, participation, choice and community.

Pedagogy

There are pedagogical implications of viewing children as citizens, seeing children 'through the lens of their citizenship' (Neale 2004: 8). In their recent research about citizenship education in secondary schools, however, Kerr *et al* (2007: 57) found there was 'still a tendency towards traditional methods of *"teaching"* students, rather than a focus upon student-centred learning'. As McLaughlin and Byers (2001: 72) observe:

> active citizenship builds on the active learning approach. The learning needs to be based in the world of the student and it involves action. If students are to learn from their own experience and to struggle with what that means then teachers will have to allow a certain amount of risk.

Active learning approaches and 'participatory pedagogies' are characterised, for example, by: group inquiry and collaborative learning (Print 2007); facilitative conversation, learner-centred teaching, and holistic, process-oriented pedagogies (Deakin-Crick *et al* 2005); collaboration, problem solving and engagement (Nind 2007); negotiation and facilitation rather than direction, and an absence of teacher-imposed targets or objectives (Babbage *et al* 1999). Writing about people with profound and multiple learning difficulties, Nind (2007: 112) argues that active and interactive learning are about 'empowerment, democracy and citizenship' and 'rehearsing and preparing learners to participate more fully in communities'. Such approaches should therefore underpin citizenship education, emphasising education *through* citizenship. Indeed Deakin-Crick *et al* (2005: 5–6) call this a citizenship pedagogy:

> A citizenship pedagogy ... will have at its core communication, facilitating and enabling, dialogue and discussion, encouragement to engage with learning, and relating learning to experience. This more conversational and negotiated style of teaching and learning involves mutually respectful teacher-student relationships where traditional authoritarian patterns of control are no longer appropriate.

Acknowledging children in this way as 'social actors in their own right' may challenge traditional patterns of hierarchy and structural organisation and the dynamics of power between adult and child, teacher and pupil (Devine 2002). The institution of school defines what it is to be a child and pupil, controlling and organising time and space and defining what is important. However, Devine (2002: 307) proposes, 'where adult-child, teacher-pupil relations are framed in terms of voice, belonging and active participation, children will be empowered to define and understand themselves as individuals with the capacity to act and exercise their voice in a meaningful manner'. This suggests a sharing of power with children and young people. For staff working with children and young people with learning difficulties, where the traditional adult-child, teacher-pupil power differential may be even greater, this may be especially challenging (Sebba *et al* 1993).

Pedagogical approach and teacher-pupil relations seem crucial, then, to the development of education through citizenship. Indeed an international study of different approaches to the learning and teaching of citizenship emphasised that 'active citizenship' could be 'understood as much in terms of an *approach to learning* as of young people's *participation* in school and community life' (Nelson and Kerr 2006: vi).

Participation

The participation of children and young people is inherent in the citizenship pedagogy described in the previous section. Indeed citizenship education can be viewed as a forum for a participation agenda. Consultation and participation are also enshrined in a wide range of legislation. For example, article 12 of the UN Convention on the Rights of the Child (United Nations 1989) gave every child the right to be heard on issues that affect them and the Education Act 2002 requires that students' views are to be considered regarding decisions that affect them in school life. It is interesting that the right to express views and for these to be considered is particularly evident for children defined as having special educational needs, in legislation and guidance at least (Department for Education and Skills 2001a; 2001b).

May (2004) problematises the notion of participation as expressed in the special educational needs Code of Practice (Department for Education and Skills 2001a), suggesting that the term is used in different ways which each imply different levels of participation, from simply taking part, through consultation and involvement, to participation as a reciprocal partner. A recent government definition of participation states:

> By children's and young people's participation we mean adults working with children and young people to ensure that their views are heard and valued in the taking of decisions which affect them, and that they are supported in making a positive contribution to their school and local community. (Departments for Children, Schools and Families 2008: 5)

May (2004: 69) might suggest, along with other definitions, that this 'renders participation as delineated by professionals and portrays it as something that is imposed on pupils'.

Cleaver *et al* (2007) express similar concerns about definitions of participation and about confusion between 'voice' and 'participation'. They prefer Treseders' (1997: 4) definition that 'participation is a process where someone influences decisions about their lives and this leads to change'. Here, participation is about making a difference and having a clear sense of agency; it is much more than 'consultation', 'hearing views' or 'listening to voices'. It is crucial to avoid tokenism and manipulation in place of genuine participation (Hart 1992). Attempts to seek children's views through formal consultation exercises can be symbolic gestures (Allan 2008) and empty exercises (Neale 2004) that rarely lead to changes in practice. Lodge (2005) also draws our attention to the purposes for student participation. She draws a distinction between participation for institutional purposes, often compliance, such as OFSTED pupil surveys and consultation about improvement in the appearance of the school, and participation encouraged and practised for community purposes, such as the improvement of learning. Aspis (2002) draws a similar distinction in discussing self-advocacy in adult learning disability settings where boundaries are often set that determine what people can advocate for and results are frequently superficial.

Much government guidance to schools (for example, Children and Young People's Unit 2001; Department for Children, Schools and Families 2008; Department for Education and Skills 2004a, 2004b) reflects a commitment to increase children and young people's participation. However, even with the commitment to make adaptations, limits to participation are evident within the guidance. In UNCRC Article 12 the views of the child are given due weight in accordance with the age and maturity of the child, and in the Education Act 2002 children's views are to be considered in the light of their age and understanding. In the SEN Code of Practice (Department for Education and Skills 2001a:14), whilst there is a clear 'principle of seeking and taking account of the ascertainable views of the child or young person' and it is recognised that support is required to enable some children to participate, it still states that children should 'where possible' participate, and that children 'who are capable of forming views' have participation rights. As May (2004) suggests, this is conditional participation: if you are old enough, mature enough, understand enough.

The Code empowers professionals to decide whether participation is appropriate for pupils, if their views should be taken seriously. 'By rendering the child's wishes revocable on account of these conditions, the law demeans the strength of their rights', May (2004: 70) argues. This is crucial to issues of access: if participation is conditional then access to community will also be conditional.

Ensuring the opportunity for participation of children and young people with profound learning difficulties is complex (and, of course, people have a right not to participate as well). The SEN toolkit suggests that:

> For a very few children with profound needs, it may not be possible to directly ascertain their feelings. Adults will need to interpret the child's

responses and agree on a way forward that takes account of their interpretation of the child's feelings and wishes. (Department for Education and Skills 2001b: 6)

Advocacy here becomes important, where another person (or people) seeks to understand and represent the child or young person with learning difficulties. There are probably more examples of advocacy and person-centred approaches with adults (Gray and Jackson 2001; National Institute of Adult Continuing Education 2006), but there is a growing commitment to such advocacy for children and young people with learning difficulties in schools through, for example, person-centred thinking (Murray and Sanderson 2007).

Choice

Advocacy and person-centred approaches are regarded as crucial in enabling people with learning difficulties to have choice and control over their lives (Department of Health 2001). Should choice-making be part of school life and part of citizenship education? Neale (2004) suggests that choice and decision-making are not the same thing as participation. He purports that young children actually prefer to make decisions collaboratively with supportive adults, but that these need to be based on transparency and open communication. In this way, choice-making seems to be viewed as a sub-part of a much larger ethos of participation. Again, we see the view that participation is not something to be 'done to' or even 'done with' children and young people, but is part of an overall philosophy, a way of working, a way of teaching, that is part of a citizenship pedagogy. To make choices, a young person 'needs not only the concept of choice and the skills to make one, he (or she) needs to see himself (or herself), and be seen by others as a choice-maker' (Griffiths 1994: 16) and the opportunities and occasions to make meaningful choices.

Marchant and Kirby (2004) suggest that children need to learn to choose, through having 'meaningful experience of real choices and being supported to understand the options and the consequences of choosing one thing over another'. They argue that:

> Adults can become so preoccupied with giving children options that they offer unnecessary, unrealistic or complex choices. Children are sometimes presented with an apparent opportunity to make decisions when their choices are in fact limited or nonexistent. Apparently open questions, such as 'what shall we do today?' can create confusion unless the child has understood that the options are painting, bricks or dressing up, rather than going to the park or going home. (Marchant and Kirby 2004: 130)

Additionally, enabling young people to make choices does not necessarily mean providing limitless choices. It is about appropriate and genuine options, sometimes using adults' knowledge of children's abilities and preferences (Kirby *et al* 2003). As Morris suggests, 'a need for support to make choices does not mean that someone cannot experience self-determination' (Morris 2005: 6). Indeed, from a capability theory perspective, children and young people with learning difficulties would be provided with *additional* opportunities and resources to participate effectively (Terzi 2007). Ware (2004: 177) points out the 'extended and intensive intervention' that is necessary to support people with profound learning difficulties to make choices.

Choices, however, must be available. Hughes *et al* (2005) state that the concept of choice in terms of what, how and when to learn (and even why), for example, is not open to many people with learning difficulties. Too often choices and options for disabled adults are limited and circumscribed (Disability Rights Commission 2005a), professionally determined (May 2004). Access to choice would seem to be an important feature of access to citizenship and community.

Community

A sense of community and concern to belong to a community are among the key factors that 'foster and sustain active citizenship' (Ireland *et al* 2006). In the study by Ireland *et al* (2006), students viewed school as the main social and participative community in their lives, though also caring about what happened in the wider community especially in relation to family and neighbourhood networks. A distinction is frequently made between active citizenship within the school community and the school in the wider community. Ireland *et al* (2006) recognised that this sense of belonging within the school community can be difficult to create and establish where schools serve students from disparate communities. For young people with learning difficulties in specialist settings the notion of local community can be particularly problematic. Often such schools serve a wide geographical area and children and young people have lengthy journeys to travel to school. Children and young people with learning difficulties frequently have limited engagement with social networks outside of school (Lewis *et al* 2007) and the school community, whether mainstream or special, may be of greater importance. When discussing access to community, therefore, it is crucial to consider what sort of community we are referring to.

Fergusson and Lawson (2003) suggest alternative conceptions of community for young people with profound and multiple learning difficulties, commencing with a very immediate community: oneself within the immediate environment (awareness, preferences, control of personal environment, identity), moving to a broader understanding of self with (familiar) others, then communities of the class, the whole school, the local community (geographically local to school, geographically local to home, local friendships) and the notion of national and global communities. In this way access to community starts from a familiar focus and moves out.

Community participation incorporates an active element, which fosters a sense of purpose and belonging and desire and ability to make a difference (Qualifications and Curriculum Authority 2008a). Ireland *et al* (2006: 56) identify several key issues that affect the extent to which young people felt a sense of belonging to their school communities, issues that link closely to themes already highlighted in this chapter and relate to all children and young people, including those with learning difficulties. So, the key issues of having a say in decisions made in school and relationships in school between teachers and students are both aspects discussed above in relation to pedagogy; levels of student engagement relate to notions of active citizenship; and belonging to a smaller community within the school community has also been recommended (Fergusson and Lawson 2003). It seems that the elements that are identified as supporting a sense of belonging in school communities are interrelated with the features of education through citizenship emphasised in this chapter. Citizenship education may therefore support access to community. Access to community as a pupil would also seem to be important in terms of promoting access to community for adults. For Duffy (2005), one of the six keys to citizenship for people with learning difficulties, along with self-determination, direction, money, home and support, is active engagement in the life of the community and the development of one's own network of relationships.

We must also note that notions of community and belonging are being transformed by rapid social and technological change and young people are frequently part of online social networks/communities (Coleman with Rowe 2005). Determining and defining the community, as perhaps schools inevitably do, may be just as limiting as professionally determined choices. We need to keep the notion of community fluid to enable self-determination of community and 'living access' rather than controlled or determined access.

Conclusion

Whilst there is some mistrust regarding the introduction of citizenship as a school curriculum subject, with perceptions of a government hidden agenda and a 'politically-fashioned quick fix' to society's ills (Greenwood and Robins 2002), citizenship education seems to offer a great opportunity for children and young people with learning difficulties with the potential to transform schooling and open up participation and access to community(ies).

A government curriculum review proposes that citizenship be taught as a discrete curriculum subject in schools (Department for Education and Skills 2007). In this chapter, however, I have argued that citizenship education, especially for children and young people with learning difficulties, must be more about a fundamental ethos of citizenship than 'just' teaching it. Citizenship education, participation and citizenship/participative pedagogy need to be 'embraced as an essential (rather than detached) process in schools' (May 2004: 70). It is not particularly about the subject knowledge of citizenship, Delors' 'learning to know' (Delors 1996), but about the authentic enacting of citizenship within classrooms, schools and in relevant wider communities; learning to do, learning to live together and learning to be. Focusing teachers who work with children and young people with learning difficulties on active citizenship, on 'living and experiencing citizenship' (Hine 2004: 40), might lead them away from prescribed curriculum content, from objectives-led behavioural teaching and functional skills-based life skills programmes and really focus on the less measurable aspects of education concerning active participation.

There are many concerns, not least concerning tokenism and manipulation. There is a distinction to be made between formal consultation, 'a one-off activity that is simply "tacked onto" organisational structures', and participation that is autonomous and automatic, 'built into routine day-to-day interactions between adults and children' (Neale 2004: 2). Deakin *et al* (2005) in their systematic review of the impact of citizenship education on student learning and achievement, suggested that the findings implied 'the need for a radical review of the system and structure of schooling so as to incorporate citizenship education strategies and to reconceptualise pedagogy as learner-centred' (Deakin *et al* 2005: 65). Cleaver *et al* (2007) similarly argue that cultural change is required at both an individual level and at a collective societal level. Within school, staff at all levels must view pupils as active participants, as meaning makers, as citizens now, rather than in the future (Lawson 2003b). As Morris (2005:34) states, 'it is not impairment which determines whether disabled people can be full and equal citizens, but socially constructed barriers'.

The Disability Rights Commission, drawing upon concepts of citizenship proposed by disabled people: self determination, participation and contribution (Morris 2005) aims for 'equal citizenship' by 2020 such that disabled people enjoy full membership of society, have control over their own lives, help shape the world we live in, are equipped to play a part, make a valued contribution and get on in life (Disability Rights Commission 2005b). In order to promote access to citizenship, I suggest it is more than participation we need to strive for. Within schools, participation can take place within adult decision-making systems, structures and processes. More, it is citizenship now, living citizenship, regarding and relating with children and young people as active citizens with political voice, the right to choose, set the agenda and take action. Just as *living citizenship* is not about curriculum content but about pedagogical approach and relationships, so *living and experiencing access* to participation and community is not just about adapting structures and systems and removing barriers but also about principled, ethical relationships. Education *through* citizenship may support these.

References

Alexander, T. (2002) Citizenship schools, *Teaching Citizenship*, 4, 32–7.
Allan, J. (1999) *Actively Seeking Inclusion*, London: Falmer.

Allan, J. (2008) *Rethinking Inclusive Education: The philosophers of difference in practice,* Dordrecht, The Netherlands: Springer.

Arthur, J. and Croll, P. (2007) Editorial: citizenship, democracy and education, *British Journal of Educational Studies,* **55,** 3, 233–4.

Aspis, S. (2002) Self-advocacy: vested interests and misunderstandings, *British Journal of Learning Disabilities,* **30,** 3–7.

Babbage, R., Byers, R. and Redding, H. (1999) *Approaches to Teaching and Learning,* London: Fulton.

Children and Young People's Unit (2001) *Learning to Listen: Core principles for the involvement of children and young people,* London: DfES.

Citizenship Foundation (no date) *What is citizenship, and why teach it?* Online (http://www.citizenshipfoundation.org.uk/main/page.php?286) (accessed 26 June 2008).

Clarke, M. (2002) Citizenship education and assessment: what counts as success?, in P. Scott and H. Lawson (eds) *Citizenship Education and the Curriculum,* Westport, US: Ablex.

Cleaver, E., Supple, C. and Kerr, D. (2007) *Participation under the Spotlight: Interrogating policy and practice and defining future directions,* Slough: NFER.

Coleman, S. with Rowe, C. (2005) *Remixing Citizenship: Democracy and young people's use of the internet,* London: Carnegie Young People's Initiative.

Crick, B. (1998) *Education for Citizenship and the Teaching of Democracy in Schools,* London: QCA.

Deakin-Crick, R., Taylor, M., Tew, M., Samuel, E., Durant, K. and Ritchie, S. (2005) A systematic review of the impact of citizenship education on student learning and achievement, in *Research Evidence in Education Library,* London: EPPI-Centre, Social Science Research Unit, Institute of Education.

Dee, L. (2006) *Improving Transition Planning for Young People with Special Educational Needs,* Buckingham: Open University Press.

Delors, J. (1996) *Learning: The treasure within* (Report to UNESCO of the International Commission on Education for the Twenty-first Century), Paris: UNESCO.

Department for Children, Schools and Families (2008) *Working Together: Listening to the voices of children and young people,* Online (http://publications.teachernet.gov.uk/eOrderingDownload/DCSF-00410–2008.pdf) (accessed 1 December 2008).

Department for Education and Employment/Qualifications and Curriculum Authority (1999) *The National Curriculum: Handbook for primary teachers in England* (Key stages 1 and 2), London: DfEE/QCA

Department for Education and Skills (2001a) *Special Educational Needs Code of Practice,* Annesley, Notts: DfES.

Department for Education and Skills (2001b) *Special Educational Needs Toolkit,* Annesley, Notts: DfES.

Department for Education and Skills (2004a) *Every Child Matters: Change for children,* Annesley, Notts: DfES.

Department for Education and Skills (2004b) *Working Together: Giving children and young people a say,* Annesley, Notts: DfES.

Department for Education and Skills (2007) *Curriculum Review: Diversity and citizenship* (Ajegbo review), Annesley, Notts: DfES.

Department of Health (2001) *Valuing People: A new strategy for learning disability in the 21st century,* London: The Stationery Office.

Devine, D. (2002) Children's citizenship and the structuring of adult-child relations in the primary school, *Childhood,* **9,** 3, 303–20.

Disability Rights Commission (DRC) (2005a) *Equal Opportunities Committee Disability Inquiry: Removing barriers and creating opportunities,* written evidence from the Disability Rights Commission in Scotland, Online (http://www.scottish.parliament.uk/business/committees/equal/inquiries/disability/evidence/DI037%20Disability%20Rights%20Commission.pdf) (accessed 1December 2008).

Disability Rights Commission (2005b) *Shaping the Future of Equality: Discussion paper,* London: DRC.

Duffy, S. (2005) *Keys to Citizenship: A guide to getting good support for people with learning disabilities,* (2nd edn), London: Paradigm.

Faulks, K. (2006) Education for citizenship in England's secondary schools: a critique of current principle and practice, *Journal of Educational Policy,* 21, 1, 59–74.

Fergusson, A. and Lawson, H. (2003) *Access to Citizenship,* London: Fulton.

Further Education Funding Council (2000) *Citizenship for 16–19 year olds in Education and Training: Report of the advisory group,* Coventry: FEFC.

Gearon, L. (2003) *How do we Learn to Become Good Citizens? A professional user review of UK research undertaken for the British Educational Research Association,* Nottingham: BERA.

Gilbert, T., Cochrane, A. and Greenwell, S. (2005) Citizenship: locating people with learning disabilities, *International Journal of Social Welfare,* 14, 287–96.

Gray, B. and Jackson, R. (2001) *Advocacy and Learning Disability,* London: Jessica Kingsley.

Greenwood, J. and Robins, L. (2002) Citizenship tests and education: embedding a concept, *Parliamentary Affairs,* 55, 3, 505–22.

Griffiths, M. (1994) *Transition to Adulthood,* London: Fulton.

Hart, R. A. (1992) *Children's Participation, from Tokenism to Citizenship,* UNICEF: Florence.

Hine, J. (2004) *Children and Citizenship,* London: Home Office, Online (www.homeoffice.gov.uk/rds/pdfs04/rdsolr0804.pdf) (accessed 30 July 2008).

Hughes, B., Russell, R. and Patterson, K. (2005) Nothing to be had off the peg: consumption, identity and the immobilisation of young disabled people, *Disability and Society,* 20, 1, 3–17.

Ireland, E., Kerr, D., Lopes, J. and Nelson, J. with Cleaver, E. (2006) *Active Citizenship and Young People: Opportunities, experiences and challenges in and beyond school (Citizenship education longitudinal study: fourth annual report),* Annesley, Notts: DfES.

Kennedy, K. (2003) Preparing young Australians for an uncertain future: new thinking about citizenship education, *Teaching Education,* 14, 1, 53–67.

Kerr, D. (2000) An international comparison, in D. Lawton, J. Cairns and R. Gardner (eds) *Education for Citizenship,* London: Continuum.

Kerr, D. and Cleaver, E. (2004) *Longitudinal study: Literature review – citizenship education one year on – what does it mean? Emerging definitions and approaches in the first year of National Curriculum citizenship in England,* Annesley, Notts: DfES.

Kerr, D., Lopes, J., Nelson, J., White, K., Cleaver, E. and Benton, T. (2007) *Vision Versus Pragmatism: Citizenship in the secondary school curriculum in England (Citizenship education longitudinal study: fifth annual report),* Annesley, Notts: DfES.

Kirby, P., Lanyon, C., Cronin, K. and Sinclair, R. (2003) *Building a Culture of Participation: Involving children and young people in policy, service planning, delivery and evaluation,* Annesley, Notts: DfES

Law, B. (2000) For richer? for poorer? for worker? – for citizen!, in R. Best (ed.), *Education for Spiritual, Moral, Social and Cultural Development,* London: Continuum.

Lawson, H. (2003a) Citizenship education for pupils with learning difficulties: towards participation?, *Support for Learning,* 18, 3, 117–22.

Lawson, H. (2003b) Pupil participation: questioning the extent?, *SLD Experience.* 36, 31–5.

Lewis, A., Davison, I., Ellins, J., Niblett, L., Parsons, S., Robertson, C. and Sharpe, J. (2007) The experiences of disabled children and their families, *British Journal of Special Education*, **34**, 4, 189–95.

Lodge, C. (2005) From hearing voices to engaging in dialogue: problematising student participation in school improvement, *Journal of Educational Change*, **6**, 2, 125–46.

McLaughlin, C. and Byers, R. (2001) *Personal and Social Development for All*, London: Fulton.

Marchant, R. and Kirby, P. (2004) The participation of young children: communication, consultation and involvement, in B. Neale (ed.), *Young Children's Citizenship: Ideas into practice*, York: Joseph Rowntree Foundation.

May, H. (2004) Interpreting pupil participation into practice: contributions of the SEN Code of Practice (2001), *Journal of Research in Special Educational Need*, **4**, 2, 67–73.

Morris, J. (2005) *Citizenship and Disabled People: A scoping paper prepared for the Disability Rights Commission*, Online (http://www.leeds.ac.uk/disability-studies/archiveuk/morris/Citizenship%20and%20disabled%20people.pdf) (accessed 1 December 2008)

Murray, P. and Sanderson, H. (2007) *Developing Person Centred Approaches in Schools*, Stockport: HSA Press.

Neale, B. (2004) Introduction: young children's citizenship, in B. Neale (ed.) *Young Children's Citizenship: Ideas into practice*, York: Joseph Rowntree Foundation.

Nelson, J. and Kerr, D. (2006) *Active Citizenship in INCA Countries: Definitions, policies, practices and outcomes*, London: QCA/NFER. [INCA = International Review of Curriculum and Assessment Frameworks Internet Archive]

National Institute of Adult Continuing Education (2006) *Person-centred Approaches and Adults with Learning Difficulties*, Annesley, Notts: DfES.

Nind, M. (2007) Supporting lifelong learning for people with profound and multiple learning difficulties, *Support for Learning*, **22**, 3, 111–15.

Osler, A. and Starkey, H. (2006) Education for democratic citizenship: a review of research, policy and practice 1995–2005, *Research Papers in Education*, **21**, 4, 433–66.

Pavey, B. (2003) Citizenship and special educational needs: what are you going to do about teaching them to vote?, *Support for Learning*, **18**, 2, 58–65.

Print, M. (2007) Citizenship education and youth participation in democracy, *British Journal of Educational Studies*, **55**, 3, 325–45.

Qualifications and Curriculum Authority (2001) *Planning, Teaching and Assessing the Curriculum for Pupils with Learning Difficulties: Personal, social and health education and citizenship*, London: QCA.

Qualifications and Curriculum Authority (2008a) *Community Participation*, Online (http://curriculum.qca.org.uk/key-stages-3-and-4/cross-curriculum-dimensions/communityparticipation/index.aspx?return=/key-stages-3-and-4/cross-curriculum-dimensions/index.aspx) (accessed 15 July 2008).

Qualifications and Curriculum Authority (2008b) *Curriculum Purposes, Values and Aims*, Online (http://curriculum.qca.org.uk/key-stages-3-and-4/aims/index.aspx) (accessed 26 June 2008).

Qualifications and Curriculum Authority (2008c) *The Importance of Citizenship*, Online (http://curriculum.qca.org.uk/key-stages-3-and-4/subjects/citizenship/keystage3/index.aspx?return=/key-stages-3-and-4/subjects/index.aspx) (accessed 26 June 2008).

Sebba, J., Byers, R. and Rose, R. (1993) *Redefining the Whole Curriculum for Pupils with Learning Difficulties*, London: Fulton.

Terzi, L. (2007) Capability and educational equality: the just distribution of resources to students with disabilities and special educational needs, *Journal of Philosophy of Education*. **41**, 4, 757–73.

Treseder, P. (1997) *Empowering Children and Young People,* London: Save the Children.

United Nations (1989) *Convention on the Rights of the Child,* Online (http://www2.ohchr. org/english/law/crc.htm) (accessed 1 December 2008).

Verhellen, E. (2000) Children's rights and education, in A. Osler (ed.) *Citizenship and Democracy in Schools: Diversity, identity, equality,* Stoke on Trent: Trentham.

Vorhaus, J. (2005) Citizenship, competence and profound disability, *Journal of Philosophy of Education,* **39,** 3, 461–75.

Vorhaus, J. (2006) Respecting profoundly disabled learners, *Journal of Philosophy of Education,* **40,** 3, 313–28.

Ware, J. (2004) Ascertaining the views of people with profound and multiple learning disabilities, *British Journal of Learning Disabilities,* **32,** 4, 175–9.

Watts, M. (2006) Citizenship education revisited: policy, participation and problems, *Pedagogy, Culture and Society,* **14,** 1, 83–97.

Chapter 8

Talking together about access

'When I am here I don't feel like I've got any problems'

Drew Bradley, Judith Clayton, Darren Grant, Claire Royall and Wayne Taylor

Introduction

We are from Choices Advocacy, an independent advocacy project in Southampton and South West Hampshire, and we were approached with an invitation to take part in the seminar series on Concepts of Access. While not knowing quite what to expect we thought it was a good opportunity. For Drew, Darren and Wayne it was our first experience of going to a university, so we were accessing something new from the start.

In this chapter we talk about how advocacy support enabled people to access the seminars at the University. We talk about this from the perspective of the advocacy staff (Judith and Claire) and from the perspective of the people with learning difficulties (Darren, Drew and Wayne). We use taking part in the seminar series as an example for showing people the issues. We also talk about some of our struggles for access. We wrote the chapter through talking together; Melanie Nind wrote notes from our conversations (first just Judith and Claire and then all of us) and helped us to structure our thoughts on paper, but the ideas are all ours.

Advocacy

Judith and Claire: The advocacy role is different from roles like home support worker, social worker and so on. The advocacy relationship is different: advocacy supporters don't give advice and they don't make decisions. Everything the person you support says is confidential; you don't say or do anything unless they want you to. You only go to their meetings if they invite you. People with learning difficulties are used to being talked about by professionals and they can expect that kind of thing so you have to be very clear that you never talk to the staff about them. These different working principles are vital to the relationship.

Learning to do advocacy isn't about formal training; it's about the qualities you bring and working from advocacy principles and values in everything you do. Training just develops the confidence and skills. With volunteer advocates it can be better when they're less experienced as they don't have so many preconceived ideas. Many people coming in who are naive to learning difficulties services assume that people have rights and make choices and they don't have low expectations. This can be helpful and important for challenging services sometimes. With new advocacy staff or volunteers we do a lot of shadowing, talking, reminiscing about similar situations, telling stories that illustrate how our principles are enacted. Advocacy is about making sure that people's views and opinions are heard and respected. Making sure people know they are being listened to.

Most people could use an advocate at sometime in their lives. Choices Advocacy was set up in 1994 to support people who have learning difficulties when they need to make decisions and understand what is happening.

Darren: Choices is really helpful; a great service. And we're not just saying that because Claire told us to! The people listen and they've got time for you. Sometimes social workers complain if you take too much of their time or phone them too often. Choices is about talking and listening. They help us to tell other people what we want. It's confidential. It's totally different from Social Services. They can advise you and give you information but they don't tell you what to do. That can be frustrating sometimes as you sometimes want answers. Sometimes I think they want to give answers too, and make things happen, but they can be stuck in the middle between us and staff.

Drew: I think it's a great service too because it is really good and helpful. I wish that now I have moved out of Southampton that you could still help me tell people what I want and help me sort out the problems I'm having, by coming to my meetings.

Meaningful participation: being there and joining in

Judith and Claire: You can't just ask the people we support what they think and expect long, detailed answers. You may have to tease it out. You might get a short statement and you hear that and ask another bit of the question. You gradually piece information together. Someone might go right off the point but there will be some purpose to what they are saying and you have to look for that. Or you might have to pull them right back to re-engage them with what the conversation is about. If you know the person really well you can be quite direct: 'Forget all that; what do you want to happen/tell people?' or you may need to be really gentle and spend several visits to slowly establish the trust.

When we were in the seminars we weren't sure at first how the guys wanted to be supported. We didn't want to be too obvious; it's better for us to be in the background. But we were worried at first that they might get left behind, so we'd have a quiet word: 'What do you think?'; 'Anything you want to say?' We wouldn't want them to just smile and nod as it can be really hard to disagree with people. Sometimes we would take what speakers had said and cut it down and rephrase it 'They're talking about…' sometimes just to reconnect them if they'd lost focus. We didn't need to do it at the seminars so much but sometimes in meetings if we think there's something being discussed that someone doesn't understand or recognize the importance of, then we'll ask the naive question to bring the facts out more clearly: 'I'm a bit confused here, can you tell me…?'

Drew, Darren and Wayne: The seminar experience was good. We didn't really know what to expect, just what Judith and Claire told us. We hadn't been to the university before. It was amazing to have the chance to be around normal people and normal conversations (whatever they are!) People treated us normally, with respect; they took us seriously. We might have been less keen to come to something at college where staff aren't always so nice. We were happy in the university seminars as we were treated like everyone else; treated like we didn't have special needs. There wasn't really anything we felt uncomfortable with.

Making a contribution: information we brought to the seminar

Drew, Darren and Wayne: We remember doing our posters for the seminar series. We went to the pub to think about it. We talked about our school times: getting locked up in the classroom, being bullied and getting picked on. There were also some good times.

At the university everyone behaved well, they were all mature and polite, not like people at college.

Judith and Claire: The guys taking their turn in leading one of the round table discussions was important to them. We went to the pub to talk about what they wanted to say and the informality of that worked really well. They were pleased to do it and they felt valued. There was a buzz about it on the way home. We'd often talk about the speakers with learning difficulties too; the interesting things they said.

Work behind the scenes: making sure we were there to take part

Judith and Claire: A lot of the support we did for the seminar series was behind the scenes. There was a lot of work in talking to the other people involved with the guys and in sorting out the transport. And when we travelled together we talked about the seminar topic and the people, to tune in ahead of getting there. Going home we'd always check how they felt about it all, mop up afterwards and explain anything puzzling them. Time together in a car always provides a good space for good communication.

At the seminars themselves our main goal was to enable the guys to be relaxed so they could participate and enjoy it. We'd do that by giving off a relaxed aura ourselves. Like the swan we'd appear to be just gliding along, but with our feet going like mad under the surface; we'd be keeping a watchful eye out, thinking ahead, doing reassurance work. We'd sometimes give the facilitators feedback, like about the number of breaks or the length of sessions. We certainly wouldn't want to be glued to the guys. We'd leave them to wander and mix; let them stretch their wings. But we'd be around if they didn't quite make it. If you have a negative experience it takes you back a bit. So we'd try to soften the impact of negative things so you can just learn from them and move on. We don't often talk openly about the nature of our support, it's more subtle than that and there's a lot of judgement involved, based on us knowing each other well. It would be good really if they didn't recognize what we did in support, rather than say we were as subtle as a brick!

Darren, Drew and Wayne: Looking back we think we would have been keen and able to take part in the seminars even without Judith and Claire to support us. But now we know that the experience was a good one. We didn't know that it would be at the start. With confidence in ourselves we might have gone along on our own, but then (as Judith and Claire remind us) our confidence has grown over the last couple of years. When we walked in on the first day we felt a bit shy because we did not know anyone. When we started to get to know people it was good. No one was rude to us or anything. If Judith and Claire couldn't have supported us we could have come along with someone else for support, someone like Rachel (Drew's girlfriend!) or Pat (a volunteer advocate) but not someone from day services or a social worker as they tell us what to do.

The kind of support we got from Judith and Claire meant that we didn't feel like we were being watched all the time. They didn't follow us around and make me (Drew) kick off! They didn't drive me (Darren) mad by asking 'Have you taken your meds today?' They weren't a bit bossy (Wayne). But they did help us with the reading, with writing it down, with making our posters. They joined in and they liked being there too.

Ongoing access: changes over time

Judith and Claire: The benefit of the seminars being more than just a one-off and coming back several times over the two years was that everyone got used to it and got to know each other. The university became a safe environment where the guys could be themselves and have their say, hence Darren saying 'When I'm here I don't feel like I've got any problems.' We were working harder at the beginning, but for the last seminar only one of us went and then I almost didn't need to be there. I reminded the guys about the arrangements and what they had agreed to in their role as seminar members, but I was not needed when we got there. If the seminars had continued we wouldn't need to be there; our role was reassurance only by then. That's so different to the start when I worried a bit about epilepsy and things if we were in different discussion groups. But the guys liked having the space and being involved.

Drew: I wish that sort of support would happen with staff.

What makes for good support?

Darren, Drew and Wayne: It's easier to think about what makes for bad support than to talk about what good support looks like. Drew hates it when people panic because it makes him panic; he hates it when people are anxiously all over him worrying about his epilepsy. Darren hates it when people tell him what to do, when they fuss round him, when they nag and when they go into his room without asking or when he is out. Sometimes people's hearts are in the right place, such as when they grab your arm when you cross the road, but they don't realize that you travel everywhere on your own every day. Wayne is now a qualified lifeguard; this has been possible because he's got a day services support person who actually knows what she's doing, but not all support workers are this good. We need people to be friendly with you when they are helping you with something difficult, not to get cross and angry.

Judith and Claire: It's important to prevent people getting into difficulties by helping to put them and others at their ease. We sometimes have a role in stopping panic or anxiety from developing. But mostly our role is enabling: asking the right questions, offering examples, different words and alternative ways of thinking something through. It's unbearable when support workers mollycoddle; as if 'I need you all to see I'm doing my job.' Someone recently got it all wrong during a consultation meeting. Instead of just writing down what the person with learning difficulties was saying about the service – hearing it, noting it, valuing it – she started to defend the service putting in her own justification. If you ask for comments you need to value the response.

Access struggles

Darren and Judith: Getting heard in the seminars was easy. Sometimes it's much harder. Darren has just succeeded in getting his own flat to live independently. With Judith's help he recalls how this has taken at least two years of struggle: first, expressing a desire to move out of the group home and having a place in mind but then getting turned down because it cost too much money. Going on the council list was going to take eight years, which was too long to wait, so he switched to a private let. Early on there was the need to track down a social worker and lots of work had to be done to convince him it was a good idea. And then there was the need for the support to find the deposit. Over and over again, 'I had to fight my corner. I think Social Services are starting to listen; a little.' (Darren)

Darren, Drew and Wayne: We have to live with rules to protect us. Rules about who can go out alone, who can sleep upstairs, not running up the stairs or standing on chairs and so on. Some of this is also about not doing things that other residents might copy. But some of it is because of staff worries about us having epileptic seizures. They questioned whether we could sign up to learn karate. We also have to have alarms in the rooms and wear chains with medical information on. These are the things we want to put an end to when we live by our own rules in our own homes. We want to be able to lock our own doors and be private.

At the Partnership Board meetings that Drew now attends, decisions are made about what happens in Southampton and sometimes votes are taken. We use cards in the meetings: red means 'Stop I want to speak', orange means 'Slow down and explain that again', green means 'Yes I agree' and yellow means 'I disagree'. In Darren's group home there's a red card shown to someone to tell him to go to his room or outside.

Things are done differently in Hampshire and Southampton and sometimes it can seem quite unfair:

Wayne: Has got three different jobs: Asda, gardening and being a lifeguard at the swimming pool. This is because he has had some good support.
Darren: Would really like help to get a job but has been waiting for someone to get back to him for a long time.
Drew: Has just started Portsmouth College and would like to get a job when he has finished. But he will have to find out who to talk to for help to do that, to be able to have his own place and live with his girlfriend.

Conclusions

'We don't need protecting'; 'We need support who actually know what they are doing.'

Darren, Drew and Wayne: Things have got to change. In this book chapter we want to tell people who read it that we want to be treated normally; we want respect. We want more staff in day services who are funny, jokey and never panicky. We want Social Services to act quicker and show more interest; not to get bored with us and stop listening.

Wayne: And that is about it . What we got so far is quite good.

Darren, Drew and Wayne: If there was some more money we would like to do some more seminars please! It would be good to talk about why we want staff to stop making rules and care plans that we don't think we need.

Chapter 9

Promoting social inclusion through building bridges and bonds

Roy McConkey and Suzanne Collins

Introduction

This chapter addresses the theme of access in relation to community participation and social networks. It uses results from recent research[1] into social
inclusion and community participation to explore four key questions: what is
meant by social inclusion? What is it that excludes people? What would make
a difference to their life? What kind of supports are required to promote
social inclusion?

The chapter illuminates the concept of building bridges and bonds (see Figure
12.2 in Chapter 12) through its focus on the role of support staff in facilitating
community access, especially those working in supported accommodation.

Social inclusion: an impossible dream?

Modern technological societies are rediscovering the value inherent in the
social participation and the civic endeavours of its citizens. The phrase 'social
capital' has been coined to describe this contribution to the overall wealth and
wellbeing of a society. A concern among leaders of the world's richer countries
such as the US and UK is that the social capital of their countries is declining.
The bonds that brought social cohesion to families and communities were loos-
ening as people lived more individual lives. But even when bonded groups
existed, they were increasingly separated from one another with fewer bridges
linking them. The dual concepts of 'bonding' and 'bridging' are the processes
underpinning the creation of social capital. The fewer the bonds and bridges in
a person's life, the poorer is the social capital he or she has to draw upon.
Likewise a society with declining bonds and bridges among its citizenry is experiencing a recession in its social capital.

This analysis has powerful messages for people with an intellectual disability.
They are among the most marginalised in our society (Emerson *et al* 2005). This
remains so, despite the drive to provide them with access to an ordinary life
rather than the segregation typified by long-stay hospitals of a bygone era. Yet
the thinking behind the policies of yesteryear lingers on and many people with

an intellectual disability remain congregated in special centres or homes with a glass wall separating them for the rest of society.

Recent reviews of services provided to this group, such as the Equal Lives Review published by the Department of Health, Social Services and Public Safety (DHSSPS 2005) in Northern Ireland have described a new vision of the values and aspirations that should underpin future provision. Foremost among these is an emphasis on citizenship and social inclusion: 'People with a learning disability are valued citizens and must be enabled to use mainstream services and be fully included in the life of the community' (DHSSPS, 2005: 6).

This intention echoes similar statements contained in international declarations of rights from the 1970s to the present day. For example:

> the equal right of all persons with disabilities to live in the community, with choices equal to others, and (States) shall take effective and appropriate measures to facilitate full enjoyment by persons with disabilities of this right and their full inclusion and participation in the community. (*Convention on the Rights of Persons with Disabilities,* United Nations 2006)

The continuing exclusion of people from mainstream society suggests that such intentions are not easily translated into practice. On reflection, one of the main lessons we have learnt is that merely providing access to services in community-based settings is insufficient to ensure people's social inclusion within those communities. It is, nonetheless, a prerequisite. There are greater opportunities for social integration when people live in ordinary neighbourhoods rather than in remote hospitals or residential centres. Hence the resettlement of patients into community accommodation was a most welcome development but one that is still incomplete in many European countries (Mansell *et al* 2004). However, the alternative accommodation offered to people with an intellectual disability lacked many of the features of an ordinary home. Groups of people lived together in the one building with communal living, dining and bathrooms and only a bedroom of their own. Many of these homes were modelled on those provided for older people, but most of the residents with learning disability were neither old nor ill.

In the closing decades of the last century smaller homes located in ordinary housing became more widespread in Britain and Ireland along with the idea of supported living. People are given the tenancy to their house, bungalow or apartment with support available to assist them as required. A growing international literature has documented the improved quality of life that these newer models of accommodation provide (e.g. Emerson *et al* 2000; Simons and Watson 1999). Even so, social exclusion still exists across these new forms of living arrangements. For example, Figure 9.1 shows the percentage of people in different forms of accommodation who had no friends outside of their residence (McConkey *et al* 2007). Although those living in campus-style settings were the most likely to be friendless, this is still so for between one-third and a half of those living in community settings.

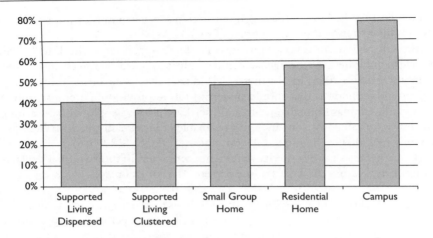

Figure 9.1 The percentage of people in different accommodation options who have no friends outside of their places of residence

Similar patterns were found on other indicators of social inclusion such as visitors to their home and activities undertaken in community settings, all of which underlines the challenges we face if we are to attain greater social inclusion of people with intellectual disabilities. This chapter explores the feasibility of a four-strand strategy for promoting social inclusion and summarises the findings of a three-year research programme on this topic that we undertook with support from the Big Lottery Fund (Collins and McConkey 2007).

What does social inclusion mean to people with intellectual disabilities?

The starting point is listening to people who are excluded. In our project we did this in two ways: by talking to groups of people and by consulting with individuals. First we invited tenants from a range of supported living schemes and some residents in residential homes from across Northern Ireland to attend one of six group meetings, with between 10 and 20 people attending each one (see Abbot and McConkey 2006 for fuller details). A total of 30 individual homes and schemes were represented in the sample. In all, 37 participants (55 per cent) were tenants in clustered or dispersed supported living schemes, 24 (36 per cent) lived as tenants in group homes and 6 (9 per cent) were residents of registered homes. In total, 45 women (66 per cent) and 23 men (34 per cent) participated, who were aged between 21 and 82 years, with a mean age of 46 years. Most were able to communicate verbally with only two participants (3 per cent) needing to communicate through staff, one with the use of a Lightwriter. The idea of 'social inclusion' was introduced by discussing photographs of people with and without an intellectual disability in different community locations.

Small groups worked together to list the different activities they did, who they were done with and the transport they used. Then together in one group, an interactive discussion identified what social inclusion meant for them, what stopped them from doing community activities and the solutions that might overcome these barriers.

The findings from group discussions

Four main themes were identified in participants' discussions about their experiences of being present in community settings: talking to people; being accepted; using community facilities and opportunities. This is how they saw social inclusion.

1. Talking to people

Participants frequently commented on meeting and talking to people: 'Yes ... I am a part of the community ... they talk to me, and I talk back to them.' 'Knowing people to say hello to when you go down town.'

Some felt that people in the community were positive towards them, and others reported that the community did not respond and talk to them, or make them feel included: 'I don't think I am included ... I want people to help me be a part of the community.'

Others felt that their own personal friendships and relationships were the best way of them getting to meet others in the community: 'I can be a part of the community because I go out with my boyfriend ... so I meet and talk to people.'

2. Being accepted

A second theme revolved around how they were treated by other people and their wish to be accepted by others: 'I'd like not to be made to feel different ... and to feel safe.'

Participants commented on how they had been singled out due to their disability, or when they had been ignored: 'Sometimes people make fun of me.' 'People talk to staff instead of talking to me ... I don't like feeling left out.'

3. Using community facilities

Involvement in the community also meant using community resources, including access to facilities and venues, as well as mainstream services such as a GP or dentist: 'It's good living near the town centre, for the shops, schools, church and my GP.' 'I can go down town to walk my dog, and meet my friends and play pool.'

The availability and cost of transport was also very important in accessing community amenities: '[We need] more accessible transport which is affordable

... and more volunteers to take me out to social events.' 'Sometimes there's not enough money to get taxis to places I want to go.'

Other participants felt there was a dearth of activities open to them: 'There aren't enough activities for us to get involved in.' 'I wish there were more voluntary work opportunities ... and more social venues close to home.'

4. Opportunities

Participants appreciated that the opportunity for social inclusion was limited sometimes by the location of their home and its proximity to facilities as well as by the availability of staff to support them: 'I feel I could go out by myself, but staff don't allow us.' 'If staff are sick, then there's not enough staff [to take you out].' '[There is] no private room in our house where you can talk to friends.'

Participants who were now living in supported living schemes felt they had more opportunities for social inclusion: 'I get doing what I want, and there's plenty of company.' 'I am living with my best friends ... like we are one big family.' 'I am given a lot of freedom, a lot of support ... the local people are very good to me. Everything I need on a daily basis, work, centres, social life, is there for me.'

Overall these participants saw social inclusion in very personal terms and each of these four themes they mentioned could be used as an outcome measure when it comes to assessing the extent to which people experience social inclusion. We will return to this point later.

The findings from individual choices

The second approach we used to defining social inclusion involved over 120 people who were living in four different accommodation options (as per Figure 9.1, but excluding campus accommodation). Each participant was invited to identify, with the help of their key support worker, up to three 'social inclusion' goals they wanted to achieve in the coming months. It was suggested that these goals would be related to doing things with other people and being involved in their communities, but also that the goals should be things that participants and staff felt they would be 'able' to achieve. Participants often requested suggestions from both the researcher and the staff member as to what goals they could chose, but as far as possible they were encouraged to identify things that they wanted to do. Some people declined to select any goals, mostly stating that they were happy with how things are. We repeated this exercise on three occasions, nine months apart, as a means of identifying if goals were achieved.

Although participants chose a wide variety of goals, for ease of reference they could be grouped into the following categories. The percentage refers to the number of people (out of the 123 participants) who selected that type of goal at any of the three time points from all those choosing goals:

Social activities (e.g. going out for a meal, or on holidays)	90 per cent
Entertainment activities (e.g. cinema, bingo, watching football match)	34 per cent
Sport / Exercise activities (e.g. play football, go for walks)	29 per cent
Increasing independence (e.g. using buses, managing money)	26 per cent
Work or training activities (e.g. placements, attend classes)	25 per cent
Increasing social contacts (e.g. meeting and visiting friends)	14 per cent
Increasing contact with family (e.g. meeting and visiting)	10 per cent

By far the most common goal was to spend more time doing things with people. These included people they lived with or who supported them as well as friends and acquaintances from outside the house. Families were rarely mentioned, maybe because some of the participants had lost contact with their relatives. The types of goals set were generally consistent across each time point.

In summary then, social inclusion for people with an intellectual disability is mainly about being with other people; talking with them, sharing activities with them and, most crucially, being accepted by them.

Barriers to social inclusion

Once we ascertain people's aspirations we need to identify the barriers that prevent them from achieving them. We did this in two ways. First we spoke with people and then we spoke with support staff.

The views of people with intellectual disabilities

When we met with people in the focus groups, we asked them about the things that stopped them meeting with others and joining in community activities. Their answers could be grouped into four themes, summarised in Figure 9.2.

Participants appreciated that their own lack of skills created difficulties for them that further reduced their confidence and motivation, and increased their

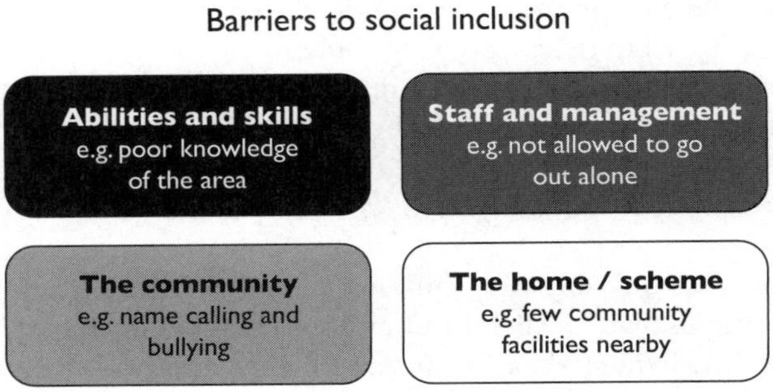

Barriers to social inclusion

Abilities and skills
e.g. poor knowledge of the area

Staff and management
e.g. not allowed to go out alone

The community
e.g. name calling and bullying

The home / scheme
e.g. few community facilities nearby

Figure 9.2 Barriers to social inclusion

perceptions of the risks involved: 'Not being able to use the bus or train or taxi on my own. Not being able to go to (town) on my own to go shopping.' 'I have to ask people if there is any activities going on. If the staff would let us know about more activities.'

However they felt that service policies and the availability of staff also inhibited community participation: 'Would like to have more staff, to get out more. Have more activities. I like getting out.' 'Because of my care needs; I would always need an assistant and they are not always available so I am limited in where I go for social activities.'

The location of the residence or the home was another barrier they identified: 'Transport is a big problem and I cannot take part in as many things as I would like to because there are not enough accessible wheelchair buses and I am charged more for buses and taxis because I am in a wheelchair. I don't think this is very fair.' 'In a smaller town I feel I could go out on my own; I'd know the area.'

They also cited various features within the local community as contributing to their exclusion: 'I wish there were more social venues close to my home.' 'Be careful who you talk to, because they could take advantage of you; knowing who it is ok to talk to.' 'Some people don't understand me, if they tried a little harder.'

These four types of barriers are echoed in other studies (e.g. Hall 2005) and reflect an underlying dependency on others to reduce social exclusion. We explored this further by consulting with support staff.

The views of support staff

Focus groups were held with a sample of 44 staff working in the four forms of accommodation in which people lived. The barriers that staff perceived were similar to those reported by the people they support. They included:

- resources, e.g. staff shortages on shifts, availability of transport, financial constraints;
- lack of volunteer/befriender schemes;
- group activities do not incorporate the needs of each individual;
- lack of confidence on the part of residents/tenants;
- priority assigned to tasks set during shifts;
- motivation of both staff and residents/tenants;
- community perception about the home/scheme.

Example comments included:

'One staff member only on each shift. Befriender schemes not that accessible, therefore getting individual clients out on their own is a problem.'
'The normal daily living tasks are done; nothing over and above this; time has to be set aside for paperwork.'
'Going out as a large group attracts unwelcome attention; seen as a threat.'

Implications

People with intellectual disabilities and their support staff were able to name formidable barriers they experienced in trying to achieve greater social inclusion. Murray (2002) and Reynolds (2002) report similar findings in research carried out in Britain. Two main conclusions can be drawn. First, social exclusion is an unintentional concomitant of the support services presently offered to people with intellectual disabilities. These appear to limit the social opportunities available to people as other facets of the service are given priority. Second, there is a need to create a welcome within the communities in which people live. Both of these failings result in a dearth of 'bridges' between the 'socially excluded' and their local communities.

What makes a difference?

Our consultations with tenants and support staff went on to identify actions that would reduce social exclusion. They needed little prompting to come up with these suggestions:

- tenants require opportunities to acquire the skills to participate more fully in communities and to make friends;
- support staff require training and encouragement to develop their job roles to embrace social inclusion;
- links needed to be made with other agencies and services that could assist with promoting social inclusion;
- resources were required to assist people to take part in community life;
- people in the community need to be made more aware of people with a learning disability and of the contribution they could make in helping them.

All of these strategies will require a radical reappraisal of support services with the focus shifting to supporting people *within the* community and not just in their homes. However, we were intrigued to discover if more immediate action might be possible, particularly if the focus was on individuals.

Goal-setting

The goal-setting exercise described earlier provided such an opportunity. Nine months after tenants had selected their three goals, we went back to discover if their goals had been met and what had helped them to do this (we call this Time 2). We did this again after another nine-month gap (called Time 3). Figure 9.3 shows the proportion of tenants in each accommodation option who reported achieving one or more of their goals.

At Time 2, 64 of the 112 participants (57 per cent) who set goals were reported to have attained them, but those living in shared and clustered

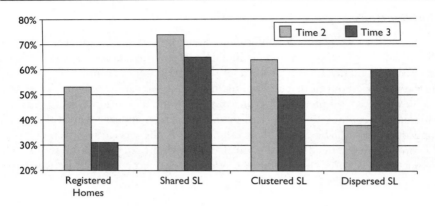

Figure 9.3 The percentage of people achieving one or more of the goals set in each accommodation option

accommodation were significantly more likely to have attained their goals than those in dispersed supported living. At the Time 3 follow-up the picture had changed. Now 38 people (45 per cent of those who set goals) had achieved their goal and the differences by accommodation options were not statistically significant, although those in registered homes were the least likely to have achieved their goals. Overall the people more likely to achieve their goals were those who had two or more friends with an intellectual disability outside of their home. None of the other personal characteristics of the tenants, such as their level of ability, was associated with attaining goals.

It was not just the achievement of outcomes that interested us but also what had assisted or hindered the tenants in achieving their goals. Across both time points, the most important factor was staff assistance, for example in arranging or booking activities (i.e. tickets to concerts and shows, or holidays), and having staff to accompany the individual to take part in the activity. Other factors were mentioned less frequently but were important for the individuals concerned. These included wheelchair access, availability of volunteers to befriend and accompany individuals, and work placements being sourced and supported.

Support and contact with both family and friends were also important in helping individuals to reach the goals they had set, particularly in terms of accompanying them to events and activities, and meeting with them socially. Others felt they had reached their goal because they had the skill or ability to fulfil a goal themselves, and were not dependent on the availability of staff.

Conversely the reasons given for goals *not* being achieved revolved around planning, for example, information on activities had not yet been gathered, a risk assessment had not been completed, or simply an activity had not been put into action even though plans were drawn up. Other times the individual had changed his or her mind or forgotten about the goal, so it had not been discussed further with support staff. In some cases, the necessary facility or resource was not available, i.e. a physiotherapy assistant to help with swimming, a suitable house for a move to supported living accommodation, or no places being available at their chosen activity (i.e. waiting lists for membership of the local Gateway Club). Less commonly mentioned but nonetheless relevant to certain individuals were behaviour problems, ill health and the individual's competence. Money was also an issue mentioned by certain people, as individuals needed to save for a holiday, or the cost of transport was prohibitive. The lack of social contacts was noted; as was people not having friends, or not enough staff available to accompany them. One individual noted an insurance reason (where a friend could not come and stay overnight) and another mentioned lack of transport available to them.

Staff priorities

If staff support for social inclusion is so crucial, what priority do they assign to tasks that promote social inclusion? From our previous research we identified 16 ways in which staff might support social inclusion, and 16 other 'caring' tasks that featured as part of their work. In all, 245 staff drawn from shared living, supported living and day centres rated the tasks in terms of high priority: 'they must be done/always get done'. Figure 9.4 shows the mean number of tasks of each type that staff in different settings rated as high priority.

In all three settings, greater priority is given to caring tasks such as giving out medication, attending to epileptic seizures and paperwork than to social inclusion tasks. Staff in supported living were significantly more likely to support social inclusion, most commonly by encouraging family visits, supporting work placements and raising the issue at team meetings.

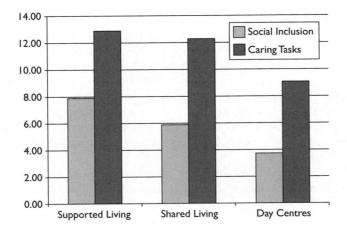

Figure 9.4 The mean number of tasks rated as high priority by staff across different services

Implications

These findings confirm the crucial role of support staff in assisting tenants to achieve social inclusion goals through assistance with planning and accompanying them to events. This support seemed to be more available to tenants in clustered or shared supported living settings who received more hours of staff support compared to those in dispersed settings. But even here, their primary role revolved mostly around care tasks.

Our findings suggest that it is possible for tenants to become more socially included once this became an explicit and shared objective for them. It was not clear why this worked for some tenants and not for others but it may come back to service supports. Robertson *et al* (2005) note that one of the common reasons why elements of person-centred plans do not get put into action can be traced to those involved in supporting the person, that is, their support staff and managers.

Other factors played a part too. Success in attaining goals will vary with the skills, abilities and support required by each individual, as well as being dependent to some degree on the location of their home setting. Finally, tenants who had friends outside of their home were also more likely to achieve their chosen goals. Perhaps it is not so surprising that those who are already socially included are those most likely to extend their social networks and activities. But it reinforces the need to get people started on this road.

The supports required to promote social inclusion

Our experiences have highlighted some key lessons for services wishing to promote greater access for people with intellectual disabilities to social networks and community activities and thereby nurture their social inclusion. The first lesson is simply stated but harder to achieve: promoting access to society is a process not an end-point. For everyone, life circumstances change as people come and go, and opportunities open and close. Hence enabling people to become more socially included is an ongoing journey that must adapt to changing needs and circumstances.

Second, inclusion is a complex process for which there are no 'quick fixes'. Rather it requires co-operative and coordinated endeavours for widening access that embraces four groups, as shown in Figure 9.5, once the underpinning government policy is in place. The individuals in these groups must work together to create the bonds and bridges that will help them to build social capital, because no one group alone will succeed to the same extent as through working in partnership.

Third, we suspect that leadership in the promotion of access towards social inclusion has to come from service staff and management. This must be done in such a way that tenants and local communities are empowered to become creative contributors to the process so that support services can gradually withdraw and leave the ownership of inclusion with them.

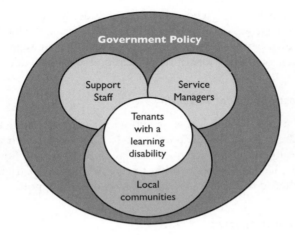

Figure 9.5 Groups involved in promoting social inclusion

Fourth, we still have much to learn as to how social inclusion can become a reality given the changes in our modern technological society that seem to generate barriers to accessing and creating social networks. But then again, the very endeavour of creating access for one section of society may regenerate the bonds and bridges necessary for building the social capital within a community.

Promising strategies

Amongst all the rhetoric, there may well some simple actions that could make a significant difference and which depend largely on a change of heart and a break with old customs rather than any radical shift in service systems. Here are some examples of the bonding and bridging that can create access to community through bringing people together.

Visitors to the home

People's home can form a natural but underused location for developing acquaintances and sustaining friendships. Tenants should be actively encouraged to invite friends and family to their home and arrangements made to provide activities in which they can participate with appropriate safeguards in place. Likewise, tenants should be supported to accept invitations that are offered to them to visit the homes of their friends (Emerson and McVilly 2004).

Person specification of support staff

Attention needs to be paid to the personal qualities and experiences that applicants bring to the post, in particular their own personal connectedness to the community where the tenants live. Staff who come from outside the area where they work should be encouraged to develop links with neighbours and the local community both in their own personal capacity as well as when they are supporting tenants. The aim is to encourage the formation of reciprocal social networks.

Create low-cost options for socialising

Support staff might develop low-cost options for people to have the companionship of others. Examples include home-based activities such as barbecues; joining in local community activities that are free; organising house swaps for holiday breaks; having visitors coming to stay or a group of friends going on holiday together so that they can share the costs of staff support.

Information and signposting

Support staff need ready access to information about their local community and the resources and opportunities that may be available to their tenants. Access to the internet by staff is one good example of how modern technology can assist with this. Also, they should be able to 'sign-post' tenants to other people or services who may be able to assist them. Links with the local volunteer bureau or community transport provision are two examples of this.

Social inclusion champion

Larger services might appoint a social inclusion champion cum coordinator on a time-limited basis to establish systems and procedures to promote social inclusion that will become self-sustaining. Their role would be to guide and motivate support staff and tenants as well as organising training events for them and the local community. Indeed building community partnerships would be a key feature of their role, as would linking with other services.

Befriending

Volunteer bureaus and community travel schemes can be used to identify people who would be willing to befriend a tenant and accompany him or her to events once the necessary vetting procedures have been completed. Support staff have an important role in sustaining these linkages, especially with tenants who may be less communicative with their befrienders. Issues around payment for expenses should be clarified at the outset.

Increasing community awareness

Service managers and staff should make contact with local politicians and the local media, newspapers and radio, so that they are aware of the particular issues that affect people with an intellectual disability. Both are in a position to create greater awareness of their needs within wider society.

Service diversity

The time has also come to rethink the traditional demarcations that exist between different forms of service provision, such as supported accommodation, respite care and day services. They all have a contribution to make in promoting social inclusion and yet their efforts are often uncoordinated if not contradictory. One solution is for a service to diversify so that it can provide a range of supports to the individual that will deliver the personal outcomes that he or she has identified. Hence supported living services might also deliver employment support and befriending schemes.

Training

Social inclusion needs to be given a higher profile in the training that staff receive both in their induction and also throughout their period of service. The knowledge and competences required to further the inclusion of tenants could be linked to assessment frameworks such as National Vocational Qualifications (NVQ) and Learning Disability Awards Framework (LDAF) as a means of ensuring a workforce that is 'fit for purpose' in supported housing. Triangle Housing Association has produced a CD-ROM Tool-Kit on Social Inclusion that provides induction training for staff on this topic.[2]

Conclusions

Models of social capital stress the importance of 'bonding' and 'bridging' as a means of creating greater cohesion within communities and societies (Bates and Davis 2004). This chapter has highlighted how these concepts may be applied to people with intellectual disabilities to explain their social exclusion. Often the bonds they forged with non-disabled peers were fragile if not non-existent, especially in congregated living arrangements (Forrester-Jones et al 2006). By contrast they are excessively bonded into service systems built around their disabilities. They live with individuals with similar characteristics and receive support from staff whose relationships with them are defined by the employing organisation and for whom the priority is often their care and protection.

The challenge is to assist people to move beyond their disability groupings and to create access opportunities that will enable them to become bonded with other social groups in their community. Membership of different groupings helps to create the social networks that typify social inclusion. This takes time and effort on everyone's part but it can be done, as our findings illustrate. Significantly, any increased risks that this may pose were managed within the procedures already established by the support services, which is as it should be.

Moreover, being in the company of others in public places is in itself an important safeguard for vulnerable people.

Bridge-building across bonded groups is equally important and requires more detailed attention than it has received thus far in our support services. Here too, we anticipate support staff taking a more proactive role in helping groups to access and connect with one another both within service systems and between these systems and local communities (Chenoweth and Stehlink 2004). Ultimately, though, this bridging may be best be done by leaders emerging from the isolated community who provide a role model for their peers with disabilities whilst opening doors into society through their advocacy. It is they, after all, who have the most to gain from greater social inclusion, as currently they are the greatest losers.

Notes

1 The content of this chapter is drawn from the research report by Suzanne Collins and Roy McConkey, *At Home in the Community? Promoting the social inclusion of people with a learning disability living in supported accommodation,* published by Triangle Housing and the University of Ulster, 2007. This gives fuller details of the research methodologies used and the findings from the different studies undertaken.

2 Triangle Housing Association CD-ROM Tool-Kit on Social Inclusion (details on http://www.trianglehousing.org.uk/).

References

Abbott, S. and McConkey, R. (2006) The barriers to social inclusion as perceived by people with intellectual disabilities, *Journal of Intellectual Disabilities,* **10,** 3, 275–87.

Bates, P. and Davis, F. A. (2004) Social capital, social inclusion and services for people with learning disabilities, *Disability and Society,* **19,** 3, 195–207.

Chenoweth, L. and Stehlink, D. (2004) Implications of social capital for the inclusion of people with disabilities and families in community life, *'International Journal of Inclusive Education",* **8,** 1, 59–72.

Collins, S. and McConkey, R. (2007) *At home in the community? Promoting the social inclusion of people with a learning disability in supported accommodation,* Ballymoney: Triangle Housing Association and University of Ulster, Online (http://www.trianglehousing.org.uk/cmsfiles/files/resources/triangleha_athome.pdf) (accessed 4 December 2008).

Department of Health, Social Services and Public Safety (2005) *Equal Lives: Review of policy and services for people with a learning disability in Northern Ireland,* Belfast: DHSSPS.

Emerson, E. and McVilly, K. (2004) Friendship activities of adults with intellectual disabilities in supported accommodation in Northern England, *Journal of Applied Research in Intellectual Disabilities,* **17,** 191–7.

Emerson, E., Mallam, S., Davies, I. and Spencer, K. (2005) *Adults with Learning Difficulties in England 2003/04,* London: National Statistics and Health and Social Care Information Centre.

Emerson, E., Robertson, J., Gregory, N., Hatton, C., Kessissoglou, S., Hallam, A., Järbrink, K., Knapp, M., Netten, P. and Noonan-Walsh, P. N. (2000) The quality and costs of village communities, residential campuses and community-based residential supports for people with learning disabilities, *Tizard Learning Disability Review*, **5**, 1, 5–16.

Forrester-Jones, R., Carpenter, J., Coolen-Schrijner, P., Cambridge, P., Tate, A., Beecham, J., Hallams, A., Knapp, M. and Wooff, D. (2006) The social networks of people with intellectual disability living in the community 12 years after resettlement from long-stay hospitals, *Journal of Applied Research in Intellectual Disabilities*, **19**, 285–95.

Hall, E. (2005) The entangled geographies of social exclusion/inclusion for people with learning disabilities, *Health and Place*, **11**, 107–15.

McConkey, R., Abbott, S. Noonan-Walsh, P., Linehan, C. and Emerson, E. (2007) Variations in the social inclusion of people with intellectual disabilities in supported living schemes and residential settings, *Journal of Intellectual Disability Research*, **51**, 3, 207–17.

Mansell, J., Beadle-Brown, J. and Clegg, S. (2004) The situation of large residential institutions in Europe, in G. Freyhoff, C. Parker, M. Coué and N. Greig (eds) *Included in Society: Results and recommendations of the European research initiative on community-based residential alternatives for disabled people,* Brussels: Inclusion Europe.

Murray, P. (2002) *Hello! Are you listening? Disabled teenagers' experience of access to inclusive leisure,* York: Joseph Rowntree Foundation.

Reynolds, F. (2002) An exploratory survey of opportunities and barriers to creative leisure activity for people with learning disabilities, *British Journal of Learning Disabilities,* **30**, 63–7.

Robertson, J., Emerson, E., Hatton, C., Elliott, J., McIntosh, B., Swift, P., Krijnen-Kemp, E., Towers, C., Sanderson, H., Routledge, M., Oakes, P. and Joyce, T. (2005) *The Impact of Person-centred Planning,* Lancaster: University of Lancaster, Institute for Health Research, Online (http://www.helensandersonassociates.co.uk/PDFs/TheImpactofPersonCentredPlanning-FinalReport.pdf) (accessed 10 December 2008).

Simons, K. and Watson, D. (1999) *The view from Arthur's Seat: Review of services for people with learning disabilities – a literature review of housing and support options beyond Scotland,* Edinburgh: Scottish Executive Central Research Unit.

United Nations (2006) *Convention on the Rights of Persons with Disabilities*, Online (http://www.un.org/disabilities/convention/conventionfull.shtml) (accessed 4 December 2008).

Part 5

Multilayered access

If we have got it wrong for people with learning disabilities, have we got it wrong for other people as well?

Duncan Mitchell

Introduction

Good health tends to be taken for granted, but it is the foundation for all other aspects of our lives. In the context of the theme of this book, health is the foundation for access to much that can be offered in society. Poor health can dominate the lives of individuals and those around them. The ultimate result of very poor health is, of course, an early death; the final denial of access! Whilst such a statement might seem melodramatic, arguments that will be presented in this chapter will demonstrate the full, tragic extent of poor health among people with learning disabilities.

The chapter is organised into three main sections. The first asks what we know about the health of people with learning disabilities. This section will present evidence that shows that people with learning disabilities tend to have poorer health indicators than the general population; they also have less health screening and tend to die earlier. An outline of some of the explanations for these inequalities will then be offered in section two, and it will be argued that there are clear structural reasons for such inequalities that affect other marginalised people and can be linked to poverty and social disadvantage. Section three will address solutions to the problem within the existing system. Starting from the position that despite the evidence, the position is very complex and that while services for people with learning disabilities are generally poor, some people report high levels of satisfaction and appear to receive care of a very high standard. Presumably if it can work some of the time then it ought to be able work all of the time. There have been many initiatives to improve services for people with learning disabilities and examples of these will be examined. The final section and conclusion will develop the theme of service improvement and will return to the structural argument that there is a lot that needs to happen before true access is achieved. Evidence suggests that single short-term initiatives will only work for the short term. Once is not enough! Real and genuine access will only happen if there is a real and genuine understanding of the issues involved, followed by appropriate and sustained action.

What do we know about access to health for people with learning disabilities?

In the United Kingdom there is considerable evidence to suggest that the health of people with learning disabilities is much worse than the general population and that commissioning of health services for people with learning disabilities has not yet addressed this (Elliot *et al* 2003). Whilst this chapter is based mainly on the United Kingdom there is evidence to suggest that access to good services is a problem elsewhere. Indeed the World Health Organisation suggests that people with learning disabilities are frequently the most vulnerable group and the most likely to be unable to access basic health and education services across the world (World Health Organisation 2001).

There are a number of sources for what we know about the health of people with learning disabilities in the United Kingdom. Among the most recent have been formal reports. One, for example, written by the Disability Rights Commission in 2006, investigated the health of people with learning disabilities and people with mental health problems. The Commission found that:

> In England and Wales people with learning disabilities and people with mental health problems are much more likely than other citizens to have significant health risks and major health problems. For people with learning disabilities these particularly included obesity and respiratory disease. (Disability Rights Commission 2006: 4)

They found that people in both groups are likely to die younger than others and that people with learning disabilities with specific conditions such as diabetes have fewer of the recommended health checks than other people with the same conditions. For example, national figures show that only 17 per cent of learning disabled women are screened for cervical cancer compared to 85 per cent of the general population, and 50 per cent have breast screening compared to 76 per cent of the general population. Furthermore there is a tendency for people with learning disabilities to experience diagnostic overshadowing in which symptoms of ill health are seen as being part of their learning disability and therefore not treated.

In 2007, the then Secretary of State for Health, Patricia Hewitt, set up an independent investigation to follow up a report by Mencap (2007) on the death of people with learning disability in hospital. The title of Mencap's report, *Death by Indifference,* neatly sums up the cause and effect of poor treatment of people with learning disabilities. People died because other people were indifferent to their needs:

> It is our belief, and that of their families, that their deaths were avoidable and that institutional discrimination is the underlying cause. We believe that they occurred because of discrimination, indifference, lack of training

and a very poor understanding of the needs of people with a learning disability. (Mencap 2007: 4)

The inquiry confirmed that 'people with learning disabilities find it much harder than other people to access assessment and treatment for general health problems'. They also found that, despite it being a legal requirement, reasonable adjustments were not being made to support equal treatment and that many healthcare staff considered that equal treatment meant the same treatments as everyone else. Other findings were that carers of people with learning disabilities were frequently not sufficiently consulted by healthcare professionals and that health care staff had very little knowledge of learning disabilities (Mencap 2007).

The real surprise behind these reports is that there is still surprise. Each time a report is published there is a sense of shock. However, there is little new because the reports reflect a trend of evidence that suggests significant problems with access to health care for people with learning disabilities. For example Thornton (2008) suggested that practitioners working in primary care teams had limited awareness of the health care needs of adults with learning disability. Alborz *et al* (2005) in a major study funded by the Department of Health found that barriers to access to health services included communication problems, inadequate and rigid procedures, and lack of interpersonal skills among general health care staff. These two examples are representative of a series of work that confirms anecdotal accounts and unpublished consultations that make clear that there are long-standing problems of access with resulting poor health outcomes for people with learning disabilities. For example, in the 1990s there was clear evidence to suggest that people with learning disabilities were 58 times more likely to die before the age of 50 than the general population (Hollins *et al* 1998).

There are therefore significant issues in terms of access to good health for people with learning disabilities. Whilst there is a general consensus that there is a problem, there is less agreement about the explanations or the solutions to the issue.

Explanations for health inequalities

There are several explanations for why such a problem of access to health services and to good health generally exists. One is that there is nothing particularly special about people with learning disabilities but that health services find it difficult to deal with people who are different from the expected norm. Similar complaints exist about blind or deaf people, people with Alzheimer's disease, or older people generally. Such a situation is exacerbated by overstretched systems and a reliance on formulaic care plans that fail to take account of individual needs. Anyone who needs more time or a different approach to care becomes a problem that professionals, working to targets, find difficult to deal with.

Other explanations suggest issues that are specific to learning disabilities in terms of communication, the additional time required, or the stigma associated with marginalised groups in general and people with learning disabilities specifically. Kerr (2004) for example, agreed that one of the potential causes of the difference between the health of people with learning disabilities and the general population was several barriers to care including mobility, sensory impairment, behaviour problems, communication and knowledge, attitudes and accessibility of services.

Lindsey and Russell (1999) advised primary carers about access for people with learning disabilities and suggest that there are several reasons why there are problems. They suggest that people with learning disabilities and their carers usually have low expectations of their own health and of the services that they are likely to receive. Some people cannot read and therefore do not respond to the written communications that are usually used to alert people to the need for health screening. Others experience barriers when waiting for services because they are confused in waiting rooms. Others need more time in consultations because they do not easily understand questions or advice that are given in ways that people are expected to use for communicating. Interestingly, a 2003/4 survey into people with learning disabilities in England found that despite a high level of satisfaction with primary care among people with learning disabilities there was a low level of routine screening. Ninety-four per cent of people said that they got on well with their doctor and three-quarters had seen their doctor in the last year. However, despite this level of contact only one in four women had had a cervical smear and only one in four had ever had their breasts checked for a lump by a nurse or a doctor (Emerson et al 2005). The fact that these self-reported figures are different to those reported by the Disability Rights Commission shows the difficulty in assessing the scale of the problem. However, both sets of figures are lamentably low.

One example of the way in which health professionals struggle with people who do not behave in expected ways is that of consent. It seems to confuse practitioners when people cannot give clear consent for treatment. Such consent requires understanding of treatment and the ability to give verbal and/or written consent. Carers report being asked to give consent for treatment on behalf of the people with learning disabilities who they support. This is despite the clear legal position that no adult can give consent on behalf of another adult. Some people with learning disabilities do not understand the treatment that they are offered and this can lead them to appear to withhold consent by struggling or refusing to sit still. This is sometimes interpreted as refusal to consent and can lead to withdrawal of treatment. This partly explains the low level of health screening because invasive actions such as taking blood are seen as problematic. Yet there are clear processes in place to help people take best-interest decisions when consent cannot be given. Health professionals should know this.

It is difficult for non-professionals to understand why, after so much evidence, there are still such gaps in knowledge. Mencap (2007) explored this in *Death by Indifference* with the example of Warren who died well before his time due to professional misunderstanding:

People with a learning disability may also find it hard to communicate their symptoms and to understand what they are being told. As a result, some people have to put up with a great deal of pain and discomfort before they get the right treatment. Sometimes people do not get the treatment they need. Warren died of appendicitis. In response to the complaint made by his parents, it was stated that the presence of his learning disability meant that his condition was 'more difficult to diagnose than in normal circumstances'. This is not an acceptable reason. (Mencap 2007: 20)

There are difficulties associated with learning disability that make diagnosis and treatment problematic. That is precisely why people with learning disabilities need more time and patience in order to ensure that they have equal health outcomes to the general population. Whilst communication difficulties are a significant issue there are also physical factors associated with learning disability that make special provision crucial. For example, there is a high level of epilepsy among people with learning disability and a higher level of hard to control epilepsy (Branford 1998). There are also higher than usual levels of physical disability among people with learning disability. Michael (2008: 14) suggested that this affected up to a third of people with learning disabilities and that there are associated risks of 'postural deformities, hip dislocation, chest infections, eating and swallowing problems (dysphagia), gastro–oesophageal reflux, constipation and incontinence'.

One difficult issue about access relates to the link between behaviour and health. People with learning disabilities are among the most inactive and sedentary members of the population (Messent et al 1999) and have high levels of obesity (Chapman et al 2005). It is quite clear that some of the health problems associated with people with learning disabilities are directly related to these personal factors. A good example of this is the rate of diabetes. Whilst there is conflicting evidence about the prevalence of diabetes among people with learning disabilities, an analysis of health checks among people with learning disability in Wales found that 9 per cent had diabetes compared to a national figure of 4.7 per cent (Disability Rights Commission 2005). There is less clarity about how to address these problems. It is difficult not to see this in the context of the wider debates about class and health that were highlighted in the Black Report in the early 1980s (Department of Health and Social Security 1980) and have continued to feature in debates about health ever since. Black argued that it was impossible to separate health from other socioeconomic factors and that it was clear that the poor and socially disadvantaged experienced worse levels of health than others.

One explanation for such comparative disadvantage is that of personal behaviour. Linked to this is the idea of personal choice and the connections between staff making choices for the people that they support in terms of diet or activity levels. According to Jenkinson (1993) people with learning disabilities can be prevented from making choices by environmental factors such as resource limitations or routine, but also from staff behaviour such as overruling choices or a more simple lack of awareness from staff of a minor activity presenting a choice-making opportunity. The staff in this context often come from the very sections of society that are affected by issues of poverty and associated poor health. A good example of this relates to diet. People with learning disabilities who live with others in supported accommodation will be dependent on the knowledge and skills of the staff employed to support them. If the staff diet depends on convenience and take-away foods then it is probable that the people they support will have a similar diet. For people with learning disabilities, therefore, their health status depends not only on their own social position but also that of the people who support them. This is compounded by personal choices that are available to people who may not have the knowledge or skills to differentiate between healthy and non-healthy options. Like anyone else, people with learning disabilities can make wise or unwise choices, but when presented with choices they need the information required to weigh up their options.

A further explanation is that the predominant cause of disadvantage in terms of health is the more general social disadvantage associated with poverty. The links between poverty and ill health have been extensively debated for over two decades. The link between learning disability and poverty has rarely featured in such debates. Graham (2005) argues that socioeconomic position is the main determinant of health, and studies of access to health for people with learning disabilities need to be undertaken within that context. The Department of Health appears to agree that there is a link:

> Access to healthcare or effective support and advice are not always available to those who most need them. This means that some groups face a double disadvantage. For example, people with learning disabilities are more likely to suffer socio-economic disadvantage or less likely to have access to effective services. (Department of Health 2008: 13)

Furthermore, even among people with learning disabilities there are differences relating to social advantage. For example, when a survey of people with learning disabilities was carried out in 2003 and people were asked about their health, one in six people said that their health was not good. However, when the figures were broken down into groups it was found that people were more likely to say that their health was not good if they were poor, lived alone, saw friends with learning disabilities less often, did not have a paid job, were older, did not live in a registered residential care home, were from a minority ethnic group or had lower support needs (Emerson et al 2005). Most of these factors are also indicative of the possession of poorer social capital and mirrors the position in the general population in which there is a clear link between social disadvantage and poor health.

The explanations, therefore, are not far from those that apply to the general population in which social disadvantage and poor health are linked. People with learning disabilities have the added disadvantage of the stigma associated with their condition. Solutions, as with the health of the general population, are not easy to find, but have been suggested, as discussed in the next section.

Solutions

The problem of access to good health services for people with learning disabilities has been acknowledged by government and also by some local services. National initiatives have tried to deal with the issue but have had remarkably little effect on the figures. Three main factors contribute to this lack of success. In the first place, initiatives have rarely been sustained beyond the immediate publicity and one of the main reasons for this is that they have not been statutory. Second, it has become clear that policies that are promoted in isolation from other factors do not lead to real change. Third, there are significant tensions related to behavioural change for people with learning disabilities. National initiatives have concentrated on improving services and have clearly recognised the problem of access for people with learning disabilities. The most recent policy framework has been the 2001 White Paper *Valuing People* that introduced two new initiatives: health facilitation and health action plans (Department of Health 2001). Prior to this, several policies were referred to or applied exclusively to people with learning disabilities. Policies such as the *Health of the Nation* (Department of Health 1992), *Signposts for Success* (Department of Health 1998), and *Once a Day* (Lindsey and Russell 1999) all reflect attempts to improve services and recognise the difficulties that people with learning disabilities have in accessing good services.

Valuing People made two recommendations in terms of health. Every person with learning disabilities was recommended to have, or at least be offered, a health action plan. To help them, they were to have a health facilitator who would be someone close to them who would help to ensure access to health services. Both policies were reviewed by the Department of Health in 2005 (Carmichael and Moore 2005). The results were mixed, particularly in terms of engagement with mainstream primary health care services, and it was clear that some areas had not made much headway with health action plans. Crucially the review found that success was more likely when health action plans were linked with other policies:

> A critical success factor for health action planning is a clear link with Person Centred Planning and other systems such as Transition Plans, Single Assessment Process (SAP) and Care Programme Approach (CPA). Unfortunately, many Health Frameworks were vague in describing how they would consider each of these to ensure an individual was not subject to a multiplicity of plans. (Carmichael and Moore 2005)

This emphasises that access to good health, taken in isolation from other factors, is difficult to realise. It is particularly the case when the other factors include policies that are either statutory or officially recorded and therefore take priority over initiatives such as health action plans, which remain only a recommendation.

We have already seen that a legal framework does now exist to force services to act. For example, the public sector disability equality duty within the Disability Discrimination Act 2005 places a legal obligation on Primary Care Trusts to take action to reduce the inequalities associated with disability. The Disability Rights Commission recommended that primary care providers should improve equity of access and treatment of learning disabled people by a number of means that include recording access needs on a patient's records, offering regular health checks, ensuring the provision of health promotion, screening and physical treatment to people with learning disabilities, and involving local disability groups in advising on improvements (Disability Rights Commission 2005). At the time of writing there have not been any cases that have challenged Primary Care Trusts or hospitals to meet the disability equality duty. This is despite the fact that the evidence from official reports is that some cannot possibly be meeting the requirements.

There have been a number of local projects that have tried to improve hospital services for people with learning disabilities. Some have been prompted by the hospitals themselves following specific complaints or series of complaints. Others have been led by local learning disability services prompted by stories from people with learning disabilities and carers about their poor care in hospital settings.

A review of such initiatives carried out in Manchester, where there were published reports (Backer *et al* 2007) found that attempts to improve services focused on the establishment of liaison nurses and liaison projects involving several staff working with the hospital. These were projects that involved workers with an understanding of learning disability from outside the hospital working with hospital staff. In some cases this also involved direct work with people with learning disabilities during their hospital stay. While these approaches recognised that people with learning disabilities need extra time and skill, they also emphasise the lack of readiness of the hospital staff to meet the needs of people seen as different. The review also considered unpublished or 'grey' literature on the subject and found that as well as the liaison roles there were a number of projects that sought to improve communication, and a need for additional training of mainstream hospital staff.

Some problems of access are the result of people with learning disability falling between different services. This is particularly the case with people who have both learning disability and mental health problems. Mental health problems are more common among people with learning disabilities than the general population (Elliot *et al* 2003) yet specialist services are not always available. The mental health special interest research group of the International Association for the Scientific Study of Intellectual Disability suggests that the presence of both learning disability and mental illness increases social exclusion because both are stigmatising conditions. This should be of concern to both learning disability and mental health services in that they ought to be equipped to identify and treat mental illness in people with learning disability.

> The combination of high prevalence rates of psychiatric and behaviour disorders, complex health needs, and the specific difficulties with respect to language development that affect the manner in which mental ill health presents and also impedes access to services, argues strongly for dedicated specialist and multidisciplinary community-based health support in partnership with individuals with intellectual disabilities, families, and providers of social and community care. (International Association for the Scientific Study of Intellectual Disability 2001)

Part of the solution must be for health services to take account of learning disability in all health campaigns. Brown (2007) makes this clear in his study of health and learning disability in Scotland. One of the recommendations is that all health activities that are targeted at the general population, including immunisations and health screening, need to be both accessible to and inclusive of people with learning disabilities. This means thinking of learning disability at every stage of the activity rather than wondering why uptake figures are so low for this group of people when it is pointed out.

The concern in this chapter is for people with learning disabilities, but the importance of getting this right goes beyond people with learning disabilities themselves: 'If services and health outcomes are improving for people with learning disabilities, they are likely to be improving for other groups at risk of health inequalities' (Department of Health 2008: 6).

These words from the Department of Health echo what many already believe: that if services get it right for people with learning disabilities they will also get it right for others. The lesson here is that there needs to be a dual approach. Initiatives such as health action plans and hospital liaison can make a difference for individuals and need to be supported. However, they will only work in the long term if people with learning disabilities are considered at all levels of decision making. Furthermore, an approach that considers difference, rather than one that assumes that everyone is the same, will have considerable benefits for all sections of society.

Conclusion

It has been shown in this chapter that there is now a legal framework that requires health services to act positively to reduce inequalities. There are also many local initiatives in place to help ensure proper treatment when people are ill, and regular health checks to help people to avoid disease. There are also a battery of reports and publications to indicate that there is a problem. Clearly there are things that can be done within the existing system, and the legal framework along with the reports, indicate the way forward. However, if the links between poor health and social disadvantage are to be taken seriously then health cannot be seen in isolation and is only part of the issue of access that is explored in this book.

References

Alborz, A., McNally, R. and Glendinning, C. (2005) Access to healthcare for people with learning disabilities: mapping the issues and reviewing the evidence, *Journal of Health Service Research Policy*, **10**, 3, 173–82.

Backer, C., Chapman, M., Mitchell, D. and Fedeczko, A. (2007) *Access to Secondary Healthcare for People who are Learning Disabled*, Manchester: Manchester Learning Disability Partnership.

Branford, D. (1998) Bhaumik epilepsy in adults with learning disability, *Seizure*, **7**, 473–7.

Brown, M. (2007) A critical analysis of the actions required to address the health inequalities experienced by people with learning disabilities in Scotland, Unpublished PhD thesis, Napier University.

Carmichael, S. and Moore, D. (2005) Action for health – how it is going?, Online (http://www.intellectualdisability.info/values/HAP_sc_dm.html) (accessed 18 November 2008).

Chapman, M., Craven, M. and Chadwick, D. D. (2005) An evaluation of health practitioner input to improve healthy living and reduce obesity for adults with learning disabilities, *Journal of Intellectual Disabilities*, **9**, 2, 131–44.

Department of Health (1992) *Health of the Nation: A strategy for health*, London: HMSO.

The Department of Health (1998) *Signposts for Success in Commissioning and Providing Health Services for People with Learning Disabilities*, London: HMSO.

Department of Health (2001) *Valuing People: A new strategy for learning disability for the 21st century*, London: Department of Health.

Department of Health (2008) *Health Inequalities: Progress and next steps*, London: Department of Health.

Department of Health and Social Security (1980) *Inequalities in Health, Report of a Working Group (the Black Report)*, London: DHSS.

Disability Rights Commission (2005) *Equal Treatment: Closing the Gap. Interim report of a formal investigation into health inequalities,* Online (http://83.137.212.42/sitearchive/DRC/pdf/10_752_interim_report_final.pdf) (accessed 4 December 2008).

Disability Rights Commission (2006) *Equal Treatment, Closing the Gap. A formal investigation into physical health inequalities experienced by people with learning disabilities and/or mental health problems,* Online (http://83.137.212.42/sitearchive/DRC/PDF/mainreportpdf_healthFIpart1.pdf) (accessed 4 December 2008).

Elliott, J., Hatton, C. and Emerson, E. (2003) The health of people with learning disabilities in the UK: evidence and implications for the NHS, *Journal of Integrated Care*, **11**, 1, 9–17.

Emerson, E., Malam, S., Davies, I. and Spencer, K. (2005) *Adults with Learning Difficulties in England 2003/4*, London: National Statistics and Health and Social Care Information Centre.

Graham, H. (2005) Intellectual disabilities and socioeconomic inequalities in health: an overview of research, *Journal of Applied Research in Intellectual Disabilities*, **18**, 101–14.

Hollins, S., Attard, M. T., von Fraunhofer, N. and Sedwick, P. (1998) Mortality in people with learning disability, causes and death certification in London, *Developmental Medicine and Child Neurology*, **40**, 50–56.

International Association for the Scientific Study of Intellectual Disability (2001) *Mental Health and Intellectual Disability: Addressing the mental health needs of people with intellectual disabilities*, Report of the Mental Health Special Interest Research Group of IASSID to the World Health Organisation.

Jenkinson, J. (1993) Who shall decide? The relevance of theory and research to decision-making by people with intellectual disability, *Disability, Handicap & Society*, **8**, 4, 361–75.

Kerr, M. (2004) Improving the general health of people with learning disabilities, *Advances in Psychiatric Treatment*, **10**, 200–206.

Lindsey, M. (1998) *Signposts for Success in Commissioning and Providing Health Services for People with Learning Disabilities*, London: Department of Health.

Lindsey, M and Russell, O. (1999) *Once a Day*, Wetherby: Department of Health.

Mencap (2007) *Death by Indifference*, London: Mencap

Messent, P. R., Cooke, C. B. and Long, J. (1999) Primary and secondary barriers to physically active lifestyles for adults with learning disabilities, *Disability & Rehabilitation*, **21**, 9, 409–19.

Michael, J. (2008) *Healthcare for All: Report of the independent inquiry into access to healthcare for people with learning disabilities*, Online (http://www.iahpld.org.uk/Healthcare_final.pdf) (accessed December 2008).

Thornton, C. (2008) A focus group inquiry into the perceptions of primary health care teams and the provision of health care for adults with learning disability living in the community, *Journal of Advanced Nursing*, **23**, 6, 1168–76.

World Health Organisation (2001) *Atlas: Global resources for people with intellectual disabilities*, Geneva: World Health Organisation.

Chapter 11

I'm in control

Gary Butler

Introduction

Gary Butler was a presenter at the Concepts of Access seminar series where he spoke about his experiences of working at the medical school, St George's, University of London. He works as a training adviser, helping medical students understand how best to work with people with learning disabilities. He has written a book about his experiences, *A New Kind of Trainer* (Owen *et al* 2004). When Gary agreed to produce a chapter for this book, he decided that he would like to talk about two things: his job at St George's, but also living with his fiancée Sharon. The way he chose to work on this chapter was to ask Jane Seale to interview him about his experiences and for Jane and Gary to work together to write up the interview as a chapter.

Having a voice and listening to others

I would like to see access for all areas. It seems to me, all the politicians do the old talk about how we are going to do this and we are going to do that. It comes and goes, then the next government comes in, says the same message, but it doesn't happen.

Towns and bridges are one thing, but access is about all parts of life as well, whether it is the NHS or the library.

I know it feels like we're going to come up against a brick wall, but if we keep pushing, sooner or later that wall is going to fall down.

I am not really coming up against walls now, because since I got my job at St George's, a lot of people have found out that I have got a voice and that I will use it if I really have to. This is even though my mates usually call me the quiet man!

The things that make me want to use my voice are when people who have a disability are still barred from doing things, even though everyone in their family knows they are capable of doing it.

People in some group homes I know, the staff promise to do things, but when it comes to the day of doing something, they say: 'Oh no, you can't do that' and all the negative stuff comes through. When I talk to my friends about this, I think: 'No, this can be improved.' But then the one-word question that pops up is: 'How?' and I say: 'You've got to keep on trying because sooner or later people are going to start listening. Don't just give up at the first hurdle.'

I've seen people give up and I've seen where they have ended up, because of it, which is a pretty sad picture. It's like when people have given up on them, like family, friends and carers and they end up in Day Centres, where they end up just sitting round watching TV. What good is that? When you are in your twenties and thirties you want to get on with life and do what your friends are doing.

Sometimes it has been frustrating, trying to access things, but that is often what comes, when you are trying something. You can't just fall at the first hurdle. Some people might turn around and say, 'That's easier said than done' and I can understand that. But whether you are in a wheelchair or able-bodied, it doesn't matter. If you want to get somewhere in life, you can do it. If other people are willing to just take five minutes out of their day to listen to you.

Everyone is always shouting about money. But you can do things without money, as long as you all pull together as a community For example, there is a place that used to be a Day Centre, but now a community support unit runs out of it and that is all based on volunteers. This works because people are willing to give up their time. So if you can give five minutes of your day to listen to someone it makes them feel more included and more wanted.

Me and my job

In this section Gary talks about how he got his job at St George's, University of London, the things that he does as part of his job and how he feels about his job.

Finding out about the job

I was inspired to apply for the job at St George's when I went to see a play there. I went with my drama group. The play was called 'A Billion Seconds'. There was another drama teacher in the audience from the theatre company that was putting on the production. Without my knowledge, she had passed my drama teacher a load of forms and the actual advert for the job. She asked my drama teacher if there was anyone in our group that could take on that role.

The following day I went to drama club and I was called into the office. I thought, 'Hello?' They usually call you in there if you are going to get a slap over the wrist so to speak. Both people who run the drama group were in the office and I thought, 'I'm really in hot water.' But they could see I was panicking and they said, 'It's ok, you are not in trouble' and that's when they told me about the job. I felt a sense of relief and when they told me about the job I thought, 'Yes, no harm in trying.' But I didn't put much hope in it.

Every time I told someone about the job, it was like, 'You won't be able to do that, it's too specialised' or, 'You are going to lose your benefits.' But my dad was working and my brother and sisters were working, and I thought, 'Why can't I?' I turned round and said, 'Oh ye of little of faith!'

I had a support worker at the time. We filled out the forms and sent them all off. The next thing I know I get a call from the Head of Department at St George's, Professor Sheila Hollins, and she invited me for an interview.

The job interview

For the interview, my dad wanted me to wear an old 60s pin-stripe jacket, but I said 'No dad forget that will you.' So I wore a denim jacket and jeans and a decent pair of shoes.

I didn't have a clue what kinds of questions they would ask me, so my support worker came with me to the interview, because it said in the notes, you can bring a support worker if you wanted to.

In the interview they asked me things like are you good with people? Are you good in front of crowds of people? That sort of thing. I've always been around people, so that wasn't a problem for me.

After the interview I had to go and work at the supermarket. I finished about 10.30. When I got home, someone in the house said, 'Oh there was a phone call for you earlier and they said they would call back.' The phone went, and I picked it up and it was Sheila Hollins on the phone telling me they were so impressed with me, I've got the job. I nearly fell off the chair I was sitting on. After the interview I thought I had no chance, because of what other people had said. But then I thought, 'No, you can do this.'

The things I do for my job

It was really strange starting work at St George's. I've known the hospital since I was born. Because I was born there I thought, 'First you are born here, now you work here, what's next?'

I do a number of different things in my job. One of the things I do is to help make health information leaflets easier to read for people with learning disabilities. I also help produce some of the *Books Beyond Words* series.[1] These are books about everyday occurrences like going to the doctor or seeing a psychiatrist. There is information for carers and support workers at the back of the book. My role is to look at the pictures when the artist has drawn them. Proof read them, as they say. We choose a subject for the book and the artist will have a meeting with us to discuss what kind of pictures they should be. Then the artist will go away and draw up a first set and if they are not right she'll redo them and then come back with a final version. We meet pretty regularly. I show the pictures to other people with learning disabilities as well, to check they understand them.

I also help teach medical students with my friend and colleague Paul Adeline, who is the other training adviser in the department. We try to talk to the students, who are early 20s upwards, about access and how to talk with people who have learning disabilities.

Teaching medical students

When I first started there would be times when I talked to the medical students, when half a dozen of them would be talking about EastEnders or what happened last night. I would think, 'What am I doing here for god's sake?' I felt like saying, 'Hello! I am here!' I thought they were rude, but I didn't want to say that in case I upset the apple cart so to speak.

Over the years they have got better and they are more interactive now. You should have seen the bunch we had the other day. They were so hands-on with us. I got a feedback form from them. They said they enjoyed having us and it was nice to see 'people in the flesh'. I thought: 'Wow! This is a turn up for the books.'

In that session, we were simulated patients, pretending to have illnesses like gastroenteritis. The students had to question me to find out what was wrong with me, take my blood pressure; that sort of thing. It was really funny. Some of the students knew what they were doing, but some were a bit clueless. I think maybe some of them hadn't met someone like me in the flesh before. Maybe they had been lectured about it, but they had never met someone in the flesh. One comment I got on the feedback form said, 'It was really nice not to have to guess what people with learning disabilities are actually like.'

When I first acted as a simulated patient, years ago, I was nervous. But I'm not so nervous now. It's like I am the expert in something these doctors don't know anything about. I heard a ward sister saying once, 'I've been doing this for 30 years and I've never come across anything like that before.'

I try to get an interactive role going between me and the students, so they are not on edge. If they are looking anxious I say, 'Don't be afraid, I'm not going to bite you.' But you still get one or two who clam up. There is an old saying that applies: 'You can't help them, unless they help themselves.' Some of the students are not confident to speak up themselves or say what is on their mind.

The group numbers vary. The largest has been 25 to 30; the smallest has been 10 to 12. The lecturers kick the session off and then hand over to me and Paul. We do it every five weeks with a different set of students, who are in the fourth year of their training.

We split the session in two. For half of the group, Paul and I talk to the students about learning disabilities. The other half of the group will go and work with some actors with learning disabilities and work through some scenarios. Then we swap over. Then right at the very end the whole group will come together and the actors will say what it was like for them. Then we will ask the students how they thought they did.

Good sessions and bad sessions

I know when we have had a good session. An example is the second week I was at St George's. I met a couple of people on the street. They recognised me from my job. It was Friday night and I was on the way to the pub. These two people approached me. I thought they were going to ask for directions, but they said, 'Excuse me, we recognise you from St George's; that was a really good talk you gave us the other day. Thanks very much.' I thought 'Wow!' I was chuffed!

An example of when it has been not so good is when I've said my piece and there are blank looks, as if I've said it Russian. Reactions like this are once in a blue moon. The lecturers say to us it is not our fault, it was just the students not paying attention and if they want to pass the course, they have to learn from us.

How I feel about my job

Having my job has been one of the best experiences of my life. Even though we are all from different backgrounds and religions, it's like we are all one big family. I've slotted in well here. I'd like to stay on at St George's as long as I can.

Working at St George's is very different to my old job at the supermarket. When I was working there it was like 'too many chefs and not enough cooks'. There were too many people who thought, 'He's got a disability, I can boss him about.' One person would tell me to do one thing; another person would tell me to do something different. This other girl with a disability left because she couldn't take the pressure they were putting her under. It was crazy. All they wanted was their money's worth out of you. It was like being in a chicken farm.

I took a risk taking the job at St George's, because I knew my benefits would go all over the place. But as long as I send their office an update now and again, I can keep my benefits on track.

I took the risk because I thought I can't live off benefits all my life. I don't want to grow old and just sit there in an armchair and be bored out of my life. I'm not ready for the old pipe and slippers scenario. Working keeps my brain ticking over. It makes life more interesting and gives you something to get up for in the morning.

My message to others about getting a job

If you want something badly, keep pushing for it. Only you can set your goals and targets. Don't worry about other people's expectations of you. Only you know what you are good at and what you are not good at. I've had so many people tell me I can't; I just switch that part of my brain off and say 'I can.'

Me and my fiancée

I originally knew my fiancée, Sharon, when she was about 5 and I was about 7.

My dad met her dad in the local pub when we were kids. We didn't see each other again until a good 20 years later.

When I saw Sharon again, I was living in a group home. At first we didn't recognise each other because we've both changed and matured. But we got to know each other and we were just going out everywhere together; to the shops, the cinema. It was a right laugh.

Sharon has got this really bubbly personality and her laugh is like a volcano erupting, it is so loud! She always brings a smile to my face.

The night I proposed

In 2001 I thought, 'Let's take this a step further.' So I took her out for a meal and proposed to her. That's when things really started happening. We had been that close, it was like a brother and sister scenario when you are really close. When I proposed I thought I had to do it without help. I took her to a restaurant which we both knew and loved because we had been there before. I ordered our food and some wine; then I got down on one knee and proposed. Sharon started crying, bless her.

When we got back to the group home that night everyone was like, 'Hey? What?' All the staff had like their eyes popping out of their heads. I don't think they could see two disabled clients living together. I heard murmurs in the background like: 'That will never last.' I thought: 'Here we go again!' Sharon didn't hear it; she was too over the moon.

Sharon borrowed a phone to call her sister and within 20 minutes her entire family north and south of the border knew. The phone kept going. Then my father got wind of it, before I had even phoned him. It was organised chaos.

After the proposal

We had an engagement party at my dad's local pub. After it all settled down everyone was trying to get used to us as a couple and not two single people. People's general perception of people with learning disabilities is that they live in group homes and go to Day Centres. That wasn't happening with us. It was an unwritten rule that people with learning disabilities don't fall in love and get engaged.

People found it hard to believe that we were in love. I've had relationships before, but they came to nothing. This one is different, because we have got so much in common; it's crazy. She knows everything about me, I know everything about her. It's the same with our families; they all know about my family and we all know what they are like. It's like we are 'normal'.

Living in our flat together

We live in a flat together now. I moved into the flat first. Sharon started coming home regularly with me and spending weekends. The staff at the group home were getting fed up with this. They had a meeting at the group home, where both my sisters were present and her sisters were present, the social worker and one of the heads of Social Services. After all the friction had died down, we said our bit.

I said, 'Sharon can move in any time she wants, she's practically moved in with me anyway, I can't see any problems.' Sharon's sister was a bit against it at first. She said, 'How is she is going to manage her money? How is she going to do this? How is she going to do that?' I said, 'One step at a time. You still hold her money and stuff like that to start off with, and then in time you put the money in Sharon's bank.' That was how I did it with my dad.

I think they thought that we wouldn't spend our money on food and bills and that I would take Sharon's money and use it. I said, 'No, Sharon's got her own money and I've got my own money.' If I'm short, I might borrow some money off Sharon, but I've always paid it back.

They were also worried about problems they thought two people with learning disabilities might have, living together for the first time. I said, 'Ok, let's turn this the other way around. What if none of the problems happen?' It hasn't happened either. We have our arguments, but tell me a couple that doesn't. Then the social worker said, 'Look there is such a thing as give and take, you have got to learn to trust these two a bit.' That was the final thing that was said and everything stopped then. I get on very well with Sharon's family, I always have done.

When Sharon moved in, she filled my flat with her stuff three times over! That was three years ago. It's been really good. Being with Sharon is the best thing that has happened to me.

Leaving the past behind

When I tell medical students that I'm engaged and living with Sharon, some of them look very surprised. I think they were thinking, 'That doesn't usually happen.' But too much of the past is being brought into the present. We need to leave all the social stigmas in the past. If we could just think from a fresh point of view and think, 'I don't see why they can't do this' or, 'Give them a trial run and see what is going on.'

At the group home meeting I said to them, 'Calm down a bit. You've got your life; everyone else has got a life. Why can't we have one?'

My message to others about living independently

If you don't have a positive outlook on life you are not going to move forward. You just need to try. You don't know until you try. People are being told you can't do this, you can't do that. But you have got to say to yourself, I can. Do your level best; if you can't do it, try something else.

Some final thoughts about what access means to me

Access was always a bit of a pain when I was growing up, because I couldn't walk very far and I was always pushed about in a buggy. But now I've improved my circumstances and my quality of life, I find I can do things if I really want to.

Quality of life is not having people telling us 24/7 what to do, when to do it and how to do it. Sharon and I bounce off each other, and if we get stuck with something we phone someone up and ask. We have independence and good ongoing support.

We have control over our lives. We have a say about how we run our lives and how we want to do things. When we were living in the group home, there were too many people who had control over our lives, we were just two balls in a football field.

Note

1 *Books Beyond Words* (www.rcpsych.ac.uk/bbw).

Reference

Owen, K., Butler, G. and Hollins, S. (2004) *A New Kind of Trainer: How to develop the training role for people with learning disabilities*, London: Royal College of Psychiatrists.

Part 6

Conclusion

Chapter 12

Access and the concept of risk

Preventing bad things from happening or making good things happen?

Jane Seale and Melanie Nind

Introduction

In this chapter we will examine the role that risk has played in shaping access-related policies and services for people with learning difficulties and the associated 'protection' discourse that has, until recently, been embedded in policy and practice. We identify the need for risk management and positive risk taking and evaluate the challenges that arise from attempting to reconceptualise risk as inherently positive as opposed to inevitably negative. We discuss how the concepts of creativity and resilience might help inform the development of positive risk-taking practices and we consider what might be required to enable access services to create and develop a positive risk-taking culture or approach to working with people with learning difficulties.

Learning difficulties and 'being at risk'

Risk has played and continues to play an important role in shaping access-related policies and services for people with learning difficulties (Alaszewski and Alaszewski 2002). People with learning difficulties are generally regarded as being an 'at risk' group and many current policy and research publications highlight the very real risks to them in terms of poor treatment by others, lack of available opportunities, and poor physical and mental health and social well-being. For example, in Chapter 10 of this book, Duncan Mitchell frames his discussion of the poor health of people with learning difficulties in the context of their being a 'high risk group' in danger of experiencing significant health inequalities. The highly influential *Valuing People* White Paper published by the Department of Health in 2001 identified three key areas of risk: access to health care, health status, and opportunities to make the transition to adulthood. For example, 'People with learning disabilities from minority ethnic communities are at particular risk of discrimination in gaining access to appropriate health care' (Department of Health 2001: 62).

Whilst the 'at risk' discourse can be helpful in terms of highlighting the need for action and making the case for different kinds of responses to the needs of people with learning difficulties and others, it can be problematic too. Roaf (2002: 55) argues that this can neglect equality issues and merely entrench discourses of need; she cites Swadener and Lubeck's (1995: 11) alternative 'vision of children and families "at-promise"'. This offers a contrast with the implied vulnerability of people with learning difficulties 'at-risk', which can lead to a 'protection' discourse where people with learning difficulties are considered in need of being protected from harm and where acts of protection can lead easily to acts of overprotection. As Booth and Booth (1998: 206) note, the 'at risk label' comes to be regarded as a 'risk factor'.

One of the key consequences of risk and protection discourses is that services designed to facilitate access for people with learning difficulties can adopt quite risk-averse policies and actions in response to identified risks that can be more perceived than real. This risk aversion was noted as far back as the 1970s. For example, in 'The dignity of risk', Perske (1972) argued that many care workers tended to be overzealous in their attempts to protect. In an examination of the perceptions of risk held by individuals with learning difficulties (service users), carers and professionals and the risk policies of agencies, Alaszewski and Alaszewski (2002: 56) found that although agencies recognised the importance of risk management, their risk policies were based on 'a restricted approach to risk' that emphasised hazard assessment and health and safety issues. This approach is also reflected in the comments and experiences of the participants of our Concepts of Access seminar series, who identified a range of events that they felt were indicative of a risk-averse approach to access. For example:

> Access is being able to go to the cinema without the threat of being carried out, because you are a fire risk.
> Access is being able to have friends over, without support workers telling us we can't 'because of insurance'. (Seale and Nind 2007: 28)

These experiences led the seminar participants to conclude that staff can think more about risk assessment and avoiding risks than about making access happen. They argued that accessing new things often involves risk and that people with learning difficulties sometimes want to take risks but professionals can be afraid to do so. These examples, given by seminar participants, suggest an approach to access that is driven either by a fear of getting things wrong and harming what is perceived as an already vulnerable group or by assumptions and preconceptions about the abilities of people with learning difficulties to cope in what might be seen as 'risky' situations.

The seminar participants identified various characteristics of risk-averse approaches to access (see Figure 12.1). These characteristics are echoed by the experiences reported by some of our chapter authors. Gary Butler in Chapter 11 and Drew Bradley, Darren Grant and Wayne Taylor in Chapter 8 for example, talk of how unwritten and written rules regarding acceptable or

Figure 12.1 Characteristics of risk-averse approaches to access

normal behaviour served to create rigid and inflexible access environments for them:

> People's general perception of people with learning disabilities is that they live in group homes and go to Day Centres. That wasn't happening with us. It was an unwritten rule that people with learning disabilities don't fall in love and get engaged. (Gary Butler, Chapter 11)

> We have to live with rules to protect us. Rules about who can go out alone, who can sleep upstairs, not running up the stairs or standing on chairs and so on. Some of this is also about not doing things that other residents might copy. But some of it is because of staff worries about us having epileptic seizures. They questioned whether we could sign up to learn karate. We also have to have alarms in the rooms and wear chains with medical information on. These are the things we want to put an end to when we live by our own rules in our own homes. We want to be able to lock our own doors and be private. (Drew Bradley, Darren Grant and Wayne Taylor, Chapter 8)

Gary Butler also talked about how access staff tended to have low expectations regarding his abilities and potential for succeeding:

> Every time I told someone about the job, it was like, 'You won't be able to do that, it's too specialised' or, 'You are going to lose your benefits.' But my dad was working and my brother and sisters were working, and I thought, 'Why can't I?' I turned round and said, 'Oh ye of little of faith!'

Risk management and positive risk taking

During the same period that the Concepts of Access seminar series was running (2005–2007), key policy documents were being published that began to adopt a different tone and focus in relation to risk, stressing instead the need for risk management and positive risk taking. The political driver for this change was probably laid by the Mental Capacity Act (Her Majesty's Stationery Office 2005: 1), which adopted a set of four principles that required those working with people who have a learning difficulty to think more positively about their abilities or capacities:

1   A person must be assumed to have capacity unless it is established that he (sic) lacks capacity.
2   A person is not to be treated as unable to make a decision unless all practicable steps to help him to do so have been taken without success.
3   A person is not to be treated as unable to make a decision merely because he makes an unwise decision.
4   An act done, or decision made, under this Act for or on behalf of a person who lacks capacity must be done, or made, in his best interests.

However, the ideological foundation for this change can be traced further back, to advocates such as Perske (1972: 195) who argued that experiencing 'the risk-taking of ordinary life' is necessary for normal human growth and development. In the consultation document, *Independence, Well-being and Choice* (Department of Health 2005: 10) there is talk about empowering the social care workforce to be more innovative and to take the risk of enabling people to make their own life choices, where it is appropriate to do so: 'the risks of independence for individuals are shared with them and balanced openly against benefits'.

Although not specific to learning difficulties, *Our Health, Our Care, Our Say* (Department of Health 2006) talks about developing a risk management framework to enable people using services to take greater control over decisions about the way they want to live their lives. *Valuing People Now* (Department of Health 2007) talks about services getting the balance wrong between protecting vulnerable people and helping people have a life, and argues that 'positive risk taking should be a part of everyone's life' (Department of Health 2007: 77).

With more recent policy documents giving high-level permission or encouragement for positive risk taking, attention is starting to focus on how access services and organisations will respond, and what positive risk taking will look like in action. Local authorities and learning disability organisations are interpreting the legislative mandate for positive risk taking in different ways. In newly developed policies and guidance, some stress the need to encourage positive risk taking in people with learning difficulties:

> By taking account of the benefits in terms of independence, well-being and choice, it should be possible for a person to have a support plan which enables them to manage risks and to live their lives in ways which best suit

them. People new to the concept of self-directed support often have concerns about the risks involved. In fact, when individuals are given the freedom to design their own care packages, it has been shown that they make sensible and mature choices that improve their quality of life and keep them safe. Risk taking should no longer be regarded in isolation with harm, but as a means for service users to become more self-reliant and to self develop. (Southampton City Council 2008)

Others stress the need to adopt a positive risk taking stance or culture within the organisation itself:

The Positive Risk Taking Group (Cumbria) was a working group tasked with the job of changing policy, procedure, practice, guidance and attitude away from a culture of avoiding risks at all costs (a risk averse culture) towards positive risk taking (a risk management culture). The group worked across 15 different organisations and has consulted broadly with over 250 people across Cumbria, over half of whom were people with learning disabilities; the policy and guidance were developed based on what people shared through the consultation and what group members (and others) contributed over the year. Thank you to everyone who has given their time and energy! (Cumbria County Council 2006)

Although positive, these moves by local authorities are still only moves at a policy level and what is not clear is how these local policy statements can be turned into action. What exactly would exemplify a positive risk-taking culture and how can access services work to change working practices so that people with learning difficulties do indeed have real freedom to design their own care packages? Drawing on the arguments used by Seale (2006) when discussing the impact of disability discrimination legislation on the accessibility of online learning materials, it is our contention that legislation and a change in policy discourse on their own are not enough to change practice. If they did, then when the Jay Committee Report on Mental Handicap Nursing and Care argued back in 1979 that 'mentally handicapped people' needed to assume a 'fair and prudent share of risk' (Jay 1979, para. 121) our access history and landscape, at least in the context of nursing, would be hugely different today than it is reality. Therefore, in the context of access-related work or practices, what is needed in addition to changing legislative drivers is twofold: first a reconceptualisation of risk that all appropriate stakeholders feel comfortable with and can use as a foundation upon which to agree acceptable levels of risk and define what positive risk taking means for both people with learning difficulties and access services; second, detailed, thick, rich descriptions of access practices that are underpinned by these new conceptualisations in order to describe and identify best practices that exemplify positive risk taking in action.

Reconceptualising risk: the challenge of different risk tolerances

The change in policy discourse challenges all access stakeholders to renegotiate their relationship with risk and to reconceptualise risk as potentially positive as opposed to definitely negative. In Chapter 9, Roy McConkey and Suzanne Collins provide a nice example of how risk can be reconceptualised when they suggest that 'being in the company of others in public spaces is in itself an important safeguard for vulnerable people'. Writing in relation to mental health services, Morgan (2004: 18), defined risk as the 'likelihood of an event happening with potentially beneficial or harmful outcomes for self and others'. He observed, however, that our relationship with risk is frequently restrictive, driven by the fear of getting things wrong. Reconceptualising risk as positive can therefore create tensions, particularly when people with learning difficulties, their families (informal carers) and access services (formal carers) have different risk perceptions or tolerances.

A number of studies have highlighted tensions between services and families in terms of attitudes to or perceptions of risk. In a dated, but relevant study, Heyman and Huckle (1993) for example, interviewed 20 adults with learning difficulties, who were living at home with informal carers and attending Adult Training Centres, about their everyday lives. In addition they interviewed informal and formal carers. Heyman and Huckle found that both adults and informal carers saw the lives of adults with learning difficulties as full of hazards such as travelling alone on the bus or crossing the road. These hazards where either perceived as risks to be calculated or dangers to be avoided. From these interviews, Heyman and Huckle classified the families of adults with learning difficulties in terms of their approach to hazards and their tolerance of risk. Adults from more risk-tolerant families were given limited autonomy in that they were able to go out locally with some freedom and therefore were able to undertake autonomous everyday activities such as going to pubs and clubs. Adults from less risk-tolerant families had 'minimal autonomy' and were only able to go out alone on specific prescribed journeys and could only engage in leisure and social activities when accompanied by carers. Adults from more risk-tolerant families appeared to be achieving more of their potential in everyday living skills (as rated by formal carers). Formal carers at Adult Training Centres were more accepting of risks for adults with learning difficulties than informal carers, and there was misunderstanding and conflict between formal and informal carers as a result.

In a more recent study Clark et al (2005) interviewed 35 people with learning difficulty and/or a family member about their experiences of living with a learning difficulty. They found that often people with learning difficulty, their family and professional staff did not have a shared understanding of the desired level of dependence or independence of the individuals, which resulted in disagreements about care objectives. They identified that a particular area of concern for everyone was around exposure to risks. For example, some families described how the expectation for risk taking was not always shared with services, which could be more or less conservative in their care of the individual.

In the description of their involvement in the development of a sexuality policy for a learning disabilities service, Cambridge and McCarthy (1997) report that extensive consultations led to overall agreement by service users, parents and staff with the new sexuality policy, although they did note some argument amongst the staff group about the need for such a policy. Cambridge and McCarthy (1997: 235) call for a balanced approach that recognises the need to manage risk in relation to protecting people with learning difficulties from HIV and sexual abuse but also provides radical responses that enable a shift from a 'culture of protection' to one of 'inclusion and empowerment'.

Reconceptualising positive risk taking: the challenge of agreeing what is central to good risk practices

Risk commentators such as Manthorpe *et al* (1997); Alaszewski and Alaszewski (2002) and Morgan (2004) echo the call for balance, but also argue that trust and clarity will be at the heart of good risk practices. For example, Manthorpe *et al* (1997: 80) argue that:

> Good risk practice means honestly trying to balance goals, acceptability and understanding between participants. However, professionals need to understand and influence their agencies' context. Issues of risk are too important to be left to individual practitioners.

Alaszewski and Alaszewski (2002: 60) on the other hand argue that since there is no consensus about risk between users, carers and professionals, it is important that welfare agencies have clear risk policies that provide users with a clear statement of how the agency will deal with risk and a framework for professionals to manage risk. The Concepts of Access seminar participants identified a wider range of characteristics for what they considered to be risk-embracing approaches to access (see Figure 12.2). These characteristics are quite different to those discussed by risk commentators. Although the concept of trust is included, other concepts are highlighted that have not necessarily been explicitly linked, in a positive manner, to risk before.

The characteristics highlighted in Figure 12. 2 are echoed by the experiences reported by some of our chapter authors. In Chapter 8, the explanations and descriptions that Judith Clayton and Claire Royall give of their advocacy role paint a picture of an approach that is influenced by a belief that success is possible, where success is understood as relaxed and confident participation. In Chapter 5, we learn how Alan Dale will be supported in his holiday trip to Cornwall by an approach that could be described as 'letting go'. The risk was

Figure 12.2 Characteristics of risk-embracing approaches to access

minimised (a carer accompanying Alan on the train to Cornwall), but autonomy was also optimised (the carer returning home once Alan has safely arrived in Cornwall). In Chapter 4, the design and consultation process involved in producing accessible signage, as described by Chris Abbott and Tina Detheridge, suggests that those involved took a 'leap of faith' to some extent in that they needed to have 'very few preconceptions about how the trail would develop'. In Chapter 11, Gary Butler describes how his social worker persuaded others to trust him and his girlfriend to manage their living arrangements safely and sensibly.

Although the introduction of concepts such as balance, trust, letting go and taking a leap of faith are helpful in reinforcing the move away from 'protection' dominated discourses of access, we would argue that much more detailed description and conceptualisation of positive risk taking is required in order to understand what conditions are required for positive risk-taking cultures and practices within access services to develop. Two particular concepts that we feel are worth further expansion and exploration, are creativity and resilience. Concepts of Access seminar participants defined being creative in two related ways. 'Being creative means seeing challenges, not problems' and 'if one approach doesn't work, trying another way' (Seale and Nind 2007: 28). Implicit in these definitions is the willingness to be flexible and try new or different things. The way seminar participants talked about this willingness suggests that a major influence on the ability of access services to be creative and flexible in their response to risk is resilience, where resilience is understood in the context of 'being brave' and not being afraid of 'looking silly' or getting things wrong (Seale and Nind 2007: 35). In the rest of this chapter we shall develop and expand on the concepts of creativity and resilience and discuss how these conceptualisations might help inform the development of positive risk-taking practices.

Positive risk taking and creativity

Alaszewski and Alaszewski (2002) titled their paper on risk perceptions, practices and policies: 'Towards the creative management of risk', but did not really explicitly define what they meant by creative or creativity in the context of risk management, other than to suggest that risk management needs to link and balance safety and empowerment. This vagueness is also reflected in policy discourses. Some learning difficulty-specific policy documents place a strong emphasis on creation, but less of an emphasis on creativity. For example, *Valuing People* (Department of Health 2001) talks about the need to create: better linkages between children living in residential care and their families; a network of personal advisers to 13–19 year olds; the potential for choice in relation to housing and the environment and the imperative for local action. There is no mention or consideration of whether the creation of these conditions requires creativity. Where creativity is mentioned in policy documents, it is either not specific to learning difficulties or mentioned in relation to access workers who are not working in health and social care settings. For example, in *Independence, Well-being and Choice* (Department of Health 2005: 70) the only mention of creativity is linked to the work of the voluntary community sector (VCS):

> We have already given examples in which the VCS has helped to develop innovative models of care, such as homeshare, and we believe that there is the opportunity in the sector to harness skills and creativity to contribute to the wider wellbeing agenda.

In *Diversity and Citizenship* (Department for Education and Skills 2007) there is an expectation that teachers will be creative in the ways in which they seek to promote citizenship amongst their groups of diverse learners and an acknowledgement that headteachers and senior management have a role in creating conditions (giving permission) for creative (risk-taking) activities to take place. These glaring omissions in the policy discourse lead to some troubling questions. Is it possible to be creative when working with people with learning difficulties? What is it about 1) learning difficulty contexts and 2) health and social care settings that mean that creativity in service delivery is not routinely expected or recognised?

In answer to the first question, examples from our chapters would suggest that it is possible for creativity to exist. In Chapter 2, Jan Walmsley talks about the creativity that has been harnessed to create accessible research methods and publications. In Chapter 3, Ann Aspinall describes the creativity that is expressed through the production of multimedia life stories. The employment of Gary Butler by St George's Medical School at the University of London, to teach medical students, (see Chapter 11) could be seen as creative in terms of the responsibilities given to Gary and the support offered to him to undertake these responsibilities. Roy McConkey and Suzanne Collins (see Chapter 9) offer some tentative answers to the second question. In their research, McConkey and Collins found that staff working with adults with learning difficulties in supported living, shared living and day centres gave greater priority to 'caring' tasks and paperwork than social inclusion tasks. The two agendas of care and social inclusion are seen as conflicting, requiring staff, according to Finlay *et al* (2008), to negotiate obstacles such as regulatory frameworks, local organisational policies, resources and existing structures. In their ethnographic study of three residential homes, Finlay *et al* (2008: 354) observed examples where residential staff missed opportunities to promote access to choice and control. The possibilities of offering or not offering access-related opportunities were conceptualised by staff in negative terms:

> In the same house staff would routinely dish the food out onto residents' plates at meal times. One day they tried putting the food in serving bowls in the middle of the tables and allowing the residents to serve themselves. Suddenly the residents could decide the quantity of food they wanted, when they wanted to put it on their plates, what parts of a meal they did not want on their plates and whether to have second helpings. Again, a simple change in practice allowed the residents to exercise a deal more control over their lives. The reason staff gave for not doing it before was that the residents were not used to doing it; they feared people would take too much for themselves, would not know when to stop or would break crockery. Rather than seeing this as an opportunity for empowerment, they saw it in terms of a perceived lack of competence.

What is interesting about this example is that the staff seek or anticipate problems not to solve them, but to predict failure. They do not reframe or reconceptualise the problem. How access staff and services deal with alternate possibilities and reconceptualise problems, or rather opportunities, would seem to be suggestive of a creative approach to access and risk taking.

Creativity and possibility thinking

In access work, positive risk taking involves developing strategies so that the risks of an access activity or option are balanced against the benefits. This might require an element of creativity in terms of how risks, problems, possibilities and opportunities are conceptualised or framed. Looking to the literature on creativity and creative thinking, we will draw on the work of Anna Craft and colleagues and their concept of possibility thinking (Burnard *et al* 2006; Craft 2002; Cremin *et al* 2006; Jeffrey and Craft 2006). Possibility thinking is a particular part of the process of creative thinking and is defined as encompassing an attitude:

> which refuses to be stumped by circumstances, but uses imagination, with intention, to find a way around a problem. It involves the posing of questions,

whether or not these are actually conscious, formulated or voiced. The posing of questions may range from wondering about the world which surrounds us, which may lead to both finding and solving problems; and from formulated questions at one end of the spectrum, through to nagging puzzles, to a general sensitivity at the other. Possibility thinking also involves problem finding. Being able to identify a question, a topic for investigation, a puzzle to explore, a possible new option, all involve 'finding' or 'identifying' a problem (using the word problem in a loose way, to mean 'other possibilities'). (Craft 2002: 111)

Finding a way around a problem has resonance with the ideas of the Concepts of Access seminar participants when they talked about 'trying another way'. Problem finding also has resonance with the ideas of the seminar participants when they talked about being creative and 'seeing challenges, not problems'. This is perhaps best exemplified by Judith Clayton and Claire Royall in Chapter 8: 'mostly our role is enabling: asking the right questions, offering examples, different words and alternative ways of thinking something through'.

Possibility thinking gives us a framework to identify what these 'right questions' might be and how addressing such questions might enhance positive risk taking. Hart (1996) has been asking similar questions in relation to the curriculum, enabling teachers to move 'beyond special needs' thinking, which leads to 'a narrowly circumscribed set of possibilities' (p x), and into innovative thinking. This, she argues, avoids the practice of individualising problems and disconnecting them from their social circumstances. Instead of relying on expert others, special knowledge or resources, teachers are required to have 'a spirit of open-mindedness and willingness to entertain alternative possibilities' (pp x–xi). Hart operationalises this as five moves: making connections (between the child and the social situation); contradicting (the traditional norms and assumptions); taking a child's eye view; noting the impact of feelings; and suspending judgement. In more recent work with teachers who free themselves of the limitations of thinking of learners as having fixed abilities, Hart et al (2004) use the concept of 'transformability'. They describe work to transform current interactions and future learning possibilities that involves working as co-agents with learners and adopting a core ethic of making the curriculum work for 'everybody'. Nind (2005) uses this and other examples to highlight the importance of creative responding to the challenge of developing inclusive curricula.

Possibility thinking and the 'What if?' questions of access

Burnard et al (2006) propose that problem finding and problem solving involve the posing, in many different ways, of the question, 'What if?' and represent a shift from asking 'What is this?' to 'What can I do with this'? In the past, the 'What if?' questions for those working with and supporting people with learning disabilities services might have included:

- What if they get run over on the way to the shops (see Heyman and Huckle 1993)?
- What if they eat too much food (see Finlay *et al* 2008)?
- What if they have an epileptic seizure (see Chapter 8)?
- What if their benefits get cut (see Chapter 11)?
- What if the administrative paperwork doesn't get done (see Chapter 9)?

In other words, access practices have been dominated by the finding of problems. Individuals and services have worried about the negative things that might happen (to the person with a learning difficulty or themselves) if the subject of the 'What if?' question happens. Now, possibility thinking in the context of positive risk taking and learning difficulties would encourage a new and different set of questions, which are perhaps best exemplified by Gary Butler in Chapter 11:

> They were also worried about problems they thought two people with learning disabilities might have, living together for the first time. I said, 'Ok, let's turn this the other way around. What if none of the problems happen?'

Possibility thinking 'what if' access questions might therefore do three things: first, challenge accepted or past thinking regarding access; second, explore the possibility of doing something new or different to promote access that would have been previously considered impossible or unthinkable; and third, focus on action or transformation. Drawing from the discussions raised in the chapters of this book, examples might therefore include:

- What if support staff were rewarded for prioritising social inclusion tasks over care tasks?
- What if we can arrange an insurance policy that meant friends could stay overnight in sheltered housing and supported living?
- What if people with learning difficulties had the power and choice to lock the doors to their rooms if they wanted to?
- What if we worked out a way for people with learning difficulties not to be financially worse off if they took on a paid job, so that talking to the benefits agency was not a nightmare?

Some questions may be contentious or cause some discomfort, but that is all the more reason to pose them, because it requires us to work through a number of scenarios:

- What if the outcomes of accessible information are not worth the effort and resources required?
- What if the watering down of citizenship-related activities for children with learning difficulties is related to concerns related to the sharing or letting go of power rather than concerns regarding accessibility of citizenship concepts?

'What if' access questions may stem from difficult 'Why not?' or 'Why can't I?' questions, but ultimately have the potential to lead to 'How can we make access happen?' questions. These kinds of questions prompt us to think carefully about defining, describing and developing risk practices.

Possibility thinking, risk taking and risk practices

Possibility thinking involves moving into original and creative spaces and taking risks (Burnard *et al* 2006; Cremin *et al* 2006). In the context of creative thinking, risk taking is part of an exploratory adventure that involves experimentation and pushing boundaries. A good example of this is the efforts made by the Heritage Forum to promote access to heritage sites. This access project took members of the Forum and staff of the heritage sites to 'spaces' neither of them had been before (see Chapter 6). Many of the forum members had little or no prior experience of visiting heritage sites and many of the heritage staff had little or no prior experience of working with people with learning difficulties. There was experimentation in terms of how to record and access the ideas gained from the visits to heritage sites but, more importantly, boundaries were pushed in terms of the challenges that heritage staff faced in thinking about how to respond to the evaluations and feedback. In pushing these boundaries, the space created was not necessarily a comfortable one. Jonathan Rix describes disappointment at some of the reactions from heritage staff and tensions experienced sometimes in managing the advocacy role.

In Chapter 7, Hazel Lawson suggests that focusing on active citizenship might lead teachers who work with children and young people with learning difficulties away from prescribed curriculum content. Moving away from the prescribed curriculum could be risky for teachers, but it could also be an adventure. We only have to look at examples from early years practice, or 'Intensive Interaction', to know what happens if the child is allowed to lead. Starting with what someone can do (rather than what they cannot) and what they like doing (rather than what is prescribed) opens up all kinds of possibilities for teachers acting as dynamic enablers and responders (Nind 2005). Both teacher and learner are freed up to develop relationships in which learning gathers its own momentum. This is not about being out of control or rudderless, not knowing where one is headed; rather it is about not having a rigid route and being willing to explore (Kellett and Nind 2003).

In seeking to understand creativity, Craft and colleagues linked learning and teaching together. They were interested in defining creative thinking so that they could identify best teaching practices that promote creative thinking in young school children. More importantly, they argued that possibility thinking is an inclusive language that brings learners and teacher together: 'Thus, teachers and learners enter a co-participative process around activities and explorations, posing questions, identifying problems and issues together and debating and discussing their thinking' (Cremin *et al* 2006: 111).

The notion is very powerful and attractive in the context of access and access practice, because it suggests that different sections of the access community can be united through a common language and a shared purpose, what Wenger (1998) in his theorisation of communities of practice would identify as examples of 'shared repertoire' and 'joint enterprise'. The common language in this case would be the 'What if?' questions that people with learning difficulties and access workers are starting to articulate and share in common. The shared purpose would be the development of positive risk-taking approaches to access, where all members of the community are expected to take positive risks and might be encouraged to do so through the valuing and facilitation of 'possibility thinking'.

Positive risk taking and resilience

Taking risks can take us outside our comfort zone and perhaps even be stressful. How people respond to this stress might influence their ability to maintain and develop long-term successful positive risk-taking practices. There are certainly examples from our chapter authors who have learning difficulties of what might be recognised as resilience in the sense of adapting, despite adversity (Jackson 2001/2002):

> I know it feels like we're going to come up against a brick wall, but if we keep pushing, sooner or later that wall is going to fall down. ... You've got to keep on trying because sooner or later people are going to start listening. Don't just give up at the first hurdle. (Gary Butler, Chapter 11)

> If Judith and Claire couldn't have supported us we could have come along with someone else for support, someone like Rachel (Drew's girlfriend!) or Pat (a volunteer advocate) but not someone from day services or a social worker as they tell us what to do. (Drew Bradley, Darren Grant and Wayne Taylor, Chapter 8).

The chapters also provide some examples of how such resilience might in part enable people with learning difficulties to take risks:

> I took a risk taking the job at St George's because I knew my benefits would go all over the place ... I took the risk because I thought I can't live off benefits all my life. I don't want to grow old and just sit there in an armchair and be bored out of my life. (Gary Butler, Chapter 11)

In this chapter, we are particularly interested in developing our understanding of how access workers and services respond to the potential stresses of positive risk taking and how this might influence their ability to maintain and develop long-term successful positive risk-taking practices. We therefore draw on the concept of resilience to explore in more detail what might influence the ability of those working in the learning difficulty field to take positive risks and handle the consequences of stepping outside the comfort zone.

Outside of the field of learning difficulties, resilience is broadly understood as long-lasting positive adaptation to adverse situations such as stressful life experiences or trauma (Luthar *et al* 2000). People are therefore considered to be 'at risk' if they are or have been exposed to stressful circumstances that can range from war to parents with mental health problems. The ability of people to deal with such risky or stressful circumstances, as evidenced by their resilience, is argued to be influenced by both internal factors (e.g. personal characteristics) or external factors such as families and the wider social environment.

In learning difficulty research, resilience is conceptualised in two very different ways: either as a risk protective factor or as a political response. Research that is heavily influenced by psychological theories of learning difficulty conceptualises learning difficulty as a risk factor and resilience therefore as a protective factor (Cosden 2003). Much work in this area has been influenced by a classic study by Werner and Smith (1992), which focused on vulnerable young people in the US, including those with learning difficulties. They identified five clusters of protective factors that could explain why some of the young people made successes of their lives and others didn't. These factors were both internal and external to the individual: temperament that elicited positive response from others; values and skills that individuals put to good use; effective parenting skills of parents; presence of supportive adults; and timely opportunities. Wiener (2002) suggests that this classic risk and resilience framework leads to three kinds of research: identifying resilient people; exploring proximal factors by clarifying how resilient qualities have been acquired (the developmental stages); and exploring distal factors through seeking to understand the experiences (e.g. educational processes) that foster activation and utilisation of personal resources' resilient qualities. Whilst it may be useful to use this conceptualization of resilience to seek to understand, at an organisational level, the experiences and processes that foster resilience, it is limited in that it views risk as something negative or traumatic that requires an 'extraordinary' survival response that some people are capable of and others are not. In the context of promoting the need for positive risk taking when working with people with learning difficulties, such a view would seem to be overly pessimistic and out of tune with the positive risk-taking discourse.

A very different perspective on resilience is that offered by Goodley (2005) who offers a more socio-cultural (contextual) framework, where resilience is viewed less as a personal characteristic and more as a political response to disabling and disempowering circumstances. For Goodley it doesn't make sense to talk about nurturing the resilience of people with learning difficulties. Goodley argues that resilience is contextualised, complicating, optimistic, and an indicator of disablement:

- Resilience is *contextualised* – for some the experience of disablement informs their resilience; for others their resilience is informed by their inclusive relationships with family and friends. For some, belonging to self-advocacy groups leads to a sensitization to disabling and enabling conditions, from which resilience grows. Therefore resilience resides in the space between structure and individuality. It is not an individual attribute but a product of the contexts in which it can emerge (Goodley 2005: 334).

- Resilience is *complicating* because it challenges medicalised concepts of impairment and adds 'some notion of resistance and challenge to commonly held views of learning difficulties' (Goodley 2005: 334).
- Resilience is *optimistic* because it encourages supporters, professionals, researchers and policymakers to assume that people with learning difficulties have the potential for resilient lives.
- Resilience is *an indicator of disablement* because 'displays of resilience' capture the wider exclusionary environment in which they have to be made.

In Table 12.1 we map out how Goodley's four aspects of resilience might be applied to access workers or access services and offer some examples of this application, drawn from contributions in this book.

Goodley's notion of resilience is attractive because it suggests that access workers and access services may develop a resilience that enables them to take positive risks, not because new government policy requires them to, but because they see the injustice and inequality inherent in learning disability services and wish to change things. We suggest therefore that resilience is likely to be required of access workers and access services in order for them to both support the positive risk taking of people with learning difficulties and to take positive risks in the access work they do. It may not be a direct response to risk, but it is influenced by access-related contexts in which risk management and positive risk taking take place (see Table 12.1).

Access, positive risk taking and the challenge of developing 'best practice'

A standard suggestion that is frequently offered as a potential solution to the identified problems of access is that support staff and access workers require more training in order to change current practices and develop new 'best practices'. For example, in reviewing healthcare for people with learning difficulties, Duncan Mitchell in Chapter 10 identifies the need for additional training of mainstream hospital staff. In Chapter 9, we learn how consultations with tenants and support staff led to one suggestion that support staff require training and encouragement to 'embrace social inclusion'. Roy McConkey and Suzanne Collins conclude, however, that this suggestion, along with others, will require a radical reappraisal of support services. We would support this argument. As positive as the actions of individuals have been that have been reported within the chapters of this book, there appears to be a general agreement that systems and services needs to change as much as individual people do. The access challenges, therefore, cannot be met solely by training individual access workers to

Table 12.1 The potential application of Dan Goodley's concept of resilience to access workers and services

Resilience as applied to people with learning difficulties	Resilience as applied to access workers or access services	Examples of access related resilience in practice
Resilience is contextualized	Resilience exists in response to negative and positive experiences of risk taking. It is a product of the contexts in which it can emerge.	The contexts in which Judith Clayton and Claire Royall (Chapter 8) work as advocates in the voluntary sector possibly means they have developed resilience and a different attitude to risk taking compared to say the residential staff described in Chapter 9 and the health care staff described in Chapter 10.
Resilience is complicating	Resilience challenges previously held views about the nature and function of access work and access services and adds some notion of resistance and challenge to commonly held views of access and accessibility	Access workers and services who are influenced by Jan Walmsley's arguments about the accessibility of information will find themselves pushing against established norms and may have to develop resilience in order to argue that in some cases blanket use of symbols or pictures does not make the ideas contained within text any more accessible. They may also need to take some risks in terms of finding creative alternative ways of conveying meaning.
Resilience is optimistic	Resilience encourages us to assume the potential for positive risk taking.	There have been times of pessimism and frustration when we have heard stories of 'failed access' from both our seminar participants and our chapter authors. But there are examples of access moments within the chapters that give rise to optimism in terms of realising it is possible for access workers and services to be resilient and take some risks: As Jan Walmsley writes in Chapter 2: 'However […] I am optimistic and have seen instances, where a combination of accessible technology and skilled human support can make a difference. This is the message people should take away from the chapter'
Resilience is an indicator of disablement	Resilience is an indicator of inaccessibility. Displays of resilience by access workers or access services capture the wider inaccessible environment in which they have to be made.	The Heritage Forum project workers have probably had to be quite resilient in the face of significant pressure from potential funders to change the focus of the Heritage project and in response to the refusal of heritage site staff to meet directly with members of the Forum who had a learning difficulty (see Chapter 6).

adopt some new skills and knowledge, for example in possibility thinking or resilience. The issues at stake, access and positive risk taking, are not resolvable by individuals working individually and in isolation. So the question therefore is: how can access services, that is, individuals acting collectively in their contexts, learn to create a positive risk-taking culture and an environment that is resilient enough to take risks and deal with consequences when the risks fail, in such a way that access workers are not afraid to take risks again in the future? To answer this question we think it may be useful to draw on the concept of expansive learning that has been developed by Engestrom (2001) and Engestrom *et al* (2007) in work on activity theory and organisational learning.

Engestrom's work focuses on the socio-cultural aspects of learning, which has resonance with our focus on possibility thinking and resilience and has also been applied by other researchers with an interest in possibility thinking and resilience. For example, Craft and colleagues invoked the socio-cultural learning theories of Lave and Wenger and drew on the concept of 'communities of practice' when discussing how possibility thinking is learnt (Cremin *et al* 2006). Edwards and Mackenzie (2005) apply the socio-cultural learning theories of Drier and Engestrom and draw on the concept of 'learning trajectories' when discussing how excluded learners develop the resilience to participate in learning.

Access, positive risk taking and expansive learning

According to Engestrom (2001) expansive learning involves a repositioning as a result of interpreting features in the world in fresh and often more complex ways. This repositioning involves new interpretations of concepts: challenges to and transformation of concepts that lead to new and different possibilities for action. This repositioning and expansion of interpretations leads learners to embrace a radically wider horizon of possibilities. In the context of access and learning difficulties, we would argue that expansive learning may happen as access services reposition themselves in the light of the transformation of the concept of risk from a negative to a positive stance and the different interpretations this brings about in relation to risk taking, creativity and resilience. Engestrom talks about expansive learning being required within an organisation when there is a change in the direction of effort (directional discontinuity). The move from risk avoidance to positive risk taking could certainly represent such a directional discontinuity.

For Engestrom (2001) it is not always appropriate to try to understand organisational development in terms of skills development, where organisational members gain competence in an established and stable set of practices. This argument is pertinent when thinking about the many calls for 'staff training' there have been in the learning difficulties field. Training usually involves experts passing on their knowledge and wisdom to novices, but if we agree that promoting access for people with learning difficulties is going to involve positive risk taking and that positive risk taking can be partially characterised as a creative activity, then the majority of people working in the field are likely to be novices. Positive risk taking is such a new and emergent practice or activity that very few experts are likely to exist. In this case, the question of how organisations learn focuses less on the search for external experts or consultants and more on understanding how organisations respond to key drivers or influencing factors. According to Engestrom, there are five key actions in the expansive learning process:

1   Conflictual questioning of existing standard practice, often invoked by 'troublesome' cases or examples.
2   Deepening analyses of the case through sharper and more articulated questioning.
3   Modelling of the new solution (pattern of activity, practice).
4   Examining the new model.
5   Implementing the model.

From the contributions to this book, we can identify examples of individuals using troublesome cases to question standard access practices. In Chapter 2, Jan Walmsley questions the practice of making information accessible. In Chapter 3, Ann Aspinall questions the use of traditional life story methods with people who have little or no verbal communication. In Chapter 4, Chris Abbott and Tina Detheridge question the practice of the government, which appears to be insisting on generalisable evidence regarding symbolisation signage that can be applied in any circumstance rather than appreciating that what needs to be applied across the board are broad principles that allow for individual solutions. In Chapter 5, Ginny Aird and her colleagues from Be Heard in Bracknell question the practices (and motives) of support workers who insist on accompanying people with learning difficulties to the cinema, even though their assistance is not wanted. In Chapter 6, Jonathan Rix and his colleagues from the Heritage Forum question the practice of heritage sites that did not seem to want to engage with them (e.g. by making visits difficult, by insisting on talking with a non–disabled member of the Forum rather than people with learning difficulties, or by seeming not to care about the results of the access surveys because they didn't proactively ask for feedback on the visits). In Chapter 7, Hazel Lawson questions the ability of schools to educate children with learning difficulties through citizenship. In Chapter 8, Drew Bradley and colleagues question the practice of support workers who don't value contributions from people with learning difficulties or who use protective rules in such a way as to prevent access. In Chapter 9, Roy McConkey and Suzanne Collins question the practice of some care/residential organisations that prioritise caring over social inclusion. In Chapter 10, Duncan Mitchell questions the practice of health care providers who seem reluctant to engage directly with people with learning difficulties, while in Chapter 11, Gary Butler questions the control that group home staff can have over the lives of people with learning difficulties.

Although we can identify examples of individuals using troublesome cases to question standard access practices, further exploratory work is needed to provide, thick, rich descriptions of how learning difficulty-related access services are attempting to deepen their analyses of troublesome cases, and model, examine and implement new solutions based on these analyses. Engestrom's work provides a method for such exploration in that it has formed the basis of a method that he uses to study individual organisations and organisational change projects. Engestrom *et al* (2007) characterise the method as 'archaeological ethnography', which extends the ethnographic method beyond situationally and temporally bound observations. They also demonstrate how the method can be used to create organisational case studies that can help to demonstrate why cases fail or succeed in their endeavours. It is this kind of information that will be invaluable in relation to access and learning difficulties. We need research and evaluation work that can address some important questions. What is it about some organisations that means they will succeed in their endeavours to develop a positive risk-taking stance to access, while others fail? Will successful positive risk taking involve, as we suggest, possibility thinking and resilience, or does it need to be understood in a different way in order for successful practices to emerge?

Conclusion

In this chapter we have reviewed the concept of risk as it has been applied to access and access services for people with learning difficulties. From this review we have concluded that approaches to access have been driven more by a desire to prevent bad things from happening than a desire to make good things happen. We have argued that access services need to develop a positive risk-taking approach to access when working with people with learning difficulties. This may require a reconceptualisation of risk that all appropriate stakeholders feel comfortable with, can use as a foundation upon which to agree acceptable levels of risk, and define what positive risk taking means for both people with learning difficulties and access services. Possibility thinking and resilience could be useful concepts that serve to drive the focus and direction of such reconceptualisation. However risk and positive risk taking is conceptualised, we will need detailed, thick, rich descriptions of access practices that are underpinned by these new conceptualizations in order to describe and identify best practices that exemplify positive risk taking in action. It is here, in particular, that more work is needed. We are not suggesting that positive risk taking is a simple or easy practice. Indeed, the application of Engestrom's ideas regarding expansive learning to the development of positive risk taking in learning disability services, suggests that we need to do more to seek to understand how services move beyond a conflictual questioning of existing standard practice to a sharper questioning that might enable new solutions and patterns of activity to be identified.

References

Alaszewski, A. and Alaszewski, H. (2002) Towards the creative management of risk: perceptions, practices and policies, *British Journal of Learning Disabilities*, **30,** 56–62.

Booth, T. and Booth, W. (1998) *Growing up with Parents Who Have Learning Difficulties*, London: Routledge.

Burnard, P., Craft, A., Cremin, T., Duffy, B., Hanson, R., Keene, J., Haynes, L. and Burns, D. (2006) Documenting 'possibility thinking': a journey of collaborative enquiry, *International Journal of Early Years Education*, **14,** 3, 243–62.

Cambridge, P. and McCarthy, M (1997) Developing and implementing sexuality policy for a learning disability provider service, *Health and Social Care in the Community*, **5,** 4, 227–36.

Clarke, C. L., Lhussier, M., Minto, C., Gibb, C. E. and Perini, T. (2005) Paradoxes, locations and the need for social coherence: a qualitative study of living with a learning difficulty, *Disability & Society*, **20,** 4, 405–19.

Cosden, M. (2003) Response to Wong's article, *Learning Disabilities Research and Practice*, **18,** 2, 87–9.

Craft, A. (2002) *Creativity and Early Years Education: A lifewide foundation*. London: Continuum.

Cremin, T., Burnard, P. and Craft, A. (2006) Pedagogy and possibility thinking in the early years, *Thinking Skills and Creativity*, **1,** 108–19.

Cumbria County Council (2006) *Cumbria Learning Disabilities Services Positive Risk Taking Policy: From risk aversion to risk management*, Online (http://www.in-control.org.uk/site/INCO/Templates/Library.aspx?pageid=224andcc=GB) (accessed 4 December 2008).

Department for Education and Skills (2007) *Diversity and Citizenship Curriculum Review*, London: HMSO.

Department of Health (2001) *Valuing People: A new strategy for learning disability for the 21st century*, London: HMSO.

Department of Health (2005) *Independence, Well-being and Choice: Our vision for the future of social care for adults in England*, London: HMSO.

Department of Health (2006) *Our Health, Our Care, Our Say: A new direction for community services*, London: HMSO.

Department of Health (2007) *Valuing People Now: From progress to transformation*, London: HMSO.

Edwards, A. and Mackenzie, L. (2005) Steps towards participation: the social support of learning trajectories, *International Journal of Lifelong Education*, **24,** 4, 287–302.

Engestrom, Y. (2001) Expansive learning at work: toward an activity theoretical reconceptualisation, *Journal of Education and Work*, **14,** 133–56.

Engestrom, Y., Kerosuo, H. and Kajamaa, A. (2007) Beyond discontinuity: expansive organisational learning remembered, *Management Learning*, **38,** 319–36.

Finlay, W. M. L., Walton, C. and Antaki, C. (2008) Promoting choice and control in residential services for people with learning disabilities, *Disability & Society*, **23,** 4, 349–60.

Goodley, D. (2005) Empowerment, self-advocacy and resilience, *Journal of Intellectual Disabilities*, **9,** 333–43.

Hart, S. (1996) *Beyond Special Needs: Enhancing children's learning through innovative thinking*, London: Paul Chapman.

Hart, S., Dixon, A., Drummond, M. J. and McIntyre, D. (2004) *Learning Without Limits*, Maidenhead: Open University Press.

Her Majesty's Stationery Office (2005) *Mental Capacity Act 2005*, London: HMSO.

Heyman, B. and Huckle, S. (1993) Not worth the risk? Attitudes of adults with learning difficulties, and their informal and formal carers to the hazards of everyday life, *Social Science
and Medicine,* **37,** 12, 1557–64.

Jackson, S. (2001/2002) Reducing risk and promoting resilience in vulnerable children, *IUC
Journal of Social Work Theory and Practice*, **4.**

Jay, P. (1979) *Report of the Committee of Enquiry into Mental Handicap Nursing and Care*, London:
HMSO.

Jeffrey, B. and Craft, A. (2006). Creative learning and possibility thinking, in B. Jeffrey (ed.),
Creative Learning Practices: European experiences, London: The Tufnell Press.

Kellett, M. and Nind, M. (2003) *Implementing Intensive Interaction in Schools,* London: David
Fulton.

Luthar, S. S., Cicchetti, D. and Becker, B. (2000) The construct of resilience: a critical evaluation and guidelines for future work, *Child Development,* **71,** 543–62.

Manthorpe, J., Walsh, M., Alaszewski, A. and Harrison, L. (1997) Issues of risk practice and
welfare in learning disability services, *Disability and Society,* **12,** 1, 69–82.

Morgan, S. (2004) Positive risk taking: an idea whose time has come, *Health Care Risk Report,*
October, 18–19.

Nind, M. (2005) Introduction: models and practice in inclusive curricula, in M. Nind, J, Rix,
K. Sheehy and K. Simmons (eds), *Curriculum and Pedagogy in Inclusive Education: Values into
practice,* London: Routledge.

Perske, R. (1972) The dignity of risk, in W. Wolfensberger, B. Nirje, S. Olansky, R. Perske and
P. Roos (eds), *The Principles of Normalization in Human Services*, Toronto: National Institute
on Mental Retardation through Leonard Crainford.

Roaf, C. (2002) *Coordinating Services for Included Children: Joined up action*, Buckingham: Open
University Press.

Seale, J. (2006) *E-learning and Disability in Higher Education: Accessibility theory and practice,*
London: Routledge.

Seale, J. and Nind, M. (2007) *Concepts of Access for People with Learning Disabilities: Towards a shared
understanding,* Accessible summary of ESRC-funded seminar series, Online (http://www.
educate.soton.ac.uk/research/field_projects/?link=project_details.php&id=174) (accessed
4 December 2008).

Southampton City Council (2008) *Positive Risk Taking: Guidance,* Online (www.southampton.
gov.uk/Images/Positive%20Risk%20Taking_tcm46–207064.pdf) (accessed 4 December
2008).

Swadener, B. B. and Lubeck, S. (1995) Foreword, in B. B. Swadener and S. Lubeck (eds)
Children and Families 'at Promise', Albany: State University of New York.

Wenger, E. (1998) *Communities of Practice: Learning, meaning and identity,* Cambridge:
Cambridge University Press.

Werner, E. E. and Smith, R. S. (1992) *Overcoming the Odds: High risk children from birth to
adulthood*, Ithaca, NY: Cornell University Press.

Wiener, J. (2002) Friendship and social adjustment of children with learning disabilities. in
B.Y. L. Wong and M. Donahue (eds), *Social Dimensions of Learning Disabilities,* Mahwah,
NJ: Erlbaum.

Index